D1546906

ALSO BY JIM SHEPARD

FLIGHTS

PAPER DOLL

Lights Out in the Reptile House

LIGHTS OUT IN THE REPTILE HOUSE

a novel

JIM SHEPARD

W · W · NORTON & COMPANY · New York · London

The text of this book is composed in Baskerville, with display type set in Kabel. Composition and manufacturing by the Haddon Craftsmen Inc.
Book design by Guenet Abraham.

First Edition
Library of Congress Cataloging-in-Publication Data

Shepard, Jim.

Lights out in the reptile house:
a novel / Jim Shepard.—1st

ed.

p. cm.

I. Title.

PS3569.H39384L54 1990

813'.54—dc20 89-8580

ISBN 0-393-02784-8

W. W. Norton & Company, Inc.
500 Fifth Avenue, New York, N. Y. 10110

W. W. Norton & Company Ltd.
37 Great Russell Street, London WC1B 3NU

1 2 3 4 5 6 7 8 9 0

ACKNOWLEDGMENTS

SPECIAL THANKS TO GERRY HOWARD,
RON HANSEN, K. K. ROEDER, AND EDWARD HIRSCH

KOMODO

BLACK CARS WERE PASSING THROUGH THE smaller streets. You could see them beneath the streetlights. You could hear them like the wind beneath your window. This was the kind of country that took things away from you, Leda had told Karel. He lay in bed listening to the cars and remembered her telling him the story of the gardener next to her on the bus who had said, "Strict rulers don't last for long," talking to himself, talking about the weather, about anything, who knew? And the man opposite him, whom Leda had not been paying enough attention to, had leaned forward and cleared his throat and said with noticeable emphasis, "I don't quite understand what you mean by that, Mr.—?" And the whole bus had gone silent.

But Leda had seen beatings. Karel had seen his room, his father, the Reptile House. The next morning he rode into the country on the back of Albert's truck and they stopped in a dense-canopied ironwood stand. Albert was breeding giant iguanas in a new experimental way for the Reptile House. The iguanas were arboreal and herbivorous, so they usually stayed in the trees, he explained, and since he supplemented their diet they remained in that one stand. He tore open one of the thirty-pound bags of feed and inverted it, spilling rich red pellets everywhere, and the trees filled with sound, the leaves in the canopy rushed with the movement, and while Karel watched, the six-foot iguanas rushed down the central branches and then the trunks, scrambling and sliding out of everywhere like black magic, like the invisible suddenly made visible at his wish.

His father sat in their tattered lounge chair watching him build his flybag. Some of the geckos and anoles at the Reptile House were not eating, and Karel thought he'd show a little initiative and raise some different food. It'd be a good thing to know if he ever wanted his own vivarium, besides. He had greenbottle and blowfly larvae.

Maggots, his father said. He had the one son in a forty-mile radius who spent his mornings playing with maggots.

He mixed the larvae with handfuls of bran and sawdust and shook them onto shallow dishes he hoped his father wouldn't notice. The dishes he put inside the flybag, a muslin bag with a narrow sleeve on one end spread over a wooden box frame. The greenbottles would pupate in a day or two. The sleeve was used for catching flies (he used a little beaker with snap-on lid) and for feeding them bottlecaps of bran and milk mash to keep them going. An old sock that he'd soaked in water he set atop the bag to provide drinking water.

"The world needs more flies," his father said. "I'm glad you're doing this."

"I like what I'm doing," Karel said. "Do you like what you're doing?" Karel's father was unemployed.

The larvae nosed around each other blindly, coated with bran dust. His father kept watching, and Karel sensed in him some desire to share in this activity at least with his son. He thought about explaining some things—the way the extra meals increased the flies' nutritional value or the way he'd have to cool them before taking them to the reptiles—while he worked, but he didn't. His father got up and went into the house.

He tied off the sleeve and carried the whole assembly to the shade. His father was crashing plates in the kitchen sink. He stood in the sun wiping his hands on his shorts while the racket continued. It was already hot. He could feel on his arms and the back of his neck an old sunburn. A small whiptail took up a basking position above the kitchen window, near the roof. The roof tiles were red clay, stained olive in the interstices. The whiptail was a few inches long and spotted, and its throat fan bulged out every so often. Its colors would pale to compensate for its heat intake as it warmed up. He thought about that kind of thermoregulation as he went into the house.

His father was sitting morosely in the chair by the window. He was holding a spoon at both ends, and a large brown ant was running up the neck of it. As it reached one end his father would reverse the spoon, forcing the hapless ant to repeat the performance. Karel started the coffee.

His father tipped and tilted the spoon. He was wearing a sock as a cravat, for the dampness, he claimed.

"Why are you afraid of me?" he finally asked, his attention on something outside the window.

Karel didn't answer. The knob on the gas stove came off in his hand. He tried to worry it back onto its spindle. He was intensely aware of his father's attention on the back of his head.

His father asked the question periodically and Karel was always unable to answer, partly because of the fear his father was talking about.

"Did you hear me?" his father said mildly. He dropped the spoon into a dish of old soapy water in the sink. "You're what now, sixteen? You can't converse with your father?"

"Fifteen," Karel was able to say. Above the stove was a calendar, with his quietly circled birthday a long way off. The calendar had a different sampler for each month. The current one read *Are There Countrymen in This House Who Don't Display the Flag on the Praetor's Birthday?*

"I'm the one should be afraid of you," his father grumbled.

Karel got the stove working. Without turning he asked his father if he really wanted coffee in this heat, and his father said yes, he really wanted coffee in this heat. Utensils pinged and clattered, and outside some crows jabbered around on the back shed.

One night a year or two after his mother died in their old house in the city, his father had stayed out all night. Karel had slept on the balcony. By mistake he'd locked the door behind him. He'd stood facing his reflection in the dark glass before settling down to sleep. The balcony had been open to the moon, and he'd noticed in the catclaw bushes at the end of the garden the thin white face of a man. The man had been watching him. The man's face had performed a series of grimaces. It had not gone away. Karel had stayed as still as possible, his stomach pitching and jumbling with the intentness of its gaze. His only strategy had been to wait for his father to return. He'd remained so still that pains had begun to shoot up his neck and lower back. Before dawn the spaces between the bushes had begun to pale and lighten and the figure had slipped away like a shadow on water. It had left a small branch wavering. Karel's father had come back after sunrise, and Karel's story had first frightened and then angered him. He had inspected the catclaw bushes and then had suspended outdoor sleeping privileges until further notice.

While his father wasn't looking he tipped the salt shaker into the coffee grounds. His father was humming a victory march without enthusiasm. The coffee took forever. Karel kept his eyes on a print his father claimed his mother had always loved of a brook and some meadows, with a pale red sky and some brushstrokes intended as birds.

"Did you hear screaming last night?" Karel asked, as if they hadn't yet spoken. "Off by the square?" He'd heard a shriek, while he lay there dreaming of Leda. In the darkness it had inhabited all parts of his room. It had shaken her from his mind and he'd had trouble reassembling her image in the darkness.

His father shrugged, playing with his empty coffee cup. "Lot of things go on nowadays," he said. He trailed off. "Nowadays" was a common euphemism for the regime.

"Did they say they might take you on for a while?" Karel finally asked. His father had gone north along the foothills of the mountains for the last few days to get some spot work in the quarries. They'd been hoping he could catch on with something steady. That was one of the reasons they had moved here in the first place. It was more or less clear that that hadn't materialized.

"They don't want to keep us around," his father said. He brightened when Karel brought the finally ready coffee over and poured some. "They want us in and out like phantoms."

"What's that area like? What did you see?" Karel asked. When his father wasn't looking he binked a sugar cube across the table toward him.

"We were bused in, bused out," his father said. "No stops, no talking. The only thing I saw on the whole trip was an oxcart with a dead driver alongside it. Is there any sugar?"

Karel indicated the cube near his cup.

His father put his concentration into the coffee, stirring by swishing the cup around. Karel went to the window and leaned out on his elbows. He didn't work at the zoo today, and the morning felt empty with possibility. Near the flybag an almond-shaped horned lizard stirred its camouflage and resolved itself back into sand. Some puffballs trembled in the heat.

He turned from the sill, and his father sighed and eased up and down in his chair. He had a hernia, which had been aggravated when he'd been taken into custody. He refused to say how. He had disappeared for three days and then had been returned. He refused to talk about any of it. One of the policemen had jingled coins in his trouser pockets while waiting for him to get dressed. It occurred to Karel, standing there, that his father was always intentionally and unintentionally creating absences or leaving them behind him.

They were both looking at one of Karel's study sheets on the kitchen table. It was crosshatched with lined columns for each reptile's common name, scientific name, size, description, voice, range, and habitat. He could make out a column: *Banded Gecko.* His father said, "I've asked you about finding me something over there. I could handle animals. Of course, that's too much to expect."

It was. Sometimes he felt more guilty at not having tried to land his father a job at the zoo. But he worried too much about his own position, and they wouldn't have hired his father anyway. There was something else, too: he couldn't imagine the reptiles in his father's care.

His father clearly didn't intend to look for a job today. He spent the morning wandering the house in his shorts with the sock still around his neck, eyeing Karel and making sad clucking sounds. He was in the dark little bathroom wrestling with the window sash and talking to himself when Karel left.

The sun was blinding. In the next front garden Mr. Fetscher sat hatless despite it, scraping potato peels into a metal bucket as if scraping potatoes were precision work. They nodded to each other, and Karel walked down the street to the Schieles'. When he got there he peered over the tall and prickly hedge but did not see Leda. Her mother came into view instead with clothespegs in her mouth. She caught his eye and he ducked below the hedge line, embarrassed to be so often caught hanging around. He headed instead toward the square, reminding himself to walk with some show of purpose. His father always complained that he seemed to just drift around when outside.

He believed himself to be in love with Leda. She wasn't really his girlfriend. When she wasn't home on weekends she was usually in the square, trapped with other girls her age in the semicompulsory League of Young Mothers. It was organized locally by a dim-witted farmer's wife whose main qualification to the regime, besides her ferocious belief in everything she was told, was her having had eleven children. They were all glumly present at the meetings, pressed into service to swell the crowd when they would rather have been anywhere else. The league was composed otherwise of twelve-to-sixteen-year-old girls. They stood around and itched and squinted in the heat. The farmer's wife performed for them household chores as they'd been done before the people had lost their sense of their own heroic history, their special characteristics and mission. She beat clothes on a rock. She threshed grain by hand. The girls were not the best audience. Whatever their enthusiasm (or lack of it) for the new regime there was a universal sense that in terms of household chores the glorious old ways were backbreaking and idiotic.

Boys loitered around the square to hoot and show off and otherwise establish themselves as annoyances. Karel usually found an unobtrusive position across from Leda where he could watch her in peace. She saw him sometimes and half-rolled her eyes to communicate how dreary and pointless she found all of this. At other times she didn't notice him. At no point did she seem to recognize or acknowledge that she was the sole focus of his attention.

She wasn't there. She'd been missing more of these things. He admired and envied her independence even as he regretted the lost opportunities to see her.

Old men contemptuous of the regime sat under the café awnings and followed the farmer's wife's efforts with head shakes and derisive low comments, hawking and spitting in the dust. She was holding up a whisk, to a purpose Karel could not make out. He decided to wait around on the chance Leda would show up late, and because he had nothing else to do.

Besides the old men in the café he could see three uniformed men lounging around a table. They wore the pale gray uniforms with black-and-white trim of the Civil Guard. The one clearly in charge was a handsome man with impressive cheekbones. They seemed uninterested in the league. One of the old men bumped the one in charge, and then said something. The other two uniformed men looked away. The one in charge seemed composed. He stood, took the old man's hand in his, and flexed it back onto itself, so that Karel could hear the cracking where he was. The old man howled and went down on his knees, and the one in charge let him go. There was a small uproar. The other old men surrounded the one in charge, who turned from them and took his seat as if he had no further interest in the incident. Karel thought something would happen but the uniformed man turned, again, and looked at the old men, and they stopped what they were doing. They helped the hurt one up. They escorted him across the square. He held his hand out in front of him and made small outcries. The uniformed man looked over at Karel and saw him watching. He did not look upset or surprised. The other two uniformed men leaned closer to say something to him, and he nodded, still looking at Karel.

Karel's face heated, and he backed into the shade. Some children on the other side of the square were playing a game involving beating each other on the arms with whip-like reeds. The dust rose at their feet like miniature weather patterns. Where the road began to lead out of town, passersby swerved to touch a begging midget for luck. Under the awning near the uniformed men a large dog, tawny in the sunlight, placed a paw on a smaller dog's back, as if to hold it still for contemplation.

He moved farther from the café and the uniformed man's gaze. With Leda gone he tried eyeing other girls. He felt the uniformed man watching with him. A blonde too old for the meeting sat on a bench in the shade with a vacant expression and her hands crossed on her knees. Her lower lip was drawn slightly into her mouth. She bobbed her head every so often against the occasional flies. He looked back at the café, and the uniformed men were gone.

He had written on his last school essay that he was not unhappy never talking to anyone or getting to know anyone well. His teacher had disapproved and commented on his unhealthy attitude. He'd thought of explaining later that like everyone else he wanted to be part of things, but had not. He was not popular in school. He had his reptiles and the Reptile House, but besides Leda, no friends. He had at some point become a hesitant, stammering speaker, and he blamed his father. He was excluded from all cliques, including the outsiders' clique. At times he would stand in a group listening to the talk and someone would say something incomprehensible or meaningless and the group would break into noisy laughter, leaving him standing there like an imbecile, like a tourist subjected to obscure jokes by the natives.

The blond girl drew her hair slowly back into a ponytail and held it, her elbows out. He envied in people like her their effortless adaptation to the world. He was always puzzling it out, trying to understand and possess by observation. He never succeeded, and he was usually left with something like a sad, studious awe for the spectacle around him.

The league meeting was winding down. He turned from the square and came face to face with the uniformed man from the café. His breath stopped, and the man lowered his eyelids and smiled. There was a badge on his chest of a sword penetrating a nest of snakes into a skull. He moved aside to let Karel by. Karel left at a trot, following two men hauling a pig by the nose and legs to a waiting cart.

He wanted to tell his father about the uniformed man, but naturally his father was gone. He spent the rest of the day in the shade of the back garden watching red-and-black diamondback beetles climb his chair leg. The street was completely quiet. The uniformed man's gaze still bothered him, and he worked to put it out of his mind. He thought about storm surges and swelling green waves in the funnel-like bay below their old house. The houses had been packed so tightly into the cliff slope that he could spit into his neighbor's window. The third floor on one side was the ground floor on the other. Red brick patios with weedy gardens stepped downward and dropped away to the port below. Lines of foam edged the beaches.

His new house was flat and dry and hemmed in by desert. All there was for him here was reptiles and Leda. Some ants were circling the flybag at his feet, interested in the bran and milk mash. He picked up the faint dry smell of sage and something else and thought of the sea smell from his old home, especially after a rain.

His father did not come back for dinner, and he made for himself a thick bean soup with some onions and a little meat. He ate it out in the back garden, listening. When it was dark enough that his plate was only a dim glow on his lap he went inside. At the kitchen table he drank some coffee, the sound of the metal cup on the saucer desolate and thin. He sighed and leafed through his reptile study sheets until he found a buried take-home essay he had neglected, due Monday. Across the top he had doodled the labials of the Komodo dragon, and along one column he'd drawn a desert iguana improbably perched in a creosote bush. He reminded himself with dismay that he had to erase all of this. Near the iguana's open mouth he'd written: *Karel Roeder. Standard Seven. Political Studies.* That was as far as he had gotten. The questions were unappetizing. He knew what his instructor wanted—only the chronically absent or stone-deaf didn't—but had no enthusiasm for organizing the material into something readable. He reread the questions the way he would read the ingredients on a can he had no intentions of opening. He read his notes for the answers, scribbled underneath as the question sheets had been passed out:

—man can live only as member of nation, therefore nation transcends group interests. Strong only as cohesive unit.

—Committee of Representatives institution that "expresses political agreement of Government and Nation." "Documents unity of Leader and Nation."

—Party inseparable from Gov.

—Party functions by finding and uniting most capable people "thru selection conditioned by day-to-day struggle."

He flopped it over. He'd finish it tomorrow. He sat at the kitchen table listening to the clock, unhappy, and when it reached ten he got up and climbed the stairs to his bedroom. He left the lidded pot with the remainder of the bean soup and a spoon and a bowl on the table where his father would see them.

From his bedroom he could make out a policeman talking in the glow of a telephone box. The town was dark except for an occasional window and a single bulb lighting the square in the distance. He turned his light out and stayed where he was in the darkness, waiting for his father, or the Schieles, or someone. He saw no movement except the lighter tones of passing clouds. He pulled a chair over and dozed and woke to see the dark shapes of dogs standing in people's front gardens and peering in their windows. When he fell back asleep even his dreams had become dull and bland, absorbed with packing and unpacking large suitcases from a trunk.

School was closed, Monday, with a curt sign posted on the chained double doors announcing it would reopen in a week. The official reason provided was unsafe stairways that demanded immediate attention. Karel's father said the real reason was the realignment of the teaching staff. Whatever the reason, Karel lay quiet in his bed Tuesday morning, his arms at his sides, in gratitude.

His father knocked once and said without opening the door that Albert had called from the zoo and had asked if he wanted to work extra hours in view of his free time this week. He could hear his father's resentment at having to pass on such messages, and he regretted it. When he came downstairs he said, "Who wants coffee?" rubbing his hands together in a parody of anticipation, but the house was empty.

He bought a small hard roll at the café and ate it on the way over to the zoo, wishing he had some juice. The zoo was on a rise along the south end of town, with a view over the square to the northern mountains. It was considered one of the attractions of the region. The new regime was enlarging its budget, and Karel hoped his apprenticeship would become a full position. The site was already bounded by an old stone wall and was being further surrounded by a moat. The moat was at that point a trench. There was to be a bigger restaurant, a concert garden, a monkey island, a new pheasantry, and expanded maintenance and administration buildings. The zoo held, besides the Reptile House, flamingos, cranes, parrots, and endless other birds, camels, llamas, tapirs, wild asses, antelope, bears, wolves, bison, ibex, wild sheep, bongos, gaurs, all sorts of deer, a mountain lion, and three monkeys. They were organized haphazardly, isolated from the looping walkways provided for visitors. In a corner of the complex a square pit represented the promised aquarium. A sign advertized its coming attractions. The centerpiece of the advertising was a lurid painting of some piranha ("the Sanitary Police of South American Rivers"). The Reptile House was next to the pit, near some neglected boojum trees. It was made of ugly yellow brick. A drab sign with an adder's head in silhouette marked the door. As a department of the zoo it was inadequately supported. In terms of commonly shared materials it always had to make do with whatever the mammal or bird staffs had discarded or could spare. Even with that, it was a model of organization and cleanliness. It held 301 reptiles in 116 species and was roofed with louvered shutters over tessellated glass to control the daylight. There was a crocodile hall and tiers for lizards, tortoises, and snakes. The louvered shutters worked badly but were supposedly to be fixed. There were some prize exhibits: a giant tortoise, a green-and-yellow crested basilisk, an impressive poisonous snake collection, including an albino krait, and two nine-foot Komodo dragons. Karel spent most of his time helping with the feeding and cleaning cages. He had less contact with the prize exhibits but visited them before and after work and was sure a promotion would mean greater responsibilities in those areas.

At the service entrance one of the older staff members looked at him indifferently when he arrived and dumped a sack of rotten turnips at his feet. Karel checked the menial work orders at the food kitchens and storehouses, the hospital, the quarantine station, and the masons' workshops. In the carpenters' workshop three men and an apprentice were standing around a box trap as if it were impossibly complex or mysterious. He could hear what he guessed to be the nearby male ibex butting heads; the sound was like great rocks being driven together.

Albert passed him from behind, carrying a sack of fish heads. He said only "Good morning," and nodded to indicate Karel should follow. They crossed to the Reptile House, white hairs atop the old man's head waving lazily in the breeze. He was wearing a white lab coat that had a footprint on the back of it. They entered the building through the rear and stopped opposite the enclosure for the giant tortoise so Albert could scrutinize its carapace at length. He eyed one side especially critically, pointing out a stretch of what looked like mold. He didn't say anything. In response to their attention the tortoise rose up on her feet, considered movement, and lowered herself down again.

"Ever feed her something like that?" Karel asked, to break the silence. He indicated the sack of fish heads.

She ate only vegetation, Albert said. Which was about the only type of food she could catch. He turned away from her enclosure and at a crossing hall handed the fish heads to an assistant heading toward the crocodiles.

They stopped again on the snake tier at a glass enclosure that seemed empty. Karel was all attention, trying to be the star pupil. What am I looking at? he thought. Albert tapped the glass. A snake appeared, a hognose, unnoticed in plain view by Karel because Karel was still, as Albert always told him, inexperienced at seeing. The old man's tapping the glass made clear that he'd seen Karel's confusion, and

Karel thumped his forehead on the pane and let it rest there, despairing of ever learning anything. The hognose, a mottled brown with an upturned nose like a shovel lip, rose and hooded its neck and hissed loudly, mimicking a cobra, and then struck at the glass. When Karel didn't move, it rolled over and played dead, its mouth agape and tongue hanging out.

At the lizard tier they stopped beside the desert iguanas. A small gecko looked on from across the aisle, waving its tail like a prowling cat. Albert gathered the long metal tube and a bag of olives left for him against the wall and prepared to enter the enclosure at the end of the row while Karel watched a brilliant yellow iguana, entranced at its way of growing torpid in intricate attitudes. Albert cleared his throat, and Karel came to himself and followed him around the back of the tier.

The old man smoothed his hair and straightened his coat, as if preparing to meet royalty, and then tapped the door loudly to clear away dim-witted individuals who hadn't registered the vibrations of his footsteps. He opened it, gestured Karel through, and followed. They watched carefully where they stepped. Iguanas scattered in various directions and then froze as if playing a children's game. Some froze on branches, others head downward on rock faces. A few squeezed into clefts in the piled shale. Albert was making tiny squeaking noises with his pursed lips. He had his sights set on a small brown lizard with a large head, clinging to a rock not much bigger than itself. He identified it as a crested anole. Not feeling good, he said, but she wouldn't hold still for the noose.

The noose was the usual way of gathering specimens, a thin bamboo pole a few feet long with a string running its length and a tiny lasso dangling from the end. Few lizards seemed to mind having the pole waved cautiously over their heads, and most were gathered this way without harm, after some admittedly exasperating maneuvering of the miniature noose. When the noose tightened they always spread their legs stiffly, as if refusing to believe they were being lifted from the earth.

"So," Albert said, "we resort to drastic measures." He held up an end of the metal tube and fitted an olive into it. He put his mouth to it like a bugle, aimed the other end at the anole, and blew hard. The olive ricocheted off two walls and the anole bounced off the rock and rolled over limp.

A larger lizard scurried to the olive and clasped it, stopping in that position.

"It doesn't hurt them?" Karel asked, amazed.

Albert shook his head, gathering the anole gently into a mesh specimen net. Its small mouth gaped, and Karel could see grain-sized teeth. "Ripe olives," Albert said. "The nomads, when they want to kill them for food, use pebbles or nails." He held the little drooping animal up for Karel's inspection. An assistant passed by and stared at them through the glass. "How would you describe her on a field report?" he asked.

Karel coughed, immediately nervous.

"You'd start with size," Albert said.

"Size," Karel said quickly, and trailed off.

"Extensible throat fan," Albert said. He pointed out the throat sac. He asked Karel if there were other distinguishing characteristics.

Karel nodded, appreciating his tone. He pointed out to Albert the coloration, the crossbands, the compressed tail with a crest supported, Albert demonstrated, by bony rays.

"She loves the sun," Albert said fondly, and prepared to leave.

Karel asked what was wrong with her.

"That we'll find out," Albert said, and he smiled, and patted the anole with his forefinger as he might pat a soap bubble.

Outside the enclosure he went on for Karel's benefit, though he'd been ready to leave. His voice was patient. He offered the information whatever Karel's capacities. She was a member of the Iguanidae family, fourteen genera, with forty-four species native to their range. She was small for the group. Did he notice the five clawed toes? Did he notice the teeth attached to the bony ledge inside the jaw? She'd only lay one egg every couple of weeks. Her mate would defend his territorial range by elaborate behavioral signals that resembled energetic pushups. When they found a mate, Karel would see.

He left Karel to the feeding, and Karel, once he'd returned from the food kitchens, sat among the iguanas and anoles in their enclosure, watching them eat their mealworms and grapes, gazing at his reflection beyond them in the glass, and smiling at passing assistants, who smiled indulgently back.

He stopped by Leda's on the way home. He was so inured to not finding her there that he was already backing away from the hedge, angry with himself for being so pathetic, when he realized he'd seen her. She was sitting in a lounge chair, holding a letter and envelope out in front of her like mismatched socks. He hesitated and then passed through the gap in the hedge to their garden. She said hi and smiled at him as if not wanting to forget something else. While he fumbled and made hand motions of hello, she slipped the letter into a flimsy overseas envelope with a dreamy precision. She was wearing a blue-and-white striped blouse with a gory ketchup stain that had not washed out, and her brown hair fanned across her cheeks. There was a faint vaccination mark on the tan of her arm. Her forehead looked damp. She said, "Well. I haven't seen you in a while," sounding like a much older girl.

"So hi," he said. His hands described a half-wave and caught themselves.

She looked at him steadily, as if she'd forgotten something about him, and set the letter aside with an odd delicacy that stirred him. He felt again reduced in her presence, and to compensate stepped forward for no reason and tipped a planter holding some pale trumpets, flopping them dismally onto the ground and spilling dirt.

"Eep," she said, bending close. She helped him gather the dirt back into the terra-cotta planter. She said her mother would die. She sounded pleased. Her eyelashes were longer at the outer corners, giving her eyes a special slant.

She settled back into the lounge chair while he tried to get the trumpets to remain upright. They tipped and drooped and packing the soil seemed not to help, and finally he left one hand cradled around the stems and tried to settle himself into a comfortable crouch beside them. She produced a bundled blue sweater and attached ball of yarn from somewhere and arranged them on her lap. Her shoulders and the back of her neck were red, and he worried tenderly about sunburn. She was focused on the sweater. There were shortages, and apparently it was being sacrificed for another project. She began winding, her hand a rapid satellite around the ball of wool, and in thin rumples and lines the sweater began to disappear. He was disheartened by her ability to shift in his presence to an abrupt and neutral lack of interest, the way dogs might in the middle of play.

"Don't worry about it," she said. "I'll tell her I knocked it over. Sit in the chair." She pointed to an undersized folding thing that always seemed to be waiting for him. It looked too small even for David, her little brother. He wondered at his most pessimistic if she intended it as a sly humiliation. He sat in it, and it flexed and tottered as it always did. The trumpets slid slowly over. He drummed a finger on his knee like a simpleton.

"How's Nicholas?" he asked. Her older brother was institutionalized locally. She thought it was unnecessary. She battled with her mother about it. She said he had a learning disorder, that was all. Karel hadn't heard her mother's side of the story. He had tried to visit Nicholas once, unsuccessfully, and remembered small groups of patients standing at the gates, staring mournfully at passing children in shorts.

Leda thanked him and said Nicholas was fine. She was pleased he'd asked.

David came out of the house carrying a comic book and sat on the sandy ground between them, puzzled at the richer color of the spilled soil. He looked over at the trumpets with interest but didn't say anything. He was seven years old and had round eyes and a thin face. Karel liked him. He had a way when nervous of hesitating with his eyes averted. He had no interest in the comic book and gave it to Karel.

The comic book was titled *The Party Comes to Power,* and featured the Praetor on the cover in armor, swinging an ax against a horde of cringing demons. Some of the demons had the exaggerated features of the nomads. They'd made the Praetor overly muscular, and he looked silly in armor. The inside had nothing to do with the cover and looked like a pretty boring account of the National Unity Party's rise to power: the two referendums, the national vote, the Praetor's appointment as Guardian of the Republic, and the announcement of the Emergency Revolutionary Defense of the Country. That had been the night Karel's father had been taken away. Karel flipped through it for anything of interest until Leda took it from him and tore it in half. She dropped both halves between them.

David looked at the mess and pinched his earlobe with his forefinger and thumb. He and Karel watched Leda work.

Her hair swayed over the yarn. She was absorbed. He watched the soft motions of her head and the quiet dance of insects behind her, and he felt a fragrant stillness, filling him with expectations of what he didn't know. He watched her expression. The yarn was speeding back and forth, the sweater vanishing from the earth.

Mrs. Schiele came outside carrying a dark brown radio shaped like an egg halved lengthwise. She said hello. She said she'd brought Leda her radio. She was a gentle and standoffish woman, full of warnings for her children about getting entangled in other people's potentially dangerous business. She liked Karel and seemed to feel he was no troublemaker, docile and intelligent enough. He wondered if his relationship with Leda could ever survive such a blow.

She complimented his haircut, and he nodded, embarrassed, running his hand over the crown of his head. His father insisted his hair be trimmed close on the sides in the current military style. It left the hair on top in a haylike mat when he washed it.

"It looks nice," she said.

Leda snorted. David picked something from the spilled dirt and held it to the light like a prospector. The trumpets by now hung horizontally over the lip of the planter. Karel willed Mrs. Schiele not to notice.

"Beautiful day," she finally sighed, and went into the house.

Leda watched her go. Then she tilted her head and peered at Karel. He was growing, she said. Was he bigger?

He said he was. He was growing fast now that they couldn't afford food. His father called him the Stork, always with some of the sadness of a poor provider. Karel thought of her questions as opportunities to talk more, and he was squandering each of them, one by one.

She asked if he wanted to hear the radio. She turned it on.

They listened to a show called *The Party Has the Floor!* The surrounding countries, the nation's enemies, the whole world could go down in flames, the speaker said. Why should the nation be concerned with that? The nation's concern was the nation, that it should live and be free.

There were bulletins from the northern border. The announcer spoke of the difficulties, the courage, and the enthusiasm of the special border patrols. They could hear singing. Some men he identified as wounded shuffled up audibly to the microphone and repeated the information that they were wounded, specifying where. One man in a preternaturally calm voice said, "I have lost my feet."

Leda shut it off. Her smile had disappeared. She said, "I visited the borderlands once, with my father." Her father had died the night of the Bloody Parade. He'd been crossing the street. She talked about him only as a quiet man who'd been an accountant for a gravel yard, who drank beer and read at night. She loved him very much, she said. She left that in unspoken contrast with her mother.

"Were you scared?" Karel asked. The northern mountains were supposed to be dangerous. They rose like walls on the horizon even from this distance. Every year hikers were lost. They died of cold and falls and snakebite before being discovered. The nomads, cause of the border troubles, were also beginning to be blamed.

She shook her head. It was too beautiful, she said. They didn't go way up. They saw a few people, but everyone was so poor.

She talked to him about what it was like. There were rounded, blunt, burned hills, between which were plains of intolerable sun glare and narrow valleys up high in the haze. There were hard dry places completely empty that they called dry lakes, and ugly and bitter pools, never dry on the hottest days, dark and ashy and rimmed with crystals. There were broad wastes open to the wind where the sand drifted in thick waves. There was this terrible pure blue of the sky. Karel could see it all and had to restrain himself from touching her. He thought: She's my age. How is it she's not amazed at herself?

He got home uncertain of what had happened and shining with the experience regardless. The house was quiet and dark. His father was sitting in the kitchen, clearing his throat in the repeated way he did when he was upset. Karel knew immediately that something involving his job hunt had disintegrated. He said a cautious hello and turned on the light. His father winced.

"You're sitting in the dark," Karel said.

His father looked at him to indicate he knew that.

He went about the busy fiction of beginning preparations for supper, with no clear idea what he was making or looking for in the various cabinets. He ended up with an unlikely array on the counter before him: a cheese grater, a large spoon, a shallow pot, a can of yams. His father gazed on the assortment impassively.

"Hungry?" Karel asked. It was dangerous to ask what was wrong, and dangerous not to.

"Look at him," his father said. The suppressed anger in the voice shook him. "Comes in like there's nothing wrong, like the world's a—" He gave up, unable to think of the word. He returned his attention to the table, as though it were the least repellent object in the room.

"What's wrong?" Karel asked.

"What's wrong," his father said.

Karel was peeved, tired of this. He rubbed his face. "Did you get turned down for something?" he asked.

"I got turned down for something, all right," his father said. He was very close to violence. "You're an imbecile, you know that? How did I get such an *imbecile* for a son?" He rode the word with such stress his head bobbed.

Karel looked at the counter, not seeing clearly.

"Your mother was right about you," his father said in distaste, as if that settled the matter.

The emotional swing from Leda to this was too abrupt, and Karel could not help tears. "What did she say?" he challenged. "She never said anything."

His father didn't respond. He seemed to have the ability to say anything he wanted and then forget he'd said it. He seemed as well not to realize Karel remembered. Karel knew when he hurt his father, he couldn't control himself and was sorry even as he did it, but his father wasn't sorry for anyone, either when they fought or afterward.

They remained where they were, wishing they had someone other than each other. "We don't have anything to eat," Karel said. "For supper." He intended it as an indictment.

His father ignored him. He folded a paper napkin into a little boat and set it on the table. "I don't want to have meals with you," he said. "For the next few days, you eat before I come home."

"Fine," Karel said. He shoved the cheese grater into the pot with a crash and left the room.

Once upstairs he heard the pop and crackle of a radio and he shouted, his anguish making him reckless, "Where'd we get money for a radio? Who has money for a radio?"

His father walked softly to the bottom of the stairs, dangerously close to coming up. "I bought it," he said. "I thought we were coming into some good luck."

Karel lay on his bed without moving, terrified. After a moment his father returned to the kitchen.

A voice furry with static spoke for the Committee for Popular Enlightenment.

"You couldn't even buy a good one," Karel said, as loud as he dared.

There was more popping and snorting of the radio being tuned. We call on our people, the voice said, for simple enthusiasm and simple pride in their national destiny, not for melancholy and sophistication.

The voice reported, as if its limitless patience were about to be overtaxed, even more provocations to the north, and added that listeners could rest assured that the government in their name intended to brook no more nonsense and to defend the country offensively along those borders.

The radio was off. There was a muffled squeaking sound, and a dull clank. Was his father eating the yams?

"Do you want help?" he called, despite himself. "Do you

want something warmed up?" His voice rang on the bare walls.

There was no answer. There was a small crash. His father rarely got cans opened without incident, never uncorked wine bottles without picking to bits half of the cork, never built things, never took things apart. Karel remembered him gazing at the flybag while Karel built it. He imagined his father downstairs, standing with dull lassitude before the yams, unable to understand the unfairness of things, unable to understand his own inertia, unable to understand at this point how his life could have gotten away from him. Years ago he'd watched his father go through the first stretch of unemployment. For whole afternoons he'd lain in bed looking at his hands or something ordinary like a chair. Karel had poked around the house, frightened and depressed, and had thought even then that if it happened again he'd leave. He hadn't gone anywhere yet. Oh, Leda, he thought melodramatically, and didn't finish, feeling selfish and childish.

He went up to the storage space above the house. The heat was stifling and close, and the single covered window seemed darker than the rest of the room. In a box for machine parts he found a woman's sun hat he didn't recognize, and a pair of shoes. His father kept his mother's things packed away. That was another reason they had moved: his father had told him once that the city had been his mother's place, their house had been his mother's house, and his father had gotten tired of trying to stick it out, and for what? The Schieles had moved after Mr. Schiele's death, and Karel, who'd been resisting his father's periodic threats to leave the city, had performed a complete about-face. He'd spoken, with some guilt at his own deceitfulness, about the possible opportunities and the lower cost of living in the desert. He had not mentioned the Schieles.

He had very few memories of his mother. One of his earliest, possibly spurious, was of a woman in warm gray and pale blue huddled near him on a tiled floor. There were snatches remaining from her funeral—an unpleasant-smelling man leaning close and telling him not to worry, another woman saying there was no doubt where his mother had gone, but not mentioning where, and a decision on his part, staring at the coffin, that she would be back by Saturday—but most of the rest was lost. He pulled a photo from a box of train and ferry tickets—why had his father saved train and ferry tickets?—and the photo, curled at the edges like a proclamation, was of the seashore, with a grainy woman by a café table in the middle distance gazing out at some boats. Her face was hidden by a hat. She was in a perfect circle of shade. The hat was not this hat, but something about it, the brim or the spray of flowers near the band, was familiar. There was nothing else in with the tickets.

He set the smaller box aside and rummaged a little more. He thought of Leda and her mother, Leda remarking distantly once while walking with him that they were happy enough in their own separate ways. He found a postcard of the desert—his mother had visited here!—sent back to the city and his father.

He knelt beside the box and turned the card over once or twice in his hands. The handwriting was careless and very adult. It was dated with the year, and he calculated he'd been two at the time. Had she left him with his father? The card read: *Simon: It's hot and glorious here, as we expected. I find blue lizards in my overnight bag. There are mineral springs and ruins to visit and travel is arduous but very inexpensive. This drawing is of a great gate from the early Empire, not nearly so impressive in person. Hope all is well—*

He sat with his back to the box for a long time, the sadness of not having been mentioned at all in a card from his lost mother growing in him like a bubble. When his father called him, he went downstairs, trailing his hand on the wall, acknowledging the truce.

Hiring was announced for a Public Works project in the area and Karel was sent to Naklo, a little town near the border, to pick up an application for his father. The zoo was not open, and he found when reporting there in the morning only a note to the staff on the outer gate: *Lights out in the Reptile House. The Civil Guard has decided to carry on a political inspection. We must, they suggest, be patient. —Albert.* So he had no convincing reason for avoiding the trip.

The noon bus dropped him at his stop an hour late. His father had gotten instructions by telephone on how to proceed from there, and Karel stood in an unfamiliar square peering at his father's scrawl. He took a numbered trolley to another part of town. He found himself growing anxious as less and less of what they passed seemed to coincide with the instructions. To double-check the number he asked a man across the aisle. The man shrugged before he finished the question.

The trolley stopped with a sway and a jolt at a narrow side street to allow a small convoy of Civil Guard buses to pass. A young man scrabbled half out of the open window of the last one, hanging upside down and waving his arms to try to get his balance. Someone had him by the belt loops. He dropped lower suddenly with a jerk and then tumbled onto the road. The woman next to Karel gave an exclamation as if she'd seen something acrobatic at the circus. The young man pulled himself onto the trolley and clambered inside. He was bleeding from the top of his head. The buses on the side street were stopped and guards were trying to get off. The trolley pulled away into traffic.

They were all quiet at the conductor's courage. He was looking at the man with his rearview mirror. The woman next to Karel took out a handkerchief and gestured toward the blood. She said, to break the silence, that it was terrible what these people thought they could get away with.

Halfway up a hill the conductor stopped the trolley. They could hear sirens and honking behind them. The young man scrambled out and disappeared between two houses.

So Karel never got to the application office. All the passengers were loaded onto another bus and driven to the local police station, where they waited to be interviewed. The trolley conductor disappeared. The woman who'd been next to Karel said, "This is terrible. This is an outrage," while they waited. Karel was interviewed next to last—naturally, he thought—by a beefy sergeant tired of the whole business whose interrogation lasted all of four or five minutes. The sergeant asked Karel what he saw, and Karel told him. The sergeant asked if the man had any confederates, and Karel said no. The sergeant asked if he could describe the man, and Karel said truthfully he hadn't seen him too clearly. The sergeant frowned, his pencil making edgy little anticipatory lines on a pad, and told him he could go.

By the time he reached the application office it was closed and he'd missed the last bus besides. He got a long and meandering ride home on the front of a manure truck, holding his breath futilely and swatting at flies even after it was too dark to see.

The next morning he went over Leda's to tell her the story. Mrs. Schiele told him that Leda was busy. He could wait in the living room. She sat opposite him with a great exhalation, as though she believed it was her unhappy job to entertain him until he drifted away from boredom. She gazed at the piano, a small black upright polished and shiny with disuse. "Do you play?" she asked, though the question seemed ridiculous. She said she once had, and left the rest to his imagination. She indicated her hands—arthritis? he wondered—and rubbed her knuckles as if to remind herself of the pain.

"What an artist the world lost," Leda said impatiently, coming into the room to flounce herself down on the fat green chair opposite him.

Her mother sniffed. "I tried to get my daughter to carry on, to have a little—"

"Oh, stop," Leda said. "So what's the news?"

Karel told her about the trolley. Mrs. Schiele was looking at him, and he realized he had a dirty arm on a lace doily that looked to be a hundred-year-old family heirloom or something.

Leda was appalled. She said that this was the kind of thing that everyone was supposed to be patient about. The NUP was always asking for patience while it consolidated its position and ferreted out those working against the unity of the country.

Her mother tsked.

"I don't know *what* I would have done," Leda said. "These people are such *pigs!*"

"Leda!" her mother said.

Leda put her hand to her forehead. She said, "What they

get away with is so outrageous it makes me want to scream."

Karel winced. She was too loud. He felt cowardly, ready to agree with anything to win her over.

Her mother got up and looked ready to leave the room. "Miss Politics," she said. "Fifteen years old and she knows better than everybody else."

"I *do,*" Leda said with some vehemence.

"So when you're old enough *you* be Praetor," her mother said.

"When I'm old enough I'll help throw all them out," Leda muttered.

"You shouldn't talk like that," her mother said vaguely. She rubbed her eyes with both hands and sighed.

"You're scared of everything," Leda said. "Daddy's ghost, this place, everyone around us."

They were quiet. Karel felt intensely uncomfortable, and politically too ignorant to know what he should be arguing.

"You listen to rumors," Leda's mother said. "This party's like the rest. You don't remember things before."

"I know," Leda said with that sarcastic look she had. "I'm too young for things."

"Why do you always twist my words?" her mother demanded.

Leda was silent.

Her mother rubbed her knuckles and the back of her hand. She was still standing in the middle of the room. She said, "You talk about border troubles and things you hear about. I'm talking about things I see, things like more jobs and less fighting and not a new government every ten minutes, things like that."

"I can't talk to you," Leda said, as if announcing the weather.

They sat quietly, Karel surrendering his hope of an invitation to lunch.

"They say in their own Party program, which they even published, what they're going to do," Leda said, sadly. "Twenty-five points."

"Who reads programs? Do you read programs?" Mrs. Schiele asked Karel. He shook his head. "The National Unity Party is something new," she said. "That's all it is."

"Well," Karel said, standing.

"What about all the troubles, all the beatings, the people who are missing?" Leda said. "You think it's just foreigners it happens to?"

"I think troublemakers who won't mind their own business are getting into trouble," her mother said sharply. "You leave trouble to the police."

"You're an idiot," Leda said.

"Leda," her mother said.

"I'm sorry," Leda said, frustrated. *"You're* awfully quiet," she told Karel.

"Oh, leave the poor boy alone," her mother said, working into an anger. "You have to badger him as well?"

"Do I badger you?" Leda asked.

Karel shook his head, his mouth half-closed.

"There," Leda said, without triumph. "See?"

"There's no sense arguing with you when you're being impossible," her mother said stiffly. She left the room.

"So don't," Leda called after her.

"You'll just disagree with whatever I say," her mother said from the kitchen.

"So test me," Leda said. "Tell me the NUP are idiots."

"I *don't* like you using that *word!*" her mother yelled. She was standing in the doorway, brandishing a large stirring spoon.

Leda quieted, frightened. Her mother left the doorway.

Karel cleared his throat. He put his palms together in front of his mouth.

Leda swung her legs around and hauled herself from the chair and suggested a walk. "We're going to go get into trouble, Mom," she called from the front step, and then shut the door behind her when her mother didn't answer.

On the walk Karel asked about Nicholas, to change the subject.

"That's one good thing," Leda said. "The NUP says too much aid goes to places like mental institutions. Naturally. They probably all escaped from one. I'm hoping they'll just abolish the whole thing and send him home."

"Where do you read all this stuff?" Karel asked. Leda shot him a look, and he didn't pursue it. "You don't like Nicholas's . . . place, huh?" he said instead. "I thought they teach them skills and things."

"I'll tell you what the kids learn," Leda said. "They learn to clean filthy things. They learn to sweep. Sometimes to count. I asked Nicholas once what he was learning and he said he was learning to be quiet."

Karel nodded sympathetically, chagrined that this topic too had exploded. He hadn't had any idea things were that bad there.

"I don't know whether to cry or hit people when I go there," she said. "It's so terrible."

"I'll go with you next time," he offered. Another, shadow part of him said, *Are you out of your mind?*

"You want to?" Leda asked, and stopped, and looked at him closely. "Thanks," she said, and squeezed his arm. "That's nice."

He was pleased with the squeeze and nursed the feeling for a while.

They continued walking, and he asked where they were going. Leda said the cave with the bats. Did he know about it? She'd show him.

How did *she* know about it? Karel asked. She said David had taken her.

The sky was red and violet in streaks. He walked along thinking of the endless number of things in this town he knew nothing about. Leda stopped opposite a shallow-looking niche in an exposed rock formation. She said, "It's late. But we won't go far." She sat on the ground and then lay back and edged sideways into the niche. She disappeared.

"Come on," she called, her voice muffled. There was some scraping. Karel sank to his hands and knees and saw a much darker slot deep in the niche, through which the top of her head bobbed. He crawled in, trying to stay low, and banged his shoulder on the rock. His exclamation of pain echoed around him. At the slot he slid over sideways and his legs tumbled down onto Leda shoulders, and he apologized until she said it was okay, already.

They settled themselves in a black oblique space as big as a car backseat. He was excited at being this close to her. She was moving stones. He spread both hands on the dark rock around him and said something inadequate to express his enthusiasm. This was amazing. She was a girl. She said, "This part's narrow," and started in feet first on her back, using her elbows on the sloping sandy floor of the tunnel. With everything but her head and shoulders in, she hesitated, and twisted around to look back at him. "You sure you want to do this?" she asked. "You won't be scared? The bats if you see them are pretty ugly."

Karel made a dismissive spitting sound. He asked her if she wanted him to go first. She shook her head and slipped into the darkness, making a light scraping noise. It reminded him of a shovel being drawn over sandy soil.

He eased himself into the hole feet first when he judged her far enough ahead. It was cold on his back, and he took a last look through the entrance up at the sky, already deep blue in the twilight, and then began edging downward.

He could just make out the rock face, three or four inches over his. He could raise his head only a little, and couldn't see over his feet down into the darkness anyway. He thought of scorpions and heavy bird spiders, and the back of his neck prickled. How was it she wasn't scared? "Hey," he said, trying to keep his voice level. "Hey." He stopped.

There was a rustling ahead and then silence. "What?" Leda said.

"How are we going to see anything?" he asked.

"I've got a candle," Leda said. Karel could hear her crawling again.

He scrabbled downward for minutes, trying to estimate the distance they were traveling, his rear and elbows thumping along. He wondered what sort of reptiles they might come across. Some skinks, some blind lizards, the sort of translucent, helpless-looking things he saw in books. It was stupid, he supposed, to just climb into places like this, but then he told himself that if Leda knew about it, it must be pretty well traveled. He kept crawling, not very reassured. He thought about finding and bringing back a new species of something, docile and unique. He thought he should have brought his hoop snare and specimen bag. He passed a part of the wall that was dripping, and he felt colder. He could smell guano. He hoped that that wasn't what he was feeling along the walls and floor. "Yick," Leda said, ahead of him.

He bumped his tailbone painfully on a ridgelike rise. He

stopped, easing down off his elbows and lying flat on his back.

"Hey," he said again. He could feel cold air sweeping up from below, over him.

"*What?*" Leda said, a little exasperated. She was much farther ahead.

"How much farther is this?" he asked.

"We can go back if you want," Leda said. The guano smell was much stronger. Then she said, "You hear that?" Her voice came up the shaft like a whisper.

He stopped and rubbed his lower back, chilled. He craned his head up as far as he could and looked over his feet down into the darkness. He listened.

"What *is* that?" Leda asked. Karel couldn't hear anything. He strained, frightened. He began to pick up the faintest puffs, bursts of air, chuffings, like someone in a distant room displacing air with sheets of paper. There was a scratching, and Leda lit her candle and the yellow glow radiated up the circular tunnel. Karel could see his feet and Leda's head, and her hand cradling the flame. The walls around him were covered with long sheetlike stretches of guano. He groaned.

"It's the bats," Leda said, and one spiraled up the tunnel with supernatural finesse, planing over her head and looping and undulating right over Karel with a whispery sound, its tiny black eyes glittering.

He was going to remark on that, delighted, when down the tunnel a huge wind seemed to be building, and Leda gave a cry. Another bat fluttered by, faster, like some black, wrinkled fruit, and he looked down and the roaring grew louder and the bat shapes exploded out from below the darkness, extinguishing Leda's candle and filling the tunnel top to bottom and roaring all around them. He jerked back and crossed his hands over his face. They were a torrent, unbearably thick and furious in the darkness, colliding with the walls, the ceiling, his head, rocketing and pinballing by and landing on him everywhere, piling up in confusion below his feet, climbing him awkwardly, stumbling as others buffeted them from behind. He felt them squirming into his pants legs and he shrieked and thrashed. The crawlers were reaching his head and arms, fighting for position and leaping into flight, tensing their little claws on his forehead and ears, propelled by his violent twisting. His cheeks were brushed and swept with fur and leathery flapping, and he revolted, turning left and right, slapping and clawing at his face. He could hear even through the din Leda's sobbing. He tried to get to her and couldn't. He turned his face to the rock and tried to submit, but they didn't let up, and he was suffocated by the smell and the sound and the overwhelming feeling of being crawled on everywhere, and he cried out for her and for help and wanted to bang his head against the rock wall until it stopped, and he stamped and kicked the walls and scraped his hands until finally, suddenly, they began to subside. He could hear again, the volume dropping steadily, and then there were only a few stragglers flitting by, or laboring up his shirt front. He beat them off, hurting himself with his violence. They made tiny squeals.

Leda was still sobbing. He shivered and shook and furiously scratched and rubbed himself. He crawled down to her and tapped her with his foot, to reassure her, and she shrieked and started crying again. He rested a foot on her shoulder, unable to reach her with his hands. Together, after a wait, they climbed back up the tunnel. The darkness beyond the cave was complete enough now that they had to negotiate their way out slowly, sniffing and choking, by touch. Outside the cave they held on to each other, sobbing, and then Leda pulled away from him and ran home.

His father helped him clean up. He was covered with scratches and dirt and guano and acrid bat urine. He explained he'd been in a cave, and there'd been bats, but couldn't bring himself to say any more, and he started crying, waving his arms fruitlessly and ashamed to be so childish.

His father patted his shoulder and sat back on the edge of the bathtub, looking at him glumly. "What a mess, huh?" he finally said. He got up and opened the bathroom door softly, as if out of consideration. "What a mess your mother left me with," he said.

He dreamed that night he was swimming under a featureless white sky in a dead-calm ocean, in complete silence. The horizon was flat and smoothed in all directions, and he had little trouble staying afloat. He could faintly hear his own splashing. It echoed claustrophobically like splashing in a bath. Brightly colored ceramic balls floated by every so often, the reds, oranges, and deep blues striking. The water was completely glassy, ripples from his exertions flattening immediately. The light seemed artificial. He gradually became aware that he was swimming near the clifflike black hull of a huge ship—a theatrical prop of some sort? he wondered—and in the far distance, while he watched, a silent and giant wave swept across the horizon, hundreds and hundreds of feet high.

• • •

He stayed in bed the next day until late afternoon. He thought about the way as a child he'd collected geckos by sliding them headfirst into empty beer bottles. He thought about the speckled lizard that came every morning onto his stone table to share his breakfast on their old patio in the city. The lizard had been fond of brown sugar, and when it drank the water he set out in a shallow dish it rested its throat on the lip.

When he got up and went downstairs his father was preparing drinks for himself and a man named Holter, whom Karel had met once before. Holter had met Karel's father while they still lived in the city and had told him about the opportunities out in the desert. Karel knew that his father hated to keep pushing Holter about it, but also resented the fact that Holter hadn't come up with anything yet, and had more or less ignored them. Holter nodded at Karel as if he lived there. It turned out he was talking about a possible job. Karel's father wouldn't say what sort of job. When Karel asked Holter, the man put his finger to his lips and mimed a shushing noise.

His father was making the horrible mint-and-grain-alcohol thing he called the Roeder Specialty. Karel stood in the kitchen doorway. The sensation of the bats' claws on his neck and arms refused to go away. He closed his eyes tightly and opened them again. His father asked if he'd seen the pestle. Karel doubted they'd ever had one. His father told Holter they needed a pestle to do the job right and then ground the fresh mint leaves into the bottoms of their glasses with a fork. The fork made an unpleasant noise on the glass.

His father held one of the drinks up to the light. The mint leaves swirled helically around the glass, creating the impression of swamp water.

Karel sat down at the table, overcome with unexpected affection and sadness. His father only wanted some purpose to his life, to be happy, to be unashamed of himself and his accomplishments. What did he lack? Some sort of energy? Will? Luck? He'd once told Karel in a café during one of his lowest periods that all he was doing was prolonging himself.

His father continued scuttling his fork around as if with enough work the drink would become appetizing. He smiled at Holter, and Holter looked at him curiously.

What sort of job was being offered Karel didn't know. He didn't like Holter. Though he knew it was wrong he hoped things wouldn't work out.

Holter extended his feet and flexed them at the ankles, looking at them with satisfaction. "I work so hard that afterward I'm too tired to enjoy myself," he said.

His father cleared his throat and asked Karel about school. He looked ready to give up on the drinks.

Karel told him flatly that he didn't think he'd like the new subjects. The same reptile study sheet was still on the kitchen table. For some reason it depressed him.

His father said he'd study the subjects he was given and like it, but Karel recognized in his voice the tone he assumed when talking tough as a way of compensating in advance for giving in.

There was trouble in the schools, Holter told them. The schools were still a problem area. These things didn't happen overnight. The Party *was* governing on an ongoing emergency basis, with the Praetor holding the government in trust until the new constitution could be worked out. It was unclear to Karel, toying with his study sheet, who was working on that problem. Holter added that anyway it was hard for anyone to imagine a constitution that would be preferable to the Praetor.

"People forget," Holter said, "how much had to be overcome simply to unify us. We'd been at each other's throats for years, a conglomeration of selfish interest groups, the plaything of other nations."

Karel's father lifted Holter's glass and the bottom fell out. He stood with the empty cylinder raised as if in a toast.

Karel was set to work mopping up. He didn't know whether to laugh or cry. Holter eyed the mess.

His father lifted the other glass, and again with a faintly musical rush the bottom and contents stayed behind, inundating Karel below with a fresh wave. The grinding had been too much for the glassware.

Holter was only with difficulty persuaded to stay.

They sat in silence, Karel squeezing out great patters of mopped-up liquid into the sink. Holter started in again: everyone had taken advantage of their good nature and internal division; for too long this country had been satisfied with too little. Did they know twenty-one percent of their country received less than eight inches of rain per year?

That was the kind of thing it was good to know, Karel's father said, and they hadn't known it.

No navigable rivers, Holter said. Few forests. And meanwhile, to the north, he asked Karel, what were their nomad neighbors doing?

Karel waited, flapping the wet dishrag. "I'm not completely clear on that," he ventured.

Holter sat back impatiently. Karel's father said, "We need more, I'll go along with that."

Holter got up, shaking his head, and announced he'd

overextended his visit as it was. He shrugged off protests. He thanked them and left, waving from the street.

They watched him go, and then Karel's father sat down disconsolately, looking at the glass cylinders.

"I don't like the Party," Karel said, after a while. He thought about what Holter had called the preventive police measures: people around town had already disappeared magically, like the objects in the flashing reflection of a rotated mirror.

"What do I care?" his father said. "What does that have to do with this?" He indicated the wet floor. "Why am I always talking with you about this? What am I even *doing* here?"

Karel put his head in his hands. He was going to take another bath. He could still smell the guano.

"I don't need lectures from you," his father said. "You can't be any help, keep to yourself." He got up and turned off the light and left the room. Karel sat where he was for a few minutes and then carried the glass cylinders and bottoms to the garbage pail and threw them out. He went to his room. He lay spread-eagled on his bed, feeling the house get darker as his father switched off the lights one by one.

When he finally got back to the zoo, a lot was changed. There were new black-and-white signs in the shape of the National Unity eagle proclaiming new rules, the zoo's history, or pertinent facts (occasionally wrong) concerning an animal group. Odd, arbitrary areas where no one would want to go such as the trash heap behind the food kitchens were now marked PROHIBITED, and walkways and benches were marked ACCESS ALLOWED. Two corners of the administration building had been appropriated for Party advisers. A huge willow older than the zoo that shaded the east end of the Reptile House had been cut down, sawn into segments, and left in a heap.

The new main sign greeting visitors was as tall as Karel and obscured the long view of the antelope and wild sheep enclosures. It read:

> *DEAR VISITOR: WELCOME to our National Zoo, West. We hope very much to give you an experience both pleasant and edifying during your sojourn with us. We ask of you the following:*
>
> *1. PLEASE, DO NOT FEED THE ANIMALS! Many of them do not know when to stop. They spend the day begging, eat too much, lose health, and die. We desire to preserve their health and encourage breeding.*
>
> *2. DO NOT TEASE THE ANIMALS. They need resting hours not only at night. Do not expect them to be active when each individual citizen passes by. Do not throw stones or verbally abuse them.*
>
> *3. DO NOT DISTURB THE ANIMALS' TRAINING. If not trained, they become bored and aggressive. They are kept chained from the evening on, since a chained animal cannot steal his neighbor's food.*
>
> *4. WE HAVE PUT UP BARRIERS FOR YOUR OWN SAFETY. If you do not respect them, you will be hurt and lose personal belongings. We will not be responsible.*
>
> *5. OUR ZOO: A GREEN ISLE IN THE HEART OF THE DESERT AND AN OASIS OF REST FOR THE PEOPLE OF OUR COUNTRY. Nomads and peddlers not allowed.*

A wooden sign on a humped and desolate area near the masons' workshops marked the future site of a huge Carnivore House that would be part of the new regime's expansion of the original "small and primitive" zoo. It would hold "exotic animals sent from all over the world, especially by diplomats serving in new colonies."

He found Albert in his office. He was very mysterious about where he'd been for the last week—Karel had seen nothing of him, despite stopping by the zoo every so often—and finally became short-tempered when Karel persisted. Did he have to report to Karel, too? he wanted to know. He indicated the papers on his desk as a measure of the work facing him. Karel shook his head, hurt, remembering another comment Albert had once made to him: "Don't keep after me. I'm not your father." He considered telling Albert about the bats, but didn't.

As if aware of his mood, Albert announced that today they'd be feeding the Komodos, and so would Karel, if Karel had any interest. It was what Karel had been waiting for, and he was disappointed the opportunity finally came this way, as a consolation prize.

The Komodos were surrounded by a new laminated-glass shield "160mm Thick to Withstand the Enormous Strength of the Animals." Albert was unhappy about it. Previously they'd been in the open, surrounded by a deep moat and wall. He was unhappy too about a new sign that said DO NOT BE AFRAID! THE PANES ARE STRONG ENOUGH! and underneath related stories about tourists on the lizards' home islands being killed and eaten, including one involving the discovery of an arm and shoulder blade with the hand still pathetically holding out a half-eaten roll. Albert felt the old precautions had been more than adequate. The two Komodos, Seelie and Herman, now looked out through the reinforced glass with an untroubled disdain for the excessive safety measures.

It was clear even to Karel that the two had distinctly different personalities. He looked at Seelie and Seelie looked back, with her lizard's oddly neutral, self-satisfied smile. After an inspection she ignored him and wandered from side to side in the enclosure, examining things she'd tramped past countless times. Like all monitors she walked well off the ground, her skin in that light like fine beadwork. Her dull yellow tongue undulated out at points of particular interest. Herman lounged against a slab of rock near the door, as always, as if too bored or stunned to move. Karel stayed where he was, his nose touching the glass: Herman had once in his presence lopped a huge shank of goat meat from a tray Albert had been setting down, the ferocity and force of the lunge all the more shocking because it had come out of such stasis.

Seelie returned to the glass and regarded him. She was surrealistically large, as though he had his eye to a giant magnifying glass. In her dark eye he could read her intelligence and her reptile's blank acceptance of torpor and violence.

Albert was preparing their meal: more goat meat, with eggs. They loved eggs. Their habitat, a reproduction of savannah grasses and brush, looked worn. It had to be maintained at a hundred degrees the year round and roofed with a special glass to allow in the enormous amounts of ultraviolet radiation the reptiles required. For all that the grass was dead in one corner.

Seelie lowered her head and scratched behind an ear opening with her foot. Her claw made a coarse scraping sound through the glass. She froze, forgetting her leg in midair. Herman lapped at nothing and tamped a patch of grass repeatedly. Seelie began to doze. Neither took any notice when Albert entered the enclosure with the tray of meat. The eggs he carried in a long-handled basket.

Karel was allowed to wait for the feeding before going back to work. It was not a small concession: it took twenty-five minutes for Seelie to work up an interest. She crawled completely over the meat and then backed up and tipped the egg basket. When Karel left she had smashed the basket and covered her face with eggshells. Herman was looking on from his sprawl.

He spent the rest of the morning cleaning the tortoise and turtle enclosures while the occupants hunkered down like sullen stones in the corners and waited with mineral patience for him to leave. He was grateful for the time with the Komodos but surprised by how little it had cheered him. While he worked he considered his last glimpse of them, their skins like polished gravel in the hazy and filtered daylight, and their clear dark eyes gazing at him sleepily and expectantly.

The next morning was Monday, and he sat staring at the corresponding date on the calendar in his kitchen, where he'd written: *School again.* He had coffee alone with some desolate lemons set in an earthen bowl before him. At school he kept to himself. On the playground there was a smallish audience for two boys who were setting mice on fire with machine oil. One mouse scampered free, trailing brown oil. As the students formed their lines it crouched in a corner of the courtyard under some discarded broken desks, licking its forepaws furiously. It watched Karel troop into the building.

Attention in class was focused on a kid named Sprute, who was wearing the black-and-white uniform of the Kestrels, the cub organization of the Young People's NUP. Karel instantly knew from his face that he'd been forced to wear the uniform by a parent who didn't know or didn't care what it meant to be the only kid dressed that way in the entire sixth and seventh standard.

Miss Hagen, while she approved of the NUP, disapproved of the violation of the dress code and the disruption it was causing. It was not clear, given the state of things, in just what ways the old rules would be relaxed, and Miss Hagen clearly resented the confusion. The class responded independent of the politics to a difference so extreme it seemed a challenge.

While his teacher confiscated paper clips and other missiles, Sprute was mocked and thumped and prodded. His papers were knocked to the floor. He sat like a soldier throughout it all. Leda, who sat in front of him, did not turn around. The kid behind him drew, when Miss Hagen returned to the front of the room, a long, slow line down Sprute's back with a pencil.

She finally suggested he go home and change. The class cheered, enjoying the uproar for its own sake.

Sprute's eyes filled with tears and he stayed where he was, sitting up straight. He looked at Karel, and Karel was moved so violently by pity for this quiet kid—where was he going to go? Home to change in front of parents who had made him dress like that in the first place?—that he said, aloud, "Let him stay."

It was suddenly quieter. He realized what he'd said and took another horrible second to realize he'd succeeded Sprute as the object of attention. He looked down in an agony of self-consciousness and stammered that it was school; who cared what people wore?

The class digested the surprise slowly. It seemed to be considering whether Karel's outburst represented common sense or an attempt to ally himself with Sprute against them. The kid behind Sprute was caught slingshotting a rubber band and was told that as punishment after school he'd have to pick the nettles out of the small rectangular lawn around the flagpole.

Karel felt bad for him but preferred their system of punishment to the one for the lower standards, where children caught misbehaving were made to wear a sign which read I AM A BAD INFLUENCE until someone else was caught and the sign passed on to that person. Whoever wore the sign Friday afternoon at the end of school was beaten. The arrangement created from Wednesday on a sense of unbearable suspense, complete with last-minute rescues and catastrophes.

They got on with the lesson. There were snorts and sneezelike sounds and badly stifled laughter.

"I'd better not see misbehavior when I turn around," Miss Hagen remarked.

"You won't," someone promised. There were more giggles.

They watched her make vigorous and glossy arches across the blackboard with a wet sponge. She outlined new subjects: *The Nation as a Community of Fate and Struggle. The Soldier as a Moral Force. Heroism. Women in War. The Community and the Struggle for Unification. Hygiene.*

Leda made a disparaging, hissing sound. No one reacted to it.

They would study the Great Trek, the march across the desert plateau to Karel's home city. It had been undertaken by the leadership of the Party in its infancy to dramatize its struggle for recognition. They would study also the example of Bruno Stitt, the fourteen-year-old who had decided to die beside his father rather than abandon him to the foreign marauders overrunning the family farm. Leda sighed audibly. There was no mention of the take-home assignment, which Karel had obviously done for nothing.

He took some listless notes, wondering what the sixth-standarders were making of this. *Answer not in material Egoism, but in joyous Readiness to Renounce and Sacrifice. Do not Stand Apart!*

Her inconsistency with capital letters struck him as evidence of sloppy thinking, though he couldn't say why. He wrote without comprehension, as usual, he thought grimly. He glanced over at Leda. She wasn't writing, and she eyed the board with a critical tilt to her head. He considered her intelligence with envy and frustration. Was she going to fall in love with someone who didn't understand what was going on half the time? Was she going to fall in love with someone who couldn't keep up? Even if he at times made the effort he learned almost nothing, and waited for the moment when a simple question or quiz would expose his ignorance in all its vastness for everyone to look upon, stupefied, as if having opened a kitchen cabinet to reveal a limitless and trackless desert.

In literature they studied Mystical Forebears, whose chantings were transcribed from rock fragments dragged from various archaeological sites. They were so stupid that everyone changed words here and there in the workbooks to mock them: "The skin of our race is roseate-bright, our complexion like milk and blood" became, in Karel's workbook, "The skin of our race will nauseate, right, our soup will be milk and blood."

They were instructed to clip and remove foreign writers from their anthologies—the new anthologies had yet to arrive from the printers—with the explanation that they as a people were the only ones capable of profound and original thought. The foreign spirit, Miss Hagen explained, was like the bee, which worked efficiently and had its place, while their spirit was like the eagle, which with its strong wings pushed down the air to lift itself nearer the sun.

Karel, irritated and lost, wrote on his paper *Bee—Eagle.*

Miss Hagen read from the booklet *Do Not Stand Apart!* There were those, she read, who found it comfortable and soothing to withdraw in a sulk to their own little chamber, to nurse their holy wounded feelings and say, "You needn't count on me anymore; I don't give a hoot about the whole thing." Because their tender sensitivities had been offended by one thing or another they spoiled the joy of achievement for the whole group. Who were these people who refused their obligations? Who were these people?

When she saw their faces she apologized for getting too complicated and promised to talk more about all of this later.

He received a note from Leda which read: *I'm glad you like the Kestrels so much,* and when he tried to catch her eye she wouldn't look.

They watched a filmstrip involving polite members of the Civil Guard teaching methods of terrace farming to grateful and simpleminded nomads. The nomads provided comic relief by doing things like attempting to eat the fertilizers. The day ended with Miss Hagen telling the story of a young boy from a school much like theirs who'd had the courage to turn in his parents, both of whom were working for outside interests. The class reaction was muted. They went home without even the enthusiasm that came from their release at the end of the day or the new opportunity to torment Sprute.

• • •

He changed and went over Leda's. When he peeked through her hedge she was sunning herself in a faded canvas deck chair. Her skirt was raised in a lazy S across her thighs. Her elbows were lifted to the sun. She seemed not to recognize him immediately. She did not move her skirt, and he imagined he saw underpants, of a dreamy pale blue.

On the ground nearby were discarded oil paints, tumbled across a palette like undersized and squeezed toothpaste tubes. David sat near the mess reading with his back to the sun while the breeze turned the pages of his book every so often, in anticipation of his progress.

She asked how things were at the zoo, and Karel told her. She said her skin temperature was about a thousand degrees. She asked if he wanted any mint tea with shaved ice. She said she had started a painting for him, and had given up. She held up as evidence a forearm crisscrossed with blue and yellow paint.

He was thrilled, and sat near the palette and examined the paint tubes for traces of his unrealized painting. The names on the tubes pleased him. Where some of the paint had bubbled out it was still moist, and the skins were resilient and yielding like the skin on boiled milk.

Leda said she hadn't gotten over the bats, and wanted to know if he had. He shook his head. She hadn't told her mother, and asked if his father had helped. Karel said he hadn't, much. She shivered, thinking about it.

She turned the radio on. It was hidden below her in the shade of the deck chair. After some staticky popping there was a howling wind, and then the overheated music of Adventure Hour.

"*This* thing," Leda said.

Karel followed along, dandling a paint tube. The story

was about mountain climbers, one of whom announced hanging over a crevasse that he was doing all of this for the people. He went on to describe the mountain he was mastering, which he called the Ice Giant. An arctic blizzard whistled behind his voice. The Ice Giant was supremely beautiful and supremely dangerous, a majestic force which invited the ultimate affirmation of, and escape from, the self.

"This is a *mountain* climber?" Leda said. Her eyes were closed to the heat.

"I don't understand any of these shows," David said.

A fanfare indicated the climber's triumph, which he confirmed by shouting, "Thus I plant our nation's flag in this wild place." There was a sound effect of the flag going in, sounding macabre, like something being stuck with a knife. Leda changed the station. She waved away an inquisitive fly.

Karel was moved by the notion of the almost-painting and felt a rush of feeling for her, a surge of excitement and longing that could have been audible as he watched her drowse. He shaded his eyes from the sun. She turned on the canvas chair and smiled. She had at that moment the face of a placid, intelligent child, someone younger than David. He was so filled with tenderness that it was only with difficulty that he restrained himself from announcing it whatever the consequences. She sighed and said she couldn't have mint tea alone.

More and more he connected unrelated elements of his life in unexpected ways to her; more and more she would appear, magically, inside a disconnected thought, slipping by without turning her head. They'd been friends since childhood, but she had had many friends, and he felt as though he'd had just her. Around her as he was now he felt the same unreasonable contentment he felt in the presence of old dogs comfortably asleep.

Most of all he wanted to talk to her about it, and couldn't. He spent so many nights burrowing through the whole thing that he was bewildered by the sight of it. Once he'd almost had the courage, walking with her in the shade of an anonymous whitewashed house, but when he'd said, "Leda," and she'd turned to face him, the directness of the clear look that returned his stare had seemed to him so adult and sensual that all he could think to say at that point was "You have nice hands." She had looked at him strangely.

Leda said, "You're quiet today." He focused on David, attempting to induce him telepathically to leave. Mrs. Schiele came out of the house in a sundress and bonnet of a matching peculiar green, carrying a glass of ice water and filling him with impatience.

"I guess I am, too," Leda said.

Her mother greeted them and settled herself into the other chair beside Leda, remarking to David that if he continued reading like that he'd grow up a hunchback. She asked rhetorically if her daughter the princess was speaking to her today, and then said to Karel, "What a battle you missed."

"That's some outfit, Mother," Leda said.

"Such a battle," her mother said.

Leda sighed and said, "We had an argument."

"Arguments like that I hope to have once in a lifetime, thank you," her mother said. The two of them were positioned identically, arms and legs straight out, eyes closed.

"What about?" Karel ventured. He nursed a crazy hope he was the cause.

"The Population Registration Act," Mrs. Schiele said, as

if talking about it once again was inevitable, and talking about it the first time had been a terrible mistake.

"Oh," Karel said, and then realized in an awful and dim way that he sounded like a simpleton.

"Karel gets worked up about these things," Leda said.

"No, I know about it," he protested, but only weakly: he knew some details. The act required registering at the post office. It assigned everyone to a racial group and said that everyone who was one quarter or more nomad had to register that way. What had they been fighting about?

Leda looked over at him. Mrs. Schiele said, "My daughter can argue about the Population Registration Act."

He was curious, but mostly he wanted her mother and brother to go away and for Leda to say "Karel," the way he'd said her name, near that whitewashed wall.

"You young people never see nomads anymore. There are a few who live outside of town," Mrs. Schiele said. "That's a shame, Leda's right. When I was her age we lived closer together. Now you have to make an effort to get to know them."

"Mother," Leda warned.

"Leda doesn't like the idea of renegotiated borders and their getting their own areas," Mrs. Schiele said.

"Now who's twisting words?" Leda asked. "I said they'll get the horrible places no one else wants."

"You're an expert, of course," her mother said. She sipped from her ice water and rolled the glass on her cheeks. "Considering all the troubles, especially after the elections, I'm sure they're happier with their own kind."

Leda made a scoffing noise. A coasting bicycle passed by beyond their hedge, whirring. Her mother was quiet.

Karel cleared his throat. "I don't see anything wrong

with giving them some land of their own that they could work," he said. It was something his father once said.

They both were looking at him. "Then you're an idiot, too," Leda said, with extra heat.

"Leda," her mother said sharply, and the blood rushed to Karel's face. "Say you're sorry."

"Why?" Leda said. "If he talks like an idiot?"

Mrs. Schiele sighed theatrically and looked over at him with a what-can-you-do? expression. Leda lay back, flushed and fidgety. Karel raged inwardly at himself, at that familiar granite feeling of stupidity.

"When I get old," Mrs. Schiele said, as though changing the subject, "I want to be taken care of by a nomad. I wouldn't want somebody else to see me that way."

Leda said nothing.

"Leda had a woman who was half nomad as a nanny," Mrs. Schiele said. "Did she ever tell you that?"

Leda made a bitter, hissing noise.

Karel shook his head, unwilling to anger her further.

"She did," Mrs. Schiele said. "She was wild about her nanny. Told her secrets she wouldn't tell me."

"You can see why," Leda said.

He experienced an odd, powerfully erotic image of interracial contact in a darkened theater, with Leda as nomad. You're depraved, he thought. You really are.

David stood and arched his back painfully, for his mother's benefit. He remained where he was. Mrs. Schiele gave no indication of intending to leave, either. It seemed to Karel that in terms of all he cared about he was moving backward.

"In the early days of my marriage we had to concentrate just on survival," Mrs. Schiele began, and Karel thought in frustration, Now why's she talking about *this?* "My father didn't approve of Leda's father, and didn't give us a bean. Still, it was exciting, we were determined to have a house, determined to have children," she said.

Leda sat up, rubbing her arms. "Mother, you must have made sense once," she said. "But it was so long ago—"

"Oh, hush," her mother said. "Karel's interested, even if you're not."

Go in the house, Karel thought fiercely.

"When I grew up, love and marriage were big things," Mrs. Schiele said. "You were told what you were doing by your parents. And it was your parents' privilege and duty to do that."

Leda announced she couldn't stand another minute of this and they were going for a walk. Her tone made it clear that Karel's comment had not been forgotten and that he was at this point the lesser of two evils. He followed her through the gap in the hedge, waving goodbye. "Have a nice time," Leda's mother called after them.

Her walk had a fluidity and purpose that suggested she knew where she was going. He found it hard to fall into her rhythm and imagined someone seeing the two of them: her glide and his uneven, constant adjustments.

"God," Leda said, "look at that," without indicating what.

"I'm sorry about what I said," Karel told her. "It was stupid."

Leda looked at him and made a lump under her cheek with her tongue. "You're so fake sometimes I don't know what to do," she said.

The comment was more crushing than the one in the backyard, and he knew what she meant: his losing efforts to keep track of her nuances and formulate strategies to win her over.

"I just like you," he finally said. At least it was honest.

"I like you, too," she said. They passed an enclosed courtyard where a black-and-white cat with an eye stitched shut stealthily climbed a ladder to the second story. He had a feeling she was waiting for him to go on. So why didn't he? Did he have any idea what he was talking about?

They passed a stone bench overhung with carpenter bees, and a terrier puppy sleeping in the sun with its mouth ajar, exhausted from a day's hysterics. "I don't know if we'll ever be really good friends, Karel," Leda finally said, looking at the dog, and he felt as though he'd watched a door close on him, locking him out of happiness.

Along the road two women sat unloading baskets of gourds and chatting. On one of the gourds an anole perched, turning his head to examine the vibrations. Leda talked about a friend from school, Elsie, and the night her mother had dozed on the couch and the two of them had drunk sweet fermented wine that Elsie had smuggled in. Elsie kept threatening to throw up and that would make them start laughing all over again, though they had to be quiet. And Elsie's boyfriend came over and tried to get in, but Elsie didn't like him anymore, though he didn't know it. He just stood at the window saying, "Let me in, let me in," in a voice muffled by the glass. Of course, her mother had missed the whole thing.

"Who was her boyfriend?" Karel asked quietly. "What happened to him?"

"I don't think you knew him," Leda said. "We shut the sunshades at one point, and when we remembered them he was gone."

They walked to the very edge of town. The dry brush in front of them extended to the hills in the distance. They turned and headed back. Leda told him more about Elsie, who was always talking about marriage and supported the regime because she liked the colors and because she'd gotten picked as a flower-bearer for the local celebrations of the Great Trek.

Leda asked if he was so quiet because of what she'd said, and he said he guessed so. She apologized.

He smelled flowers somewhere, and sage. Leda said that actually she was worried about Elsie and he said he thought it was a phase, and that Elsie would probably grow out of it. Leda said she thought that was really true and a good point.

She indicated a cloud she thought was shaped like the outline of their country, and not only could he see no similarity but they couldn't even settle on exactly which cloud they were looking at. She talked about a dream she kept having involving a tunnel inset with luminous windows. In the windows she could see coral, sea urchins, and champagne bubbles. She asked him why he supposed blue was a common color among reptiles but not among other animals. She asked him if he thought he wanted to work with reptiles when he grew up. He talked to her about exploring someday in the plateau deserts, about finding new species and setting up a Reptile House where they had everything they needed. She asked what sort of things they needed. He told her about gravels and drainage and vivarium design and food storage, registering her responses and noting with pleasure the way she opened her mouth a little the instant before laughing.

She told him her mother admired his steadiness and devotion to the Reptile House. She said she really liked her mother more than it seemed sometimes. She told him about her nanny, whom she remembered as having a beautiful voice and being magical with injuries and animals. Not an old woman at all, pretty, with dark eyes and hair and a coffee smell. She used to tell Leda she was working to make money for her family. She talked along with the radio to improve her language and told stories about her brothers in the desert while she folded sheets and pillowcases. Leda's mother just fired her one day, to save money, it turned out, though no one told Leda. Her mother said later she hadn't considered the change important enough to merit discussion. Leda had been home sick from school for two weeks afterward and no one could figure out what was wrong. Everybody had been worried. She figured all the money her mother had saved firing the nanny had been turned over to the doctors. She loved her nanny and told her everything, as her mother said, all her secrets. Now all she had was her journal. When Karel asked what kind of secrets, she said she couldn't say, or they wouldn't be secrets.

An article in *The People's Voice* interested him: in the southern swamps the Civil Guard was using snapping turtles tied with rope to retrieve corpses. He tore it out to show Albert. It got him thinking about his old life in the city. It was in the city that he'd first seen a snapping turtle, in a traveling exhibit. It had had a big effect on his growing love of reptiles.

Summers he and Leda played as often as he could talk her into it at the beach. She had other friends but liked him too. They were walloped by breakers when the waves were good, after storms, and scavenged along the shoreline when the sea was calm. Their favorite place was an underwater rock shelf filled with jellyfish slipping by on the action of the waves. They swam furiously with no style but a lot of splashing. Leda thought it was very funny to carry starfish out of the surf on her arms. The sand dried immediately after a wave's departure. When they buried each other they would leave their faces bare, and arrange crosses of pebbles atop their chests.

He remembered the pointed gables of the beachfront hotels and the green cypresses, and one hotel, the Golden Angel, with a painting they both loved in the common room. The subject was a cavalry charge they couldn't identify. It involved a chaotic spread of chargers all in near-collision and all about to burst the plane of the painting and trample the viewer. Whenever they'd had too much sun, the hotel manager, a tubby man with a bald and sunburned head, would allow the two of them, sandy and barefooted, a few moments in the room on the condition they sit on none of the furniture in their damp suits. They'd crouch or kneel on the thick red carpet in front of the painting. The horses' nostrils were dragonish and the eyes oversized with fear and excitement. The dragoons riding them were as relaxed as strollers in a summer garden. The dying or about to be trampled infantry below looked thoughtful and melancholy, as if overrun while unexpectedly drowsy.

Behind the Golden Angel through an alley of oyster shells and cat droppings they found the Seaman's Hostel, where they could get free fish broth and sermons about children alone in a world like this, and farther up the hill the Sea's Trade, a little open-air restaurant that looked down into the harbor where the gulls pecked garbage from around the ships, and where when they had some money they could eat pastries stuffed with pink shredded fish and prawns sprinkled with lime juice and crayfish and young eels that Karel always swallowed in too-large pieces, and a weak wine with some melon that made them feel like teenagers. At night there was a fair and a wheel of fortune with a leather flap slapping against nails and they could buy warm fried fish wrapped in newspaper, and ride on wooden bulls with gilded horns on a merry-go-round in and out of the harsh lights of the ticket booth.

And they loved a place his father called a junk store that featured bins of sheet metal with low glass dividers separating tiny toys: hand-painted soldiers, tin buses, rubber lizards, tiny puzzles, miniature knives and pliers, ocean liners with wavering hand-painted waterlines. White horses, golden dice, purple dolphins.

He had a dream in which Leda led him into a beautiful emerald darkness and talked to him about underground rivers far in the earth, dark caverns dripping with crystalline water. She whispered something so close to his ear it tickled. She pointed to the volcanically unstable island on the horizon known to them popularly as the Roof of Hell. He could see waterspouts like great spirals of glass taking the sea into the clouds. In the harbor she pointed out enormous whirlpools, racing cavities like inverted bells, pulling the sea down into the earth, leaving the surrounding waters weirdly domed.

After that dream he lay there trying hard to remember more, especially about Leda at that age, but found that the details had started to disappear and that he could no more make her return that way than he could have altered elements of the cavalry's charge in the painting they loved. Ultimately all that came back was pieces: her shout, her bare shoulders on the merry-go-round, a yellow shirt he wanted, until he was left only with the dark reach of shadow in the troughs of waves and a glimpse of their discarded shoes on the beach.

• • •

The house was quiet. He looked at the newspaper photo of the snapping turtle. I might as well not have a father, Karel thought. He went downstairs and his father was hungover and reading the rest of *The People's Voice* in search of temporary jobs, wincing at the noise when he rattled the paper. He was holding a pen in his teeth and looked blearily over at Karel and said good morning.

"It's afternoon," Karel said harshly. "I've been home from school for hours."

His father looked hurt and returned his attention to the paper. "I think I got into some trouble last night," he said.

Karel didn't answer. He noted the coffee cup still in the sink, alone, and said, "Didn't you eat anything today?"

Something large upstairs groaned and clanked.

"I think the pipes're gone," his father said. "We're not getting any water." The plumbing shrieked and roared hollowly in response like prehistoric animals in the distance.

Karel went over to the window and looked out. Sprute was leading a group of six or so small boys down the street. One of them was also wearing a Kestrel uniform, with an additional white sash. David was in the group. Karel went outside.

When they reached him he stopped David. The group stopped with him, to wait. Karel asked what was going on. David said he'd been invited to the party following Harold's initiation. Harold was the other boy in uniform. The party had been outlined in great detail by Sprute, who'd been recruiting at the playground. There were going to be picture cards in color with the Party eagle on them and little bundles of white almond candies and for each guest a statue of a boy and eagle together lifting the flag, and cakes and juices and games. Harold's parents and the Party together were paying for it. David had already learned the virtues of the Kestrels: Undoubting, Undivided, Rock-Ribbed, Stern, Simple, Brave, Clean, and True. He showed Karel two pennants he'd already been given just for agreeing to come along: one involved yet another eagle; the other read, in script, *We Are a Universal People; There Will Always Be a Springtime for Our Greatness.* A small bird—representing springtime?—was stitched onto the corner of the second one. No, his sister did not know where he was.

Karel pulled him out of line. He told Sprute that they had to go home and that Sprute had plenty of kids anyway. He mollified David by not only explaining how much all of this would upset his sister but also by taking him for candy and buying him a week's worth of sugared violets and waferlike crackers covered with powdered sugar.

He marched him home, stopping every so often when David dropped something and had to pick it up, and presented him to Leda. She was beautiful. She stood in the doorway in a dress of red linen. She'd been about to go to a friend's birthday party. Karel registered wistfully that he hadn't been invited and then explained everything.

Leda took in her breath and clasped David with his back to her as if he'd been saved from savages. His front was a snowfall of powdered sugar.

While Karel spoke she listened intently, and when he stopped she didn't say anything. Her hair was swept up and pinned back and there was a black ribbon around her neck. When she moved her dress flared at the bottom. Instead of thanking him she leaned over her brother, who ducked his head, and kissed him, her kiss tasting familiar and faintly sweet.

He got home much later, having dawdled through half of town touching his tongue every so often to his lips in the dreamy hope that some of her flavor would return. His father was gone. The kitchen chair was on its side, but the house was otherwise undisturbed. Mr. Fetscher appeared at the door of the adjacent house slowly when Karel knocked, and gestured him in, where he told Karel with a mix of sympathy and irritation that the police had come, or the Security Service—somebody—and had taken his father away.

At the station the local police seemed genuinely ignorant of what had happened. At home he went from room to room, from the storage space under the kitchen to the attic, searching for his father or clues or anything at all. He found nothing and couldn't tell how much clothing or what personal effects were missing. He sat on the bed in tears and turned on the radio on his father's folding bedside table and listened to a lot of garbled, excited talk and fanfare before he realized that what they were saying was that war had been declared.

With nowhere else to go he returned to the zoo. On the way he checked in again at the police station, which was a madhouse, and the café. The café owner hadn't seen Karel's father and wondered if he'd enlisted, or had been called up as some sort of worker. He took Karel inside off the patio and gave him a bitter drink tasting of lime. Karel sipped it while gazing around at a place his father spent time. Did he drink things like this when he wanted to get away from Karel? Was he friends with these people? Were they looking at Karel and thinking, This is the kid he told us about?

The café owner had his back to him and shifted a bottle along the mirrored glass as if transmitting significant information. He had no answers to whatever question Karel asked. Karel's leg bobbed independently on the stool and he wanted to break something. He touched his glass to the dark wood between them and made patterns of condensation rings: a seven, a lazy S.

At the zoo only Albert was working. Albert's assistant, Perren, told him that the nomads, not content with systematic abuse and provocation, had staged a major raid on a customs hut near the border. They'd killed an elderly official who had been simply tending his pitiful little garden when they struck. Eleven nomad bodies were available as evidence. How they had been killed was not clear. Exactly what their strategic thinking had been was not clear. But the incident had been the last straw and was being handled, the government announced, with grim resolve.

Perren was playing with two creamy white slowworms, small, legless lizards. They twirled and wound around his fingers like a caduceus. He lifted one to each earlobe while Karel watched, and they clamped on with their tiny jaws and hung like earrings.

Perren said twelve divisions of the army that had been in the area on maneuvers and four squads of the Special Sections behind them had struck at six that morning and were already encircling the only large city, which he called "the capital."

While Karel waited for Albert to give him a few minutes the old man offered a cotton swab of medicine with maddening patience to a recalcitrant pit viper. Karel made tsking and peevish noises with his tongue on his teeth and crossed and recrossed the hallway next to the viper's glass enclosure with his hands on his head and his elbows out. Opposite them the puff adder struck at the same spot on the pane over and over with his nose and then shot up to the wire netting and down again.

When he finally heard the news, Albert expressed his

sympathy so dryly that Karel was forced to conclude with surprise and dismay that this sort of grief was not transferable. Albert said he thought Karel's father was probably all right, but as to where he was, who knew? In this mess he'd be untraceable, at least until things settled down. He really couldn't have picked a worst time to disappear, Albert remarked. He led Karel down the hall. When he reached his office he turned and saw Karel's face and seemed genuinely sorry. He said that Karel should come back with him, to his house. Maybe they'd think of something; if not, at least they could have lunch. Had he eaten anything? Karel hadn't, and was hungry.

Karel had never seen Albert's house. He'd barely spent time in his office. The house was on the other side of town. A block or two before it they came to a roadblock, staffed by two soldiers. What the roadblock was supposed to be guarding was anybody's guess. Albert misunderstood at first and thought the road closed. He led Karel a few streets over to an alternate route, which was also closed. Puzzled, he returned to the first roadblock. He stood looking at it as if to verify its existence while Karel waited in a misery of impatience. The soldiers at the barrier looked at them suspiciously now that they were back. When they finally crossed to the striped sawhorses, one of the soldiers, a thin teenager with a swollen eye, leveled his weapon at Albert's chest and left it there.

"What is this?" Albert asked pleasantly.

"Do you have identification?" the older soldier said. He was a corporal and had his breast pocket lined with candy bars.

"To go home?" Albert said. He began halfheartedly to fumble through his pockets.

"You live here?" the corporal said.

"You saw me go by this morning, when you were unloading these things," Albert said. "I wondered what you were doing. The gun is unnecessary."

From his wallet he extracted a card, his membership in the Herpetological Association.

"What is this?" the corporal said, after a pause. He held the card as if it were an attempt to humiliate him.

"It's the Herpetological Association," Albert said. "I'm an officer. We study animals, reptiles. Lizards?"

"Why are you loafing near here?" the younger soldier said. Karel speculated on his swollen eye.

"Everything can be explained," Albert said. "I work at the zoo—"

"If you move rapidly like that my friend'll kill you," the corporal said. Karel felt a chill at the back of his head. The corporal handed the card back. "And who's this? This is your son?"

"I was looking for more identification," Albert said. "No."

"This is not your son?" the corporal said. This seemed to open whole new vistas of problems.

"He works for me," Albert said, near despair. "He was coming over for lunch. I'm very tired."

"Is that a hobby of yours?" the corporal said. "Inviting young boys over for lunch?"

The younger soldier guffawed.

Albert was silent. He peered down his block. The corporal looked over another identification card and speculated to the younger soldier what Albert would do or had already done with Karel. The younger soldier turned his head to use the good eye to listen. He said to Karel, "What are *you* looking at?" The corporal laughed.

The younger soldier hawked and spat and then moved aside and let Karel and Albert pass.

"Happy hunting," the corporal called. Albert turned back to look, and then led Karel to his house.

In the entryway Karel cleared his throat and commented, to change the mood, on a fat, flowered tea cozy half covering the telephone. The flowers had smiling faces.

Albert turned on the radio and sat at the kitchen table. He rubbed his eyes with his palms. He said, "You want to know about the tea cozy. So. There's a man named Kehr. From the Civil Guard. He knows many surprising things about me, it turns out." He got up and went through the cabinets and pulled out a box of crackers and a jar of olives, which Karel hoped wasn't his idea of lunch.

"People have been here to look at my phone," he said. He pointed to his ear, and Karel gaped at the tea cozy, amazed.

"Or it could've been a neighbor," he said, sighing. "I was supposed to have been listening to foreign broadcasts, and the idiot next store could've said something. We go at it every so often. She beats her rugs over the fence while I try to nap."

"You listen to foreign broadcasts?" Karel said.

Albert made a disgusted noise and refused to answer.

Karel considered the tea cozy. Suppose his father had said something stupid or wrong somewhere? The more he thought about it, the more miraculous it seemed his father had stayed out of trouble this long.

"What would they do to you?" he asked. "If they thought something like that?"

Albert dumped the olives into a dish and brought out bread and cheese. When he lifted the bread from the cabinet the shelving lifted with it and Karel saw that it had a false bottom, a secret space. Albert glanced at him, and Karel had looked away in time. "Turn me over to somebody like our friends at the roadblock," he said. "Or one of the centers."

"To be reeducated?" Karel asked.

Albert looked at him sharply. "That's one way of putting it," he said.

"Suppose that happened to my father?" Karel said.

Albert sliced the bread and then the cheese, and arranged the slices with a hurried sense of the right way to do things. "Your father didn't seem particularly opposed to this regime," he said finally.

That was true, Karel reflected. He felt better.

Albert indicated the food and took a piece of cheese to demonstrate.

Karel laid some of the thicker cheese slices on a piece of bread and ate standing up. The cheese was very sharp and the bread was dry, a day or two old. He was thirsty. He asked what Albert thought about the war, and Albert said only that the war was obviously what the majority wanted.

"You think?" Karel said.

"By the majority I mean the Praetor," Albert said.

When Karel asked him after a pause what he thought the nomads wanted, he said, "To be left alone."

One of the olives tasted horrible, and he wasn't sure if he should spit it out. It made him more thirsty. He sat down without being asked, chewing endlessly and eyeing the water faucet. Albert poured himself a glass of water while Karel watched and drank the entire thing and put the glass in the sink.

After lunch they went into the shaded and gloomy living room, and Albert surveyed his sofa. It looked like he was getting ready to nap. He suggested Karel try his neighbor, who was working for the new transportation board and might have issued Karel's father a travel pass. She'd be home now, for lunch.

So Karel went next door and followed her around like a dog waiting for an answer to his question. She was directing workmen laying in plaster sculptures in her rock garden. When she finally put her attention to Karel she announced she had no idea what he was talking about, and that no Roeder had been through her office, and how had he found out where she worked in the first place?

On the way back he could see from the street Albert talking intently with a young man in the living room, the two of them sitting forward on the sofa and nodding. Albert had his two index fingers together and moved them apart to demonstrate something. When Karel knocked and came in the young man stood up and looked at him and then thanked Albert for the directions. Albert wished him luck, and the man left.

Trying to find the square, Albert said. He asked how things had gone. He said again not to worry, the thing to do was to check at home and give it a little time before getting excited. He'd written a number on his palm, and when he saw Karel notice it he made a casual fist.

The house smelled of mildew. Albert settled back on the sofa and closed his eyes and draped an arm over his face. Karel could see his nose in the crook of his elbow. He said things were a mess everywhere and transportation was impossible. Karel's father was probably sitting in a café somewhere worrying about *him.* He brought up the Komodos, which were refusing to reproduce in captivity. He asked Karel if he had any ideas. When Karel didn't answer he guessed that all of this clumsy coming and going by the

Civil Guard wasn't helping. He talked about Seelie as now so aggressive that the prospects of artificially impregnating her were fading fast. He frowned, finally, and abandoned the subject.

He lay silent for a while, perhaps hoping Karel would leave. He seemed relaxed, but his foot jiggled impatiently. Karel felt he had nowhere to go after this, and looked around the room hopelessly. There was a plaque above the sofa framing a silhouette of a rattlesnake's head. There was a mounted photo on the lamp table of Albert kneeling beside a netted tortoise. Some skeletons were jumbled together across the room in a breakfront. He'd imagined endless interesting things in Albert's house, and none of these gave him any pleasure. He stood uncertainly beside the sofa, unhappy where he was and with no idea where he could go.

Albert outlined some of the characteristics of the anguid family of lizards. Karel wondered if he thought it therapeutic. He talked about individuals who were willing to give up part of their tail to an attack, or would smear the attacker with excrement. He moved to the differences between the snake families Elpidae (fixed fangs) and Viperidae (retractable fangs). He gave the Helodermatidae one last try. Did Karel know that they tracked prey by tasting the ground with their tongues?

Karel sighed so Albert could hear him. Albert gave up, his arm still over his eyes. He sighed as well and lay still.

"I'm going to go," Karel finally said.

Albert made an approving noise.

"You think the government needed him for some special secret job?" Karel asked. He thought there was a better chance his father was on Mars.

Albert cleared his throat and made an unhurried chewing sound. He said, "There are a lot of people you meet who can get a penknife and some string and rewire a house. Fix your watch. Build a birdcage. Your father is not one of them."

Karel felt the heat on his cheeks from the harshness and truth of the comment. He was ashamed of feeling shamed. He said, "You shouldn't say that. You don't know. How do you know?"

Albert shrugged, as much as he could lying on his back. He apologized. Outside a small translucent gecko pressed itself against the glass of the living-room window. He could see light through it, and its pale palms and belly somehow suggested to him both vulnerability and mercy.

Albert explained that he was under a lot of pressure recently and was upset because he'd been notified that the zoo as a newly designated Educational Institution would be under the jurisdiction of the Committee for Popular Enlightenment, which was under the jurisdiction of the Civil Guard.

Karel rubbed the back of his neck. He thought now that Albert had never really been considering his problem. It occurred to him that possibly no one was going to help.

Albert said, "I'm getting too tired to be careful. I'm sitting here in my house with a tea cozy over my telephone. I'm sitting here worried about what I can say to a boy who works for me."

Karel blinked. He had the impression the house was settling, easing apart. "Do you think I'd get you in trouble?" he asked.

Albert said, "They're taking so much away I'm wondering what I'm trying to save."

"You mean the zoo?" Karel said.

Albert finally took his arm off his face and rubbed his eyes with his fingertips. It made a faint and unpleasant sound. "Whatever I'm doing now won't undo all the time I was doing nothing," he said. "How long ago was it I knew there was a hundred percent turnover at the centers? What did I do then? How sure did I have to be?"

"What's that mean, hundred percent turnover?" Karel asked, frightened.

"It means bad things have been going on," Albert said. Karel resented his tone. "And your boss here took a long time to figure it out."

In the kitchen there was a clinking, as though the dishes were taking care of themselves.

"I have mice," Albert said.

"You didn't know then," Karel said. "About what was going on."

"It's sad, is what it is," Albert said.

"I'm going home," Karel said. He made show of moving his feet on the rug. "I have to find my father."

"We should have a new motto, on the flag," Albert said. " '*We Are Mute. We Are Shameful. We Are Miserable.*' That's how it should go."

Karel let himself out. Albert told him to take some olives with him. At the blockade, the two soldiers laughed at him and told him his shirt was on inside out, a comment he did not understand.

His father was not home. The radio announced the nomad capital had fallen. There were few casualties and fewer prisoners. The nomad armies had melted away before their forces like snow beneath the sun, and now were broken and scattered through the mountains. A passing officer was apprehended and asked about the nomad situation.

"They're broken," he said. "And scattered through the mountains."

The radio announced the anniversary of the Bloody Parade, and Karel winced, for Leda's sake. The festivities planned for their town included a parade, band concerts, and orations. These would be expanded to celebrate the victory. The Bloody Parade had been the first coup attempt by the Party. It had been a measure of the Republican government's unpopularity, Albert had told Karel, that an abortive coup was seen for years as the NUP's greatest achievement.

He spent two useless days banging on doors in the neighborhood and rechecking with the police. On the evening of the second day he sat in his kitchen with the lights out listening to the groans of the plumbing and the parade cranking up in the distance.

There was not going to be any question of avoiding the thing. He got up and banged his chair against the table and went out, unable to sit still any longer and hoping to come across his father maybe having simply and miraculously lost track of the time.

The Schieles' house was dark. Poor Leda, he thought. He walked to the square. They'd put up a lot of new flags of thin cloth that flailed around in the wind. He hit the crowds and started working his way through them. Booths created standstills every few feet where hawkers told fortunes with dolls of little girls that rose or sank in jars of water, or white mice that dragged string through various chutes marked "Yes" or "No" or "It Needs More Thought" or "He/She Loves You." He was taken by the crush past a booth involving a blind violinist and a bald baby in a smock and was unable to figure out what they were doing—selling? begging? entertaining?—even after hearing suggestions from other puzzled passersby. Along the parade route people began holding their positions on the side of the road whether or not they blocked access to the booths. He stopped for a while at a table rooted like a breakwater and looked at a large multicolored parrot whose entertainment value seemed to be based only on his ability to shift his weight from foot to foot. Behind the parrot a vendor was selling plaster busts of the Praetor and auto parts.

Farther on, cheeses carved into likenesses of the Praetor were displayed in delicatessen windows. Sausages were arranged around them. He watched the crowd for his father but still felt he was wandering around stupidly, like a puppy who'd been smacked on the ear. He passed Holter, and Holter said that that was some news about his father. They were separated in the crowd and Karel said "*What?*" and Holter nodded and smiled and said he thought so, too, before disappearing. Karel fought his way after him in a frenzy of anxiety and frustration. He'd been wearing a light blue jacket. At an intersection of two alleys a lieutenant in the Civil Guard blocked the way, stooping over to examine the arm of a little boy who seemed lost. The lieutenant asked the boy if he knew what happened to little boys who stole things, and the boy said no.

The alley emptied back into the square, where stages had been erected around the central well. A band on one struck up the old drinking song the Party had adopted as its anthem. It sounded to Karel like a horn section falling down the stairs.

The people behind him started shouting and air horns sounded on the side streets: something else was going on.

He fought his way to a streetlamp, pulled a younger boy down, and shimmied up. He scanned the crowd in all directions. There were three people above him higher on the pole, and it swayed and lurched. His palms were skinned. He could not find Holter.

The parade had started. It took a few minutes to reach him. While he waited he sucked on one palm and then the other. Both were burning. A cart passed, carrying a bust of the Praetor covered with flowers. It was followed by ten of the town fathers portraying the Old Guard and one the Praetor. They marched along reenacting the Bloody Parade every thirty yards or so by walking into a hail of tossed flowers. When the flowers hit, the Old Guard staggered and lay down, while the Praetor marched on. He paused every so often to allow the group to re-form. Behind them young men with glasses and uncertain expressions carried a banner that said JUNIOR SCHOLARS OF THE HOMELAND. Behind the banner two men rolled a large silver-and-glass thing on wheels shaped like soup tureen and said to contain the Praetor's legacy to the future, a short autobiography in verse. It was topped by a silver baby kicking up its heels. A small band followed, identified as the Flutes of the Political Orphans, and then jugglers, and more local officials, and at the end rowdy unofficial marchers. Karel checked everybody. At the very end two members of the Young People's NUP called to each side over and over: *We are a universal people—*

We are a rersle-rersle riesle, the crowd responded, tailing off.

There will always be a springtime for our greatness—

There will always be a ringtine rerer rateness, and they were past, a lot of the crowd following, with or without Holter, he wasn't sure, and then there was only one more person, bringing up the rear: the mayor's small son in army fatigues, sitting reverently on a tiny pony.

He had a last chance, though: the races and contests. He worked his way over and squeezed into a spot high on the largest temporary grandstand, feeling it tremble from the weight of the numbers scaling it. People near him were shouting at everyone else to stay off. Fights started at the bases of the aisles. The stands collapsed regularly and Karel remembered an engineer saying in the newspaper after one of the bigger disasters that as a people they just weren't very good with wood.

Nobody could hear the opening. It was a reenactment of the Marta Siegler story. Siegler, played by a young girl, was seduced by a foreign grain salesman, killed him with a threshing machine, retired to a nunnery, spied for her country, and was stabbed to death resisting the advances of a crazed youth who was actually her half brother. She reappeared to her murderer in his jail cell with her arms full of lilies, offering forgiveness and causing him to repent. He then became a member of the Civil Guard. The three parts of the story were titled Purity, Forgiveness, and Repentance on easels beside the action.

Afterward the regional Party head gave a speech. Karel didn't follow it. His palms still hurt and he figured with his luck they were probably infected. He tried to keep scanning the crowd. The speaker said that the great issues of the day were settled not with words or speeches but with iron and blood. The crowd's applause had some sarcasm to it that the speaker didn't seem to catch.

After that there were poetry contests—one of the Praetor's most despised innovations—and races of cripples around the stages, which some in the crowd seemed uncertain about. During the pauses the Kestrels led them through the cardinal virtues. The stands swayed and creaked. On the main stage there was a boxing match between two women and then fireworks, and gifts were shaken down from nets stretched above the grandstands—fruit and papier-mâché eagles—and hundreds of birds were released, pheasants and guinea fowl and smews and ravens, with a thunder of flapping wings from cages below the stage. In the uproar Karel slipped down from the grandstand and rushed around with lights booming over his head and birds exploding up before him like the bats from Leda's cave. He slipped on plums and cherries rolling underfoot. He checked all of the light blue and near-blue jackets he could find, and never found Holter.

On the way home he looked in on the Schieles (still no lights) and then found himself staring blankly at his dark front door. Occasional fireworks were still booming in the distance. Mrs. Fetscher called him from next door. She was silhouetted against her lighted doorway. When he got there she nodded him into the house, something she'd never done before. He thought, She has terrible news about my father. But in the foyer he saw with a shock the uniformed man from the Civil Guard he'd seen in the café. The same supporting officers were with him. They all looked at Karel as if they expected him. The uniformed man was looking at him as well. Karel took a closer look, despite himself, at the badge with the nest of snakes and skull. They stood around Mr. Fetscher in a semicircle.

"You are—?" the uniformed man said.

"This is a neighbor," Mrs. Fetscher said. "He can swear my husband was home yesterday, working in the garden."

Karel blinked, not sure he could.

"That's true," Fetscher said. "I waved to him. I remember thinking, that poor boy."

"Umm-hmm," the uniformed man said. "My name is Kehr," he said to Karel. "You are—?"

"Karel Roeder," Karel said.

Kehr nodded. He said to Mrs. Fetscher, "Why is he a poor boy?"

"His father's disappeared," Fetscher said. "Though it might be anything—"

Kehr looked back at Karel. "What's your father's name?" he asked.

"Simon," Karel said. He thought about the old man's hand from the café and the cracking sound. "Do you know anything about him?"

"No," Kehr said. "Mr. Fetscher, get your things."

"But Karel can swear," Fetscher protested.

"I'm not interested in what he can swear," Kehr said. He was absorbed with his cuff. "You'll only be gone overnight. Collect your things."

Fetscher continued to protest and was led away by one of the supporting officers. The family dog, a small black-and-white mongrel with rumpled ears, followed them into the bedroom. The supporting officer opened a small suitcase on the bed and began to demonstrate how to put clothes in it. Fetscher relented and began packing, still pleading his case. The dog stood on the bed and unpacked things—folded undershirts, shorts, an eyeglass case—as fast as the harassed Fetscher could pack them.

"Stop that, Eski," Mrs. Fetscher scolded.

There was a cautious knock on the door and the neighbor from across the street, Mrs. Witz, peered in.

"What do you want?" Mrs. Fetscher said. "Can't you see enough from across the street?"

"I came to see if there was some trouble I could help with," Mrs. Witz said, wounded. She had dressed up. Her five-year-old, Sherron, stood behind her and kept peeking around. "If you'd like me to leave—"

"Who is this?" Kehr said. "Is this your son?"

Mrs. Witz looked at Karel in horror. "Oh, no," she said. "This is my daughter, Sherron." She brought Sherron out in front of her, holding her by the shoulders. Sherron's feet left the ground when her mother maneuvered her. "And you are—?"

"A servant of my country," Kehr said. He stroked an ear with some weariness.

"I didn't catch your name," Mrs. Witz said.

"Would you please leave my house?" Mrs. Fetscher asked. Her voice was heading toward shrill.

"What's going on out there?" Fetscher called. He was told to keep packing. There was the muffled sound and yelp of the dog being cuffed.

"Is there any sort of trouble?" Mrs. Witz asked.

"None whatsoever," Kehr said. He looked at Karel briefly and turned his attention to the bookcase and two knickknacks, ceramic crocodiles with open mouths. One held stick candy and the other matchsticks. Kehr's jawline and collar were perfect, and Karel felt shabbier in his presence.

Mrs. Fetscher asked if Mr. Kehr would like some of the sugared wafers she'd been making when he arrived, which, she remembered with a worried look toward the kitchen, were probably ruined by now.

Kehr declined. Mrs. Witz suggested Sherron might like some. Sherron looked toward the kitchen dubiously.

Sherron was fat enough as it was, Mrs. Fetscher snapped. Mrs. Witz glared at her.

"But this is some kind of mistake," Fetscher called from the other room. There was the brisk sound of clasps being shut.

"We do not hunt for crime," Kehr said. "I do not have the details." His subordinate looked aimlessly around the room, arms folded.

Fetscher returned with a small plaid suitcase, trailed by the other subordinate and Eski, who wagged her tail festively.

Kehr checked a pad and repeated Fetscher's name. Fetscher nodded. His wife touched his arm. Eski stood, with her front paws on his thigh.

The escorting subordinate asked if he was a salesman and Fetscher cried out, new hope breaking over him. See? he said. There *was* a mistake! He was a butcher.

"Do you often take walks, Mr. Fetscher?" Kehr asked.

Fetscher looked around the room, dumbfounded. He looked at the others, and Karel, as if it were their responsibility to help. Everyone backed up a step.

"What kind of question is that?" Mrs. Fetscher finally said, after a silence.

"Please come with us," Kehr said.

But he was a butcher, Fetscher said frantically, repeating himself to avoid making another mistake.

They made way as Kehr and the others led him out. Sherron stood straight with her feet together, as if at a ceremony. "Where will I reach you, Tommy?" Mrs. Fetscher wailed, and no one answered.

Eski, sitting now in the middle of the foyer, looked at Karel with an excited and irritating expectancy, as if he were the one who was supposed to do something. The last Civil Guard officer when he passed said to Sherron, "See that you're a good girl," and in response she smiled and showed him a handful of marbles.

For a week he met with Mrs. Fetscher over their fence each morning to exchange the fact that they hadn't heard anything; then she disappeared, not answering the door for three days, and Mrs. Witz when she caught him passing the house told him that Mrs. Oertzen had made a mistake, turning in the wrong Fetscher, and that this Fetscher had on top of everything else had a fatal accident. He'd lost his head and had fallen against the wall. They hadn't been able to wake him. Mrs. Fetscher was in a bad way. They were going to bring her something later. The funeral was on Thursday, if Karel was interested in attending.

School was suspended again. He roamed the neighborhoods during the day. At night he listened to the radio, which didn't help but at least broke the silence. He entertained the hope he'd learn something of use. The war was at a standstill and the news concentrated on fifth columnists and shirkers. The head of the Civil Guard promised that when final victory occurred the Party would return its attention to all those of that sort who had slipped by. Karel stopped listening. He ate some mealy peaches. He turned the radio back on and suffered through a long playlet involving a simpering character who made trouble for everyone and who was finally identified as a profiteer and a corrupting intellectual spirit. They shot him and after the theatrical sounds of the gunshots he made a surprised 'Oh!' as if he'd found something in his shoe. Somebody else gave a talk about saving wood palings. The only concrete news Karel heard was the announcement broadcast on all channels that for the duration of the emergency the administration of justice was now out of the hands of civilians and entrusted to the bureaus of the Special Sections of the Civil Guard.

He slept in his father's room. He rummaged through the closet, kneeling on the floor, setting aside piles of shoes and old newspapers. He found things he could not have said belonged to his family: folded brightly colored tablecloths, a musical instrument made from a gourd, copies of *Guardian of the Nation,* a magazine "dedicated to the preservation of civilization and race," a chessboard of copper and dark wood, a cigar box full of chess pieces, a loop of wire, a photo of a desert path, a leather shoe repair kit. There was nothing in all of it that seemed like part of his life, and he remembered his mother's letter, and imagined desolately a historian peering into his parents' history and finding no trace of him whatsoever.

The next morning he found a letter without postage from his father under the front door. He looked up and down the street as if it had just been dropped off, and then opened it. It said his father was well, and that Karel shouldn't worry. There was great news. All would be explained soon. There was more money for food under the top step below the landing. It added in a P.S. that Karel should call a plumber if he hadn't already.

He sat slapping the letter against his cheek, mystified and angry. Had his father dropped it off? Had a friend? He checked beneath the step and found more money than his father had ever claimed to have had. He stood staring at it. How long had his father been lying to him? What was he saving this for? Where had he gotten it?

He almost destroyed the letter. He was considering it

when Albert showed up. Albert poked around the house as if looking for someone and then said he'd just stopped in to see what the news was. He'd never visited before.

Karel showed him the letter. Albert took it and before opening it mentioned that the zoo was once again shut down. He shook his head while he read. He refused to speculate on what was going on. He agreed Karel had a right to be angry.

They sat in Karel's kitchen contemplating the letter until Albert finally asked if Karel was going to offer him anything to eat.

Karel laid out a few things—a hard-boiled egg, some carrots, some fennel—after giving the old man an incredulous look. He was determined not to apologize for not having anything else. What did I get over there? he thought. Olives? Old bread? Albert looked at the vegetables and egg and made a disappointed chewing noise and then went to the sink to wash up. He noted the water wasn't working.

"I know that," Karel said, banging a dish down. "I live here." The egg rolled onto the table.

He should have that fixed, Albert told him.

They ate without speaking. Karel thought, If I could go to a country where there were no people, I'd go.

Albert asked him if there was any salt. They looked at each other. It occurred to Karel that he was in a country like that now.

"Pretty quiet next door," Albert observed.

Karel crunched his carrot.

"A newspaperman I admire," Albert said, "or admired, from your home city, wrote in one of his last columns the day after the Party took over, 'Are we a joke? Are we a bad dream? Whoever hears our speeches has to laugh. Whoever sees us coming had better reach for his knife.' "

Karel nodded. The egg and the carrots were gone. Albert was acting peculiar, and Karel had the feeling he wanted to ask something.

"Well, I'm still here," Albert said finally. "After some of the indiscreet things I said in your presence the other day. I assume that means you don't aspire to National Greatness."

"I don't aspire to anything," Karel said bitterly.

"Very wise, in our country right now," Albert said. Karel wished he would leave. He had a headache, he was out of food, and he was having trouble imagining a subject that wouldn't depress him.

Albert said, "Perren joined the Party."

Karel suddenly realized that Albert's earlier remark meant he thought Karel was capable of turning him in.

"Said it was something he had to do," Albert said. "That it was in the best interests of the zoo."

They were silent, Karel toying with the rhyme in his head: *had to do, of the zoo.* "So will it help?" he finally asked, out of some sense of obligation as host to extend the conversation.

"Hey," he said when Albert didn't answer. "You really think I would've turned you in?"

Albert looked at him closely. He gave a small shrug. "Before today I would've said that Perren wouldn't've."

Karel looked away, and then got up and cleared the table. When the old man didn't move, he was forced to sit back down.

"And they go on about uniting the country," the old man said.

Karel tipped the empty dish to show everything had been finished. You should talk, he almost said. His father was gone. Albert was turning into a jerk. He had no friends. He had a fleeting image of Leda with her head turned to listen more acutely to something, and then an image of her lips lifting to his, and then she faded entirely.

He was sad and frightened and upset about his father. Albert was going on about the regime. The white hairs in his ears moved when he talked. Karel didn't want to listen anymore and asked suddenly if he remembered the beaches from the city. Did he remember the beachfront hotels? The huge trees, and the way the gables would stick out?

The old man looked at him, a little miffed, and then put his mind to it. He did, he said. He remembered especially the tall white one.

"The Golden Angel," Karel said.

The Golden Angel, Albert repeated. Rebuilt. Destroyed years ago with the rest of the cove by the tidal wave after the eruption on that island, part of the volcanic archipelago.

"The Roof of Hell," Karel said.

"Right, the Seprides, the Roof of Hell," Albert said. He drummed his fingers on the table and cast around the kitchen for food.

"What happened?" Karel said. "When it blew up?"

Albert lifted salt from the plate with his moistened finger and ate it. "You don't know this story," he said, as though that were news to him.

"I don't know this story," Karel said.

Albert made a face as if his life lately were an endless string of small surprises. One June morning, boom, he said. The entire cove of the city had been destroyed, two thirds. There'd been the usual warning phenomena: tremors, water levels in wells changing, domestic animals refusing food and getting excited, birds and rodents migrating inland. Cattle moved to high pasture. The tide went out completely and abruptly. A lot of people knew at that point but hoped the high ground would protect them. What else was there to hope? There'd been a grammar school right on the waterfront, and Albert imagined the children at the classroom windows, awed, looking at the stranded fish and the muck of the exposed harbor bottom, amazed by the beached and listing ships. And then the wave came in piling up on itself, shoaling and rearing on the shallow harbor shelf to sixty or seventy feet. Albert's father had told him all this. His father had been on higher ground. His father, Albert said, had never forgotten things: the way whole buildings were driven through the ones behind them like parts of a collapsing telescope, the thunder of the walls disintegrating booming up the cove, the far-off screams, the wash of bodies and debris back down the harbor.

His father dreamed about the wave the rest of his life, Albert said. In the dream they were all whirling and singing, shouting and falling, his father, his brothers, an elderly aunt, his mother, with the wave rising behind them like a curtain. His father, Albert said, lost his whole family to that wave. He'd been playing where he wasn't supposed to be playing, in one of the high quarries, and their house had been lower down. He used to say he could still hear the sound of their roof going. He used to say, *Oh God of mercy, all those roofs and all those people just like that.*

On Saturday he found Leda folding sheets and towels in her kitchen. Her mother and David were out and her mother had given her two thousand things to do. She suggested a walk.

On the front step she slipped out of her sandals and laced up some light ankle boots. He watched the lacing proceed before asking her where she'd been. He hadn't seen her since he'd brought David home. And they kissed, he wanted to add.

He couldn't see any difference in the way she acted toward him. Maybe she'd forgotten it already. Here he was mooning about it even with his father gone.

They'd gone away, she said, to stay with their aunt. It was hard on everybody. It brought back her father and all. Karel summarized for her disconnected parts of the parades and performances.

She got up and rocked back on her ankles to display her tied shoes. "I thought you could show me how you go noosing," she said. "Catching little lizards with the fishing pole."

He agreed. He said while they walked to his house, "I don't think I'll ever be able to predict what you're going to say."

She seemed flattered. The street was crowding for the market day. He didn't know how to tell her now about his father. He'd waited so long it would sound funny.

"My father's missing," he finally just said.

"Oh," she said, and stopped so suddenly in the street that people behind them shied away in alarm.

"Well, I got a note from him—he's all right," Karel said, stumbling. "He's not in any trouble. I don't know where he is."

Oh, Leda said, annoyed he'd scared her for nothing.

Before, he'd been worried, he tried to explain. There'd been no note or anything. He still didn't know what was going on.

She nodded, peering at him. They were at his house and she stopped. Oh, forget it, he thought in disgust. I'm never going to make myself clear to anybody.

While she waited outside drawing shapes in the dust on the side of his house, Karel rummaged around upstairs for the nooser. He tested the action in front of her before they left, pulling the metal loop so the tiny hangman's knot of string shrank and grew. She arched her eyebrows to show she was impressed.

"How does it work?" she asked, as if determined to be interested.

"This is it," he said. "This is all it does."

They walked to the south end of town. They avoided the street that led to the cave with the bats. Leda appreciated the sunlight beneath the wild olives and remarked on the smell of the dusty gravel. Where the town ended some barren hills began, at the foot of which refuse was dumped. Jackals and mangy dogs picked and haggled over the piles and watched them climb the first slope. It got steeper quickly, scree and larger rocks giving way in short cascades beneath their feet.

"Yuck," Leda said, watching one dog carefully. It was watching her as well. Something filthy and limp was hanging from its mouth.

"They're all right," Karel said. As they got higher the rocks increased in size.

"Are there scorpions here?" Leda asked, holding a foot in midair.

"I guess," Karel said. "I haven't seen one during the day."

She completed her step. "I don't like scorpions," she said.

They climbed, leaning forward and making huffing noises, until they reached another steeper slope abutting theirs.

"Here," he said, and in a minute or two, flipping over flat

stones, he found a lesser earless lizard, gray with pale blue along its spine. It skittered a foot or so away and froze with a quizzical expression.

Leda was facing the panorama of the town below them. She said, "It's *pretty* up here."

"I thought you wanted to watch," he said, and lowered the noose slowly over the lizard until it looked condemned by a tiny lynching party. He yanked the noose and his hand must have jerked: the lizard was magically gone.

"Huh," Leda said.

"It usually always works," he said. His armpits were sweating and the sun was hot on his back.

"Well, keep trying," Leda said. "It looks hard."

"It isn't, really," he said, irritated with himself. "It's not supposed to be." He crouched beside some chia blooming in indigo clusters above the slope. There was something there, too, maybe a horned lizard, but as he maneuvered the bamboo rod through the tangles it disappeared.

"Huh," Leda said again.

When they'd disappeared they were right nearby, often downslope, Albert had taught him. While he searched the area in a crablike crouch she gazed back at the town again, shading her eyes with her hand.

"Did you hear about Mr. Fetscher?" she said.

"I was there," he said. He overturned a rock slab to confront a Jerusalem cricket, tomato red and enormous, grotesquely humpbacked.

"You were?" Leda said. She turned, shadowed by the sun. "Oh, God. Look at that thing."

He shooed it away, and it left unhurriedly, dragging itself audibly over the shale.

She watched it clamber over a rock with distaste. "So?" she said. "What happened?"

Karel shrugged. He piled some rocks. "They took him away."

She made a face.

"Did you hear what happened after that?" he asked.

"I heard what they said." She watched him ease a fan-shaped rock up. Nothing underneath. "What do you think happened?" she asked warily.

"Right here," he said. "Look."

She crouched immediately beside him. Her face was more tanned with shade and he could see the tips of her teeth as her mouth opened slightly in anticipation. He held the noose over a head-sized stone concealing a tiny horned lizard smaller than the first. He could hear her breathing through her mouth while she watched him maneuver the rod.

She said, "You never answered."

He lowered the loop and the horned lizard's head turned, as if listening for far-off music. "I think they killed him," he said.

"So do I," Leda said. She was looking at him intently, and her eyes had the directness of the eyes of figures he'd seen in old mosaics. He could pick up the sun smell of the hairs on the back of her neck. It was as if as a child she hadn't been spared anything, as if her mother had never changed the subject when she'd entered the room.

"I may want to run away," she said.

"Where?" he said. Not: With me?

"The city," she said.

He closed his eyes at a horrible thought. He said finally, "Are you with me only because you want me to help?"

She told him no as if that were a peculiar notion, and the simplicity of her answer flooded him with relief. He waited for her to go on, unsure what to say. "You can't get on the train without a seat reservation and a permit to leave our area," she said. "I need three."

"Three?" he asked.

"David and Nicholas and me," she explained.

"What about your mother?" He sat on the scree, but she maintained her crouch.

"If my mother would go I wouldn't need to run away," she said.

"Do you think it's going to get worse?" he asked. He still didn't know where his father was, and now all this was happening. His unhappiness had crystallized into that one thought, *run away with Leda,* and he worked on the courage to ask her if he could go.

"My mother was talking with my aunt," Leda said. "Near Naklo they found eighty people, women and children. The Special Sections are killing everybody after the army passes." Naklo was on their side of the border.

"Maybe they were . . ." Karel said. He trailed off.

"They're just killing people," Leda said. "And we say, 'Oh, that's awful. What do you think happened?' And we don't *do* anything."

Karel dangled the noose, squeezing and relaxing it. Leda put her finger through it and started a gentle tug-of-war. "Everybody thinks they don't have to do anything and this'll pass, like the weather," she said. "Stay quiet and let everything happen and it'll turn out okay in the end just because the days are going by." She slipped her finger from the noose and examined it. "Well, every time the days go by I hear something worse."

She looked up at him for confirmation, and he nodded.

"You want to keep walking?" she said. "My knees hurt."

She stood and stretched. They walked carefully back down the slope.

What would she do after she ran away? he wondered. What do you do after you run away? How would she live?

She couldn't talk to Elsie or Senta about it, she said. Kids in their class just sat there, like little birds with their mouths open, waiting for worms. Elsie memorized even what she didn't understand.

They did believe a lot in memorization, Karel said, meaning the school. It was a principle or something.

"Habit's our principle," Leda said. She cupped her hand over a stalked puffball as she passed it. "Our *first* habit is not asking questions."

He trailed his nooser as though trolling and thought, What good is asking questions? but then remembered the number of questions he'd wanted to ask his father, and Leda.

"We have to fight them," she said. "To do that, we have to fight ourselves."

He nodded, openmouthed. He said, "Where'd you get that?"

"I read it," she said. "In a newspaper you get in certain places that the NUP *hates.*"

He was impressed. This was another of those times he felt four years younger.

They were on a road skirting the town and leading through dry scrub. A black-and-red bird darted and swooped over their heads—they were probably near a nest—and a family of jackrabbits still far away were spooked into flight, leaping as they ran.

"I get scared," Leda said. "People are doing what they're doing because they're scared, so they're not doing the right thing. It's like they didn't pay enough attention and then they weren't brave enough, and now they don't know *what* to do."

We could go back, Karel was thinking. We could go back to the beach and the Golden Angel.

"Does your mother think the same thing?" he asked.

"My mother's waiting," Leda said. "Sitting there like a lump waiting for someone to change everything or tell her what to do."

Karel was quiet.

"It's like she's caught in this—box, of just being pleasant about everything and hoping for the best. I said to her at Elsie's birthday party, 'Just say what you think. Go ahead.' You know what she said? She said, 'Leda, that's impossible.' She said, 'I don't even think I'd know what to say.'

"So," Leda added, and then stopped. They sat under a gnarled and peculiar tree he couldn't identify. She found a clump of long-leaved phlox and took the pale, star-shaped flowers between her fingers.

"Tell me about your father," she said.

He didn't know where to start. He tented his sweaty shirt away from his chest to cool off. He found himself in the shade of the strange tree telling her of the times they'd gone to the beach. He'd been five or six. He remembered the bathing huts with their damp pine smell and changing and not liking being barefoot on the splintery and unsteady boards, and the sound at the end of the day of the wet sandy suit dropping onto the wood. He remembered his inability to copy the swimming strokes that his father demonstrated for him in front of the whole beach. It occurred to him while he talked that his father's power came just from being his father, not from anything he'd earned. He told another story, of his father buying him wafer candies, as many as he wanted.

Leda had her chin on her knees and the hem of her skirt stretched between the two. She said that it didn't seem so bad, just sad. He was taken aback by the mixture of compassion and perspective.

She said as she got up and they kept walking that she thought starting a family, taking care of kids and showing them what was right, was the biggest accomplishment that anybody could do, and that most people didn't really do it as much as it just happened to them with their being around at the time.

He agreed. He was happy with how much better he felt, and moved to tenderness by the patience with which she tossed her hair back with a turn of her head. On the outskirts of town they knelt in a stranger's open back garden like saboteurs, hidden by a screen of shrubs and grunting along the furrows of a strawberry patch. They edged along keeping an eye on the neighboring houses, gobbling the berries and smelling the plants and earth under the hot sun while an irrigation hose trickled uselessly into a culvert.

They came into town on an unfamiliar street. A dog foamed and snarled at them along the length of a ramshackle corral. Nothing seemed to be keeping it where it was except its own sense of where it could or couldn't be. Leda gave it as wide a detour as possible.

The street led to the Retention Hospital, where Nicholas was kept. Leda was pleased with and Karel skeptical about the coincidence. She suggested they visit.

"Can you visit on Saturday?" he said. "Just like that?"

That's *when* you visit, she told him. She was going to go later anyhow.

The hospital was walled the way the zoo was. There was an iron gate. The ironwork read WORK AND USEFUL THOUGHTS ARE THE HOMES OF FREEDOM AND HAPPINESS.

They rang the bell. A boy with his leg in a complicated harness of wood and leather, all straps and slings, watched them carefully. Two other girls who looked to be twins stood by and seemed to be exchanging information about the boy. He knew it was unfair that he expected exotic horrors here, pinheads who would say "Why aren't *you* like this?" or frightening people who would feel better only if they knocked him down and sat on his chest. He was ashamed.

"Come *on,*" Leda said, and rang again.

A nurse crossed the yard to the outer gate as if demonstrating how to walk erect. Leda mentioned in a low voice that this woman, Mrs. Beghé, was a jerk.

They smiled like conspirators. Mrs. Beghé was almost beautiful, with dark blue eyes and straight blond hair. Her chin was too small. Above her breast a plastic pin said Beghé, with the accent drawn on.

"Call her Mrs. Begg," Leda whispered, while the woman opened the gate with an impossible key the size of a spatula. "She loves it."

But as they passed by the woman rested her eyes on him and he had a fleeting sexual fantasy: an abandoned room white with bedsheets or towels, Mrs. Beghé arching her back, reaching with her hand spread behind her to scratch herself.

He followed them to the reception area. While you're visiting the sick brother of the girl you love, he thought dismally. His mind was a sinkhole, the mesh trap in the filthy steel tub in the back of the butcher's.

Mrs. Beghé asked them to sit, and left. Leda said, "She hates me. I'm always giving her problems."

The right half of the reception area was roped off under the slogan from David's Kestrels pennant: WE ARE A UNIVERSAL PEOPLE, etc. On a freestanding placard there was an architect's drawing of a proposed new National Museum, to be erected on this site.

"Hey," Leda said. "Maybe they *are* going to shut this down." She got up and walked over to the sign and peered closer.

In the drawing over the front of the building he could read the words IN OUR CREATION THE WORLD SOARS.

"What's that mean?" he asked.

Leda had already moved to the next exhibit. "Some of these things people think make sense just because they've heard them a thousand times," she said.

He followed her a little way, hoping they weren't going to get in trouble.

More drawings showed what the museum would look like. Until a solution was found for the inmates, the National Museum of Folk and Art would share the building with the hospital, occupying the east wing.

"That makes more sense than they think," Leda said.

Along the corridor there were sample exhibits: the various Armed Forces in Ceaseless Motion and a marble family group with the family kneeling around the sitting father, who spread his hands over them, palms downward. "Must've been just passing through," Leda said bitterly.

Mrs. Beghé was waiting for them with Nicholas. He had a long face, like David's, but otherwise didn't appear to be Leda's brother.

"How are we, Nicholas?" Mrs. Beghé said, in the encouraging way people address invalids. "Are we happy to see Leda? And so early?"

"Hi, Leda," Nicholas said.

Leda hugged him. Karel felt stupid standing around the reception area. Leda introduced them. Mrs. Beghé explained that because of the work for the museum they'd have to have their visit in the dining room, which was quiet this time of day. Leda agreed. Nicholas was clearly disappointed at the lost opportunity to get outside.

"We could come back," Leda said. She stopped and looked at him closely. "Nicholas? Do you want us to come back, later, and we can all go outside?"

Nicholas rubbed the back of his neck and gazed at Karel helplessly. He thought about the question while they all waited and finally said no. Mrs. Beghé led the way through the inner doors. Karel scanned Nicholas furtively for differences.

A harassed orderly in the corridor was mopping at a large stain and rinsing his mop with water dirtier than the floor. Writing on the walls extended all the way down the hall. It looked to be one long story or message. The corridor smelled of urine. A young man in olive pajamas followed them and pressed his hands to his head and asked for sweets.

The NUP might be doing a lot of good things for the country, Mrs. Beghé said, but not for this hospital. Leda and Karel didn't respond.

They were led into a dining room filled with long rows of splintery pine tables covered with clear plastic. Mrs. Beghé said she'd return when they'd had a nice visit and left them alone, shutting the door with annoying care in an effort to be silent.

Color photographs of food were hung around the room: roast lamb with pineapple rings, mounds of cherries, white asparagus in butter, pastries, lingonberry tarts, kiwis and cream. Some of the pictures had old thrown-food spatters on them. Leda gave Nicholas some chocolate biscuits she'd brought, and he thanked her.

He offered one to Karel, who said no. He considered them conclusive proof that their stop at the hospital had been no coincidence.

A small group entered and sat on the opposite side of the room: a girl riding a tricycle with orthopedic attachments on the pedals, and two older boys. The tricycle squeaked and creaked until she got off. One of the boys was blind and being steered by the other. He didn't have glasses on his eyes. Karel closed his and practiced being blind, touching the plastic sheeting in front of him. Another nurse brought the three children a tray of food.

Leda was talking to Nicholas about the museum. She said she hoped now he'd be able to come home. "Mom wants you back, she does," she said. "She just doesn't know it."

Nicholas thought that was fine. He leaned forward and whispered into his sister's ear. She smiled.

"He tells me secrets," she said. "I tell him secrets, he tells me secrets."

Karel tried to smile. "Like your nanny," he said.

She nodded, pleased at the connection.

She asked her brother what else was new, and he told her he'd been allowed as a special treat Thursday to flush all the toilets at once with a master lever.

The blind boy across the way was eating in big bites. It bothered Karel that the boy was so used to his situation, that he'd grown into it and was no longer conscious of it.

"They should give more money here," he said finally. "Somebody should complain."

Leda looked at him and made a face.

"What's the matter?" he said.

"As long as you say 'somebody' it's easy, right?" she said.

He made a helpless fuming noise. "All you do is tell me what I should be doing," he said sullenly.

She ignored him and talked with her brother. It was as if they'd moved four seats down. Karel played miserably with the sheeting and pulled some of the tacks. A tiny boy with a shaved head passed the doorway lugging dark liquid in a pail. The weight made him walk in a hurried and stiff-legged way and the liquid slopped out metronomically.

Leda showed her brother a trick you could do by inverting your interlocked fingers. They were having fun, and Karel sat there. Mrs. Beghé at some point showed up and explained they'd had a nice visit, and that their brother would certainly look forward to the next Saturday.

Leda hugged her brother at the inner door while Karel and Mrs. Beghé looked away in opposite directions. When they passed into the reception area Nicholas waved through the glass. Leda waved until he turned and shuffled down the corridor, backlit by a window at the end of the hall in a dispiriting image of incarceration.

Karel led the way for once, into the courtyard. He mused that Leda had her answer for why she'd been born—for Nicholas, for David—and she went day to day living for the moment when they'd be happy, when the hidden justice would be found and released. They passed the deserted play area and a flopped-over bicycle. A little girl with one side of her head shaved and stitched watched them leave. Mrs. Beghé let them out. They waited, for no reason. The little girl pressed her fingertips to her mouth and signaled to them something lost and intricate with the complex movements of all ten fingers, sketching an unreadable alphabet on the air.

The local policeman handling the six-block grid where Karel lived was an elderly sergeant named Grebing. Karel knew him from hanging around the café. He was a harmless old man. He did his best to avoid trouble and cultivated a hearing problem partially for that reason. He liked to cadge fruit from the market stands.

Grebing was doing his best with what *The People's Voice* called spontaneous outbursts of patriotism. The outbursts took the form of late-night vandalism. The victims were those who had been or might have been supporters of the Republic, those in the town records who had voted against the party in the very first referendums. Grebing usually arrived in time to assist in the clean-up. The newspaper openly lamented such lawlessness, however well-intentioned, and listed in its sympathetic account of the damage done to each home the home's address, usually with the comment that it had not been entirely destroyed. Following such announcements it usually was.

The radio announced the local police were being directed by the Security Service to assist in the firmer measures soon to be instituted. Grebing, apparently, was handling Karel's grid.

He pedaled past while Karel watched from his window. His cap sat high on his head; it looked as if he'd forgotten his and borrowed someone else's. He coasted to a stop at the Fetschers' front hedge. The chain rattled. He got off the bike and it fell over with a crash. He stopped and then decided against lifting it, and tore his sleeve on the handbrake straightening up. Karel could hear the sound where he was.

A light went on in Mrs. Fetscher's house. Grebing struggled with the latch of the low gate and closed it behind him.

Karel left the window and went outside. A bat swooped and fluttered above his head in the dark. A truck engine coughed.

At her front door Mrs. Fetscher was looking at Grebing. Her eyes were flat and her expression suggested there was nothing more to say.

"Karel, come here," she called.

Karel came around into her yard, stepping over the gate. There was a rustling in the cactus bed near his feet.

"Sergeant Grebing is arresting me," she said. Her voice was neutral.

Grebing protested. He was trying to tuck the torn part up his jacket sleeve. It was protective custody, to keep her safe from the hoodlums.

"I thought he had news of the investigation about my husband," Mrs. Fetscher said. She ran the palm of her hand across her forehead. "He informs me otherwise."

Grebing, embarrassed, held out the sheet of paper for Karel to see. "I think it's a small thing," he said. "These people are supposed to gather at the Town Hall. It's a small thing."

"I'm going to call my sister," Mrs. Fetscher said. She seemed to be looking at Karel. "I assume you'll wait."

"Might I wait inside?" Grebing asked.

"No," Mrs. Fetscher said. She left the doorway.

Grebing lowered his head and stepped back and forth in place while he waited. He glanced at his bike and then at Karel. He looked as if he thought there was a chance he had something to worry about in that regard. It was colder now, and he shivered, maybe to demonstrate his unsuitability for this kind of work. He had no weapon.

Mrs. Fetscher returned. She was holding Eski up by her chest and carrying the other piece of the matched suitcases her husband had taken. Eski's ears bobbed.

"I don't know if Eski can come, Mrs. Fetscher," Grebing said.

"Eski can come," she said.

Grebing knitted his eyebrows with sadness, thinking probably of the upcoming reprimand. "Is that all you'll need?" he asked. "You may be—"

"That's all," she said. To Karel she added, "My sister will be coming in a week or so. You'll help her if there's anything she needs?"

Karel told her he would.

"By then you'll be back, I think," Grebing said.

She led them to the gate. She stooped and set Eski down. While the dog urinated she cleared away with her free hand some peppergrass from the walkway. She said, "Karel, you'll give these flowers some water?" She said goodbye. Grebing offered her his bike and she said, "You ride it." He did, weaving slowly and erratically along in an effort to maintain a slow enough pace for her, circling her like an suitor while Karel watched. She kept walking, back straight, with Eski's ears bobbing over her shoulder, all the way down and into the square, and out of sight.

The next morning Karel was in his kitchen early, making coffee even though there was no sugar. He washed the brown ring out of his cup and thought about things he could have done for Mrs. Fetscher. He imagined a protest that stopped everybody or his hand on Grebing's arm, and thought these were things Leda might do, not him.

With the coffee ready he didn't want any. There was nothing he felt like having for breakfast anymore.

Someone banged at the back door. When he opened it, Leda looked at him critically. "You just get up?" she asked.

"Yes. I just got up," he said. He wiped his eye. "It's early."

"We have to go back and see Nicholas," she told him.

"You want some coffee?" he asked. He didn't remember if there was another cleanable cup or not.

"We have to go now," she said.

He looked at her, conscious of horrible early-morning breath. It dawned on him that he was still in tattered shorts and a T-shirt that had egg on it. His hair, too, probably looked like a rat's nest. What she was saying at that point formed in his mind, like letters becoming visible through disturbed water.

"You want to go where?" he said. "We were just there yesterday."

"We have to go back," Leda said. "My aunt called. She wasn't going to, she told me, but she was worried. Something's going on."

He looked at her blankly. They stood facing each other in the doorway.

"My aunt?" she prodded. "With the son in the Civil Guard? My cousin?

"Yeah," he said. "What's going on?"

She rolled her eyes. "I don't *know.* She said her son told her that one of their units had gone to Nicholas's hospital, the whole thing was supposed to be very secret, last night."

"What would they go there for?" he asked. He tried to tuck in his shirt.

"*Kar*el," she said.

She waited for him to dress right where she was, in the doorway, and called out, "Can't you find your clothes?" when he didn't reappear immediately. He barely had time to lock the door, and he followed her in silence for a while, feeling taken for granted and peevish. He told her finally about Grebing and Mrs. Fetscher.

She nodded, ahead of him. Had she already known? She walked faster.

At the iron gate they were told by a new nurse with no nametag that Mrs. Beghé had had an accident and was recuperating. The news increased Leda's agitation geometrically.

"Where's my brother?" she said shrilly. "Where's Nicholas Schiele?"

"Hsh," the nurse said. "You can't visit anyone today."

"Where's my brother?" Leda demanded.

The woman winced and made conciliatory petting gestures at the noise. She suggested they come back Saturday.

"Where is he?" Leda shouted. The woman looked over her shoulder and back at them, biting her lip, and then produced the spatula key and opened the gate. She stopped Leda when she tried to push by. *"I'll* fetch him," she said. "You wait here."

"What happened here last night?" Leda asked.

The woman looked at her carefully. "You're concerned, I know," she said. "I'll fetch him. I'm sure whatever happened, happened." She was one of those adults Karel was always meeting who believed if they said something it had to mean something.

They waited in the courtyard. Leda said to herself, "I should go in there," but stayed where she was.

A few of the patients were out, standing around, and looked at them curiously. Windows of the reception area were broken, and there was a tricycle wheel near the door. Otherwise things looked the same.

Karel looked at the patients, full of doubts. Suppose something had happened? What could they do about it? Make things worse?

An impossibly short girl walked up to them and stared, holding her doll by the foot. The doll's head thumped through the dirt. Why was she in here? he found himself wondering. He could see nothing wrong with her.

"Did some men come last night?" Leda asked her, bending over. "Did something happen last night?"

The little girl smiled, and righted the doll and twisted its head decisively, as if she knew all about it.

"Here we are," the nurse said, leading Nicholas out of the reception area. He looks as tired as I am, Karel thought. Probably got him out of bed, too.

Leda flew to him and hugged him. He hugged her back with one arm, rubbing an eye with the other hand.

"Hi, Leda," he said. "You must've made a big stink." He smiled.

Leda looked over his shoulder at the nurse. "Can we talk for just one second?" she asked.

The nurse, with an expression meant to convey that there was no end to the extent to which she could be taken advantage of, withdrew to a safe distance and remained there, wounded.

"What happened?" Leda said. "You're all right?"

"I'm okay," Nicholas said. "I don't know what happened. I was asleep."

"You don't know anything?" Leda said.

"A lot of people are gone," Nicholas said. "Mrs. Beghé, both Willems."

"Who took them? Where'd they go?" Leda said. "Are they coming back?"

"Willem's brother said the Civil Guard," Nicholas said. "I don't know, because I was asleep. Willem's brother said he was pretending. They took the girl they just operated on. Andrea." He pointed to his head.

Karel said, "The one with the head that was shaved? Like this?"

Nicholas said that was the one, and Karel felt his stomach shift.

"Are they coming back?" Leda said. To the nurse, who had come closer, she said, "What happened here? Is he safe?"

"Everything's fine," the nurse said. She seemed to feel that was her signal to come back. "And you're to get out of here now, before I get into more trouble."

But Leda was not to be budged until two orderlies appeared and carried her out of the courtyard. A third escorted Karel by locking his arm behind his back. Nicholas waved to them before being led back inside.

She watched her brother disappear from outside the gate and told Karel they were going to the police. He asked why.

"You don't understand *any*thing, do you?" she demanded. "Don't you get it? The Civil Guard took them, I don't know why. But suppose nobody says anything? Suppose it's a test? Suppose they want to see if anyone *cares* what happens to these people?"

"I *thought* of that," Karel said, but he hadn't. "I just meant what's the point of going to the police."

Leda didn't answer. Then, halfway there, she said, "I don't know what else to do. At least they're not the Civil Guard. Maybe they can do something. Maybe they know something."

But his hopes in that regard sank immediately when they entered the station. The crush he'd seen following the declaration of war was gone. The local police's supersession by the Civil Guard and Security Service had clearly turned the station house into a backwater. The waiting room had one other customer, a shy fat man sitting as if hoping he was camouflaged by a nearby potted plant.

The sergeant on duty was eating either an early lunch or a late breakfast. It was spread before him on a sheet of waxed paper, and he eyed them when they came in as if part of his daily routine involved having his meals ruined.

Leda walked up to his desk and said, "I'd like to find out what's going on at the Retention Hospital."

The sergeant gazed over at Karel as if trying to connect him to an unpleasant memory. He had an unappetizing way of rinsing his mouth with milk before he swallowed it. He said, "Is it about the stolen plants?" He motioned for Karel to sit down.

"No, it's not about stolen plants," Leda said. "It's about missing people."

"A girl was in here before about stolen plants," the sergeant said. He folded a small wedge of sandwich into his mouth. "With everything else that's going on," he said, mouth full.

"It's not about plants," Leda said, exasperated. "People are missing, kidnapped, from the hospital."

"Kid-napped," the sergeant said. "Hold on, here." He moved his lunch aside by lifting the corners of the waxed paper and shifting the square over. He scanned papers that had been beneath it. Leda waited.

The fat man, as if a host, indicated for Karel a bowl of nuts on the table. Karel shook his head.

The sergeant looked up sharply and shot Karel a look. Karel attempted to return it or straighten out any misunderstanding until he realized the stupidity of what he was doing and stopped.

"Kidnapped," the sergeant said with a little more feeling,

as if it were one of those familiar and tragic stories one was always hearing: placid dog attacks baby in crib.

Karel paged through a glossy photo magazine called *Community Life.* It was full of beautiful black-and-white pictures of well-oiled and gleaming machine parts and thighs and backs, dramatically lit. There was a two-page spread of a woman high diver in a black bathing suit, her body an arcing T over a tiny pool below. He shut the magazine, and the fat man gestured that he'd like to see.

Leda was explaining the situation to the sergeant, who said finally, "You'll want to speak to the lieutenant," and left to fetch him.

The lieutenant was thin and deferential and conscious of his posture. It looked as if he resented being called out here for this. He gave the sergeant looks while he listened to Leda. The sergeant, settling back down to his lunch, refused to notice.

"So," the lieutenant said, pleased it was only a girl, "this isn't about a plant?"

"No, it isn't about a *plant,*" Leda said, and her voice rang through the room. The lieutenant made the same patting conciliatory motion the nurse had made. He asked what was going on then, and Leda, grimly, her teeth set, explained it again.

"Ah," he said. "The Civil Guard." He nodded. Leda stared at him. He was sorrowful, as if this were all a regrettable local custom or inevitable process that couldn't be prevented. The Civil Guard just did things, he said, and informed the police afterward, if at all. Relatives complained, the police had to write to them, fill out forms, it all took forever. He said he'd complained many times and could show Leda the correspondence on the subject. He said they'd do their best in this case. He asked exactly who in her family was missing.

"No one," Leda said.

"No one?" the lieutenant said. The humor left his face in a way that frightened Karel. "What're you doing? You think we have time for games?"

"My brother says people were taken from the hospital," Leda said stubbornly. "I'm not related to them."

"Concerned citizen," the lieutenant said. The sergeant grunted.

Leda looked at him. Everything was quiet. "I think you know what happened to them," she decided. Karel thought, Oh, God.

The lieutenant looked at her a moment more, and then made a show of arranging papers on the counter, indicating the interview was over.

"I could go to the mayor," Leda said helplessly. The mayor was notorious for his timidity.

The lieutenant gazed around the room for the next citizen in trouble. The shy fat man lifted a hand hopefully.

The lieutenant said quietly to Leda, "You know, a town of three thousand, a country fighting for its life—all that doesn't stop because someone's crying about a missing person."

"You know something, don't you?" Leda said.

The lieutenant stood. He returned to the back room. Leda left without waiting for the sergeant to get up. Karel stared into the eyes of the fat man opposite him and thought, How am I ever going to keep her out of trouble?

BASILISK

DAVID CAUGHT UP TO THEM ON THEIR WAY TO THE mayor's office and told Leda that their mother was worried and angry and wanted Leda home *now.* Karel was relieved. Leda told him she'd come by later to plan strategies. David asked to plan strategies for what and Leda asked him how he got so dirty.

There were four trucks and a donkey cart around Karel's house when he returned. The trucks were open-backed and empty and the cart was being unloaded by a few privates from the Civil Guard.

His house was filled with boxes. It smelled like a rabbit hutch. The privates were unpacking cartons marked FRAGILE in the living room and straw and excelsior were all over the floor. There were stacked cages of rabbits and chickens in the hall, and the chickens were making a lot of noise.

The uniformed officer from the Fetschers', from the café, was sitting at the kitchen table. Parts of Karel seemed to constrict as he stood there. He flashed on the way he and Leda used to invent the scariest possible nightmares while safe on the beach in the sun, and had the sense that that was what this was: some sort of play nightmare.

The man was considering a deep open box in front of him. Two chickens were bumping and scraping around inside. Karel remembered his name but the man introduced himself anyway, as Special Assistant Kehr of the Civil Guard.

"Who do you assist?" Karel asked, and the man smiled.

"I should explain," Kehr said. He started peeling the white inner skin from sections of an orange. Each section took a while. When he judged one properly stripped he eased it into his mouth with an in-the-sun squint at its sourness.

He was going to be billeting himself at Karel's house on national business. He hoped it would not inconvenience Karel seriously. He had laid in some supplies. He reached into the box in front of him to demonstrate, and one of the chickens screamed. In the hall cages the rabbits padded sideways, nervously.

"There's no room," Karel said. "I live here with my father."

One of the subordinate officers from the Fetschers' and the café stopped into the kitchen to listen. The other came into the house and remained in the background in the living room. He lit a cigarette on the window seat. The smoke hung around him in a gauzy and unpleasant way.

"Your father's not going to be using his room," Kehr

said. When he saw Karel's face he raised a hand against foolish assumptions. "Right away," he clarified.

"What's happened to him?" Karel said. "Is he in trouble?"

"None whatsoever," Kehr said. "At some point we can talk about him. Of course, I asked his permission to make these arrangements, and he granted it."

"You talked to him? Where is he?" Karel asked. "Where is he? How do I know he said that?" He realized that that was stupid question.

Kehr looked at him. The officer in the kitchen leaned against the lintel of the doorway and guffawed quietly. "You don't," Kehr said.

The rabbits rummaged and tumbled around in their cages, the sound like someone's drumming fingers. "What are you going to be doing here?" Karel asked.

"That's the nation's business," Kehr said. "Unfortunately, not yours. We'll expect you to do the cleaning you normally do." He looked around the kitchen. It was a mess. "And help a little with the dinner. That's at seven."

Through the window Karel could see neighbors outside, standing around and speculating. "Why are you letting me stay?" he asked. "Why don't you just kick me out?"

"If you'd like, we will," Kehr said mildly. He was becoming more interested in some papers on the table. "Do you have a place you'd go?"

Karel thought of presenting himself to Leda, and her mother: *The NUP threw me out.* He didn't think he had the courage.

"Of course, I assured your father you wouldn't be displaced," Kehr said. "In these troubled times."

"What am I supposed to do?" Karel said.

Kehr leaned back and brushed his palm down his chest like a man sweeping away crumbs. His tunic was lighter than his trousers, and there was a golden pin of a winged hammer on his collar and another of a winged anvil on his breast pocket. The embroidered oval beneath with the sword penetrating the nest of snakes into the skull Karel had seen.

"You have nothing to do but not interfere," Kehr said. "Which in these times is not easy."

The interview seemed to be over. Karel hesitated in the doorway. The officer leaning on the lintel regarded him levelly.

"It's a particularly bad time to be a vagrant," Kehr said. "With the turmoil in the streets and the various bureaus and Special Sections in such competition with each other, and no clear lines of jurisdiction. . . . I should introduce you to my assistants," he said. "They'll be staying as well. Assistants Stasik, here, and Schay at the window."

Neither made any gesture. This seemed to be a joke to them. Karel maneuvered through the boxes and went up to his room.

It looked unchanged. His reptile study sheets and the long-abandoned scraps of a letter to Leda were the first things he checked. They hadn't been moved. From two canteens he kept near the bed since his father had left he drank a cup of water, a cup of warm pineapple juice, and another cup of water. He thought he should get one of those sweating metal pitchers with removable caps. He lay on his bed and listened to boxes and furniture being moved below, the noises punctuated by the occasional chicken in distress sounding like one of the laugh boxes from the amusement shops of his old city.

• • •

He went back downstairs after a half hour or so wait. "I need to know about my father," he said.

"Why are you bothering me already?" Kehr said. "Do you want our relationship to get off on the wrong foot?"

Karel sat down. Everything was going wrong. "It's just that I haven't heard anything from him at all," he said. "I don't know what's going on." He realized with some horror that he was close to tears.

"You didn't get a letter from him?" Kehr asked.

Karel looked up guiltily. "No," he said.

Kehr raised his hands as if standing figurines on his palm. "You feel you've been badly treated," he said. "And maybe you have."

Karel felt the self-pity well up in him and had to look away. Most of the boxes and both assistants were in the spare room off the living room and the door was shut.

"It's now one-thirty," Kehr said. He laid two papers carefully over one another as if matching the edges of puzzle pieces while Karel watched. "The animals have been stacked in the back near your storage shed, which you will clear out for them. At three we'll talk."

So Karel spent an hour and a half piling the junk from the shed into a heap behind it and arranging the rabbit and chicken cages so they'd get the most of the light and breeze from the doorway. The rabbits hunkered down and watched him with a blank alertness. He caught Mrs. Witz peeking over at him from across the street, but when he stood up to talk to her she went inside.

At three he came back to the kitchen. Kehr was still sitting at the table. They were alone in the house. There was a large olive field telephone dangling a bundled and corded tangle of wires on the kitchen counter. Beside it there was a stack of thin blue books tied with string. They were titled *Psychological Operations in Partisan War.* On the cover of the top one the words were placed one under the other with rows of heads between each. The heads had holes in the foreheads.

Kehr was finishing up with some papers held down with a paperweight that looked like a small hipbone. While Karel got a drink of water and then sat opposite him he rearranged other objects on the table (a set of files, the notepad from the Fetschers', a small cup) as if they were required for what was to follow.

So, he said. Karel put his glass down. Kehr picked it up and took a sip himself. What were Karel's politics?

Karel said he didn't have any.

"Tell me the story of your mother," Kehr said.

Karel stared. His temples and cheeks felt cold. He felt a vista had opened to afford him a view of just how little he understood what was going on.

"What do *you* know about her?" he said. "Did you talk to my father about her?"

"She left you when you were very young," Kehr said. "She had artistic ambitions. She died young."

My father talks to him about her and won't talk to me, Karel thought.

"She was, I'm to understand, a very intelligent woman," Kehr said. "Strong-willed."

"How do you know all this?" Karel asked.

"I know a good deal," Kehr said. "You talk. Then I'll talk."

So Karel talked about his mother, to this Special Assistant from the Sixth Bureau. He told him what he could remember. He withheld his most specific memory, of his mother embracing him on the tile floor. He was surprised how much it distressed him to talk about this.

Kehr sighed, looking at him. He seemed sympathetic. "Your mother was associated with one of the groups opposed to the NUP in the early days," he said. "Artists' political collective. Not very astute, not very dangerous." There were other details, he added, they could talk about some other time.

"That's it?" Karel said. "That's all you're going to tell me?"

"Some other time," Kehr said. "As I said."

They sat in silence, looking at each other.

"What are you doing here?" Karel asked. "What do you want from me?"

Kehr explained he was organizing Armed Propaganda Teams for the area. He had other duties as well. The patch Karel was staring at with the sword and the snakes was an antipartisan badge.

Karel looked back at his eyes. "Where'd my father go?" he said. "Did you take him away?"

"Your father has not disappeared," Kehr said. "As far as we're concerned, no one disappears. We maintain a comprehensive criminal registry. All citizens are recorded there. No one loses himself."

"The radio's always talking about somebody you're looking for," Karel said.

"They're like beans in a coffee grinder," Kehr said affably. "They get stirred around, and sometimes the big ones displace the little ones, but they all move into the grinder."

Karel pondered the image.

"Your father," Kehr said, "happily for everyone, chose another route. Your father chose to serve his country and joined the Party. He joined, in fact, the Civil Guard."

Karel's mouth was dry. "Why would he do that?" he asked. "Why wouldn't he tell me?"

"You're asking me to speculate," Kehr said. "As for the first question, I imagine he wanted to be part of a movement in which somebody like him—a failure in the eyes of his social class, in the eyes of his family, in his own eyes—can start from scratch. As for the second, I have no idea. But maybe he explains." He produced a letter from the pile and held it out to Karel.

While he read it Karel felt the same shame he'd felt when Albert had criticized his father. His father's letter was handwritten, and the penmanship if anything was worse than he remembered:

> Karel,
>
> I know I didn't handle this in the best way possible but it had to be done this way for reasons you will soon see. Special Assistant Kehr has been good to me and you should cooperate with him. I've discovered two things I can do well: organize and facilitate. Right now I spend a lot of time outside town. I'll try to visit soon. I've given Special Assistant Kehr some money to buy a quarter of a ham or better. Make sure you eat right or you'll get sick. See you soon—
>
> Your father S. Roeder

"The ham we already bought," Kehr said.

"This letter was sealed," Karel said.

"Magic," Kehr said. He shrugged.

"He didn't tell me anything," Karel said. "He didn't tell me why he did it."

"He did it for the reason people like him do it," Kehr said. Karel could hear the impatience and contempt in his voice. "To get a job, to keep a job, to get a better job."

"He didn't have to," Karel said.

"No, he didn't," Kehr said. "No one has to display intelligence or ambition. He certainly hadn't before that."

Karel stood up. "I don't want to talk anymore," he said. Stasik and Schay came out of the spare room and looked in on them both. Kehr nodded at them and they left the house.

Karel was fingering the edge of the table. "He just left," he said. "He made all sorts of promises, that he wouldn't do what my mother did, that he'd get a good job. Then he just left."

Kehr was looking at him silently, as if he'd expected something like this. "Broken promises helped make this country what it is," he said.

They remained where they were. Karel occasionally sniffled.

"Sometimes I think it's my fault," he said. Why was he telling Kehr this?

Kehr looked unimpressed with his generosity.

"Why'd you hire him?" Karel said. "If you think he's so dumb?"

"He doesn't work for me," Kehr said. "And I certainly didn't 'hire' him. He works for the Party. He's in a different bureau. Your father I assume impressed people with his mediocrity the way others do with their talent. You know him as well as I do." He sat forward. "It's important we see these things with clarity. Your father when we found him was working for a brick manufacturer and had just dropped a load of bricks four stories. He was available.

"Since then he's been working for the Fifth Bureau," he

said. He shrugged. "I'm told he's had surprising success. The details of which I won't burden you with."

He went on about himself. The information did nothing to lift Karel's spirits or clarify his sense of what was going on. Kehr described himself as an idealist, which he defined as a man who lives for an idea, and not a businessman. This set him apart from many of his rivals in the Party, including his chief rival in the Security Service, a man he didn't name but characterized as a hedonist and a shopkeeper. When Karel contributed that he thought the war was against the nomads, Kehr agreed that that was in fact the problem. Karel was very astute, he said: what had been conceived of as a healthy competition that would foster competitive spirit and loyalty to one's outfit had in fact gotten out of hand. But power in these matters had not been strictly delegated yet, or set, Kehr said, and it remained to be seen over the next few months and years just who would control what in terms of the security of the nation. But that was neither here nor there. He asked Karel why it was, he thought, that he was not involved in any way with the Party.

Karel was taken aback. "I don't know anything about it," he said.

Kehr opened his mouth and poked around his molars with his tongue.

"You know, on the radio they talk about the program and everything, but I don't follow it," Karel said. Why was Kehr bothering with him? What did he want?

"Mmm-hmm," Kehr said. He seemed to be in no hurry. Karel rubbed his hand over his face as if he wanted the skin to come off. Here he couldn't get ten minutes of talk out of his father and this complete stranger who looked busy and important enough to Karel seemed to have all the time in the world.

Kehr suggested that Karel in the future ignore the Party program, since it was conceived largely as a public relations gesture to those outside the Party. This was a movement, not a Party; it wasn't bound to any program. Karel nodded blankly. Kehr sighed and indicated that the interview was over and that they'd talk again soon.

It was hot and sticky that night and flies crisscrossed the kitchen under the light. He stood over the stove and made a dinner of broiled chicken and fried broad beans. He'd gotten the instructions and ingredients from them. Schay stood around beside him the whole time. He spoke once, to warn him that Kehr didn't like that much oil.

Karel didn't eat with them. When they were finished he said he was going out, and Kehr let him go. He headed to Leda's to tell her what was going on and keep her from walking in on everything. He ran into her on her way over.

She announced she'd had no luck pursuing the missing inmates. He was a little insulted she'd tried without him. While they walked she said she didn't understand people anymore, that whenever she heard the celebrating on the radio she felt like going out into a deserted field and lying down by herself.

Karel told her about Kehr and left out the part about his father. She was shocked, and then angry for him, and then sympathetic. She put her hand on his waist. They sat on the Oertzens' stone wall. Behind them dishes clattered in dim windows. Leda seemed to be thrashing this out for herself. She asked if he thought Kehr's being there was connected to the missing inmates. He said he didn't know. She thought even if it wasn't, considering who he was he'd know something. She said she thought that Karel had to be careful but this was a great opportunity: Kehr had access to all sorts of information. This was a really rare opportunity. Karel sat on the wall feeling as utilitarian as a rake or a hoe. They talked about her mother, and Nicholas, and then before leaving she kissed him for the second time ever, on the corner of his mouth. The pressure was moist and warm. The kissed spot was cooler when she drew away. He walked her back to her yard and then continued home alone, musing on the quiet fervor and unfailing warmth that she always displayed toward the Karel she thought he could be.

He didn't see her for the next few days. He didn't see Albert either, or tell him what was going on. He worked around the house and followed orders—what Schay mockingly called "household tips"—and had no more talks with Kehr. He registered impressions: of showing them a bad section of plumbing and being surprised at his anxiety at their lack of approval; of coming downstairs early one morning and finding Stasik in sandals and a frayed robe in the back garden, oiling his forearms and face; of passing his father's room, now Kehr's, and the way Kehr left the door open as he dressed, pleased to be seen at it. Kehr did the same thing at night, catching Karel catching a glimpse of him folding the edges and sleeves of his tunic away into Karel's father's cupboard. At one point Karel came upon Schay going through the accumulated laundry, his hands buried in a pile of socks and shorts. Kehr at meals sat and chewed for minutes, and regarded Karel, smiling, as if remembering something mischievous from long ago.

• • •

Two units of the army were garrisoned in town and just outside of town as well. They brought with them a medium-sized camp following, and the square was impassable at busy hours. An avenue of poplars where Karel and Leda walked was leveled, bulldozed, and metaled over and then surrounded by fences for reasons no one could guess. Around town Karel saw vans full of goats, wagonloads of pigs packed shoulder to shoulder, trucks with covered load beds that gave off *moo*s. He could see cows' eyes through the slats. Everywhere, day and night, there were sleeping soldiers, dozing against the wall, in the shade, in cafés, on piles of equipment. At night he thought he could hear them from all parts of the town and from within his house, stirring and sighing in their sleep, dreaming whatever they dreamed.

The rumors were that all of this was in preparation for a visit by the Praetor himself. Kehr refused to confirm or deny anything and only looked amused at Karel's curiosity. *The People's Voice* ran a retrospective article on the Praetor's early years which mentioned the possibility, though it stressed that because of security considerations and the many claims on his time nothing was certain. The article was headed with a picture of him dozing under a grape arbor. Inside they ran a more official portrait: shirt open, jaw set, staring off past danger and personal concern to a distant goal. He had thin hair and dark, blank eyes. The biography provided nothing new. He'd worked laying telegraph lines as a boy and developed a passion for things mechanical. In school he'd been the leader, organizing his peers in political discussion groups. With the Republic came disorder and hunger, and he'd been unemployed at a time when "death and mess had become the natural order of things." He never drank but had been a solitary presence, great with books. Karel hadn't studied his life and even he knew the details by heart. He also knew through Albert and Leda the other versions everybody knew: that as a child he'd been renowned for hating everybody; that he gambled on everything and refused to pay when he lost; that he once knifed a schoolmate; that he discovered out of school that he didn't like hard work and so went around with a gang of friends harassing shopkeepers and dressing so eccentrically, with a white yachting cap, winged collar, green army breeches, and a blue workshirt, that he was known in his hometown as the Circus Performer. He'd had a beanlike growth trimmed from his forehead. (That, Leda told Karel, was a particularly delicate secret: he was so vain that before assuming power he'd responded to charges that he dyed his hair by holding a series of public baths so the people could confirm he was a natural blond.)

According to both versions he achieved his first serious political notice when he was twenty-three and the press picked up his proclamation that the streets of his country were "fields of crime" and that the Republic was to blame. It was said that he disciplined traitors to his new movement by asking them to sing the national anthem at the top of their lungs and then shooting into their open mouths. He had killed, Albert said, more people than the typhus, and in towns that had been particularly hard hit the standard curse—when someone was alone, or felt completely safe, which was less and less often—was "May his lungs collapse."

• • •

It turned out the Praetor was not visiting, though one of his closest friends—one of the old OAS (Secret Army) fanatics from his original entourage—was. The visitor's name was Subsecretary Wissinger, and he had as far as anyone could tell no real role in the government. He was on a tour visiting all the towns of the frontier, *The People's Voice* mentioned with a noticeably deflated lack of interest. His work was to discover the truth about morale and the spiritual ethers of the people. He would be giving an oration, presiding over a spontaneous celebration, and dedicating a new sculpture of two men on a bench whispering while a third in uniform overhears. Karel had not seen it yet.

He asked Kehr if that was one of the reasons Kehr was in town, and Kehr said no. The rival Security Service was handling the visit. He would not be attending the festivities and did not recommend Karel did so, either. Karel was surprised and a little impressed at his independence. Leda would have told him they all thought the same way and acted completely predictably.

Kehr told him that this was not an element of the Party of which he was particularly proud. In the old days they were signing people up wherever they found them. Still, the lowest agents fostered an anarchy that the higher ones were then pledged to eradicate, the way a doctor might give you a disease so he could cure it.

Karel went anyway. Soldiers formed a cordon around the square, and Security Service men, dressed in a way they hoped was unobtrusive, drifted through crowds that pretended not to notice them. They were immediately noticeable as the only people acting casual. One kept a close eye on a string of four-year-olds brought out to hear the speech. The four-year-olds hung on to a rope tied between two adult leaders and shuffled along like a miniature chain gang.

There were only a few booths, near the entrance to the square, with canvas flaps that could be tied shut once Wissinger began to speak. One advertising a butcher's consortium said UNITED MEAT FOR ALL and featured a line of pale calves' heads holding lemons and carnations in their teeth. One booth was called SUPPORT FOR THE MASSES and displayed a pyramid of hernia trusses tied with little flags and colored ribbons.

He recognized a lot of classmates. Besides the local NUP most of the people in the crowd were children and teenage boys. The smallest children milled around a fenced-off area entitled ORIGINAL VILLAGE OF THE RACE in which two men in blond wigs and winged helmets banged on an anvil and a woman scratched at a washboard. All of this was overlooked by a painted backdrop depicting a sunset with nomad hordes on the horizon.

Nearer the stage there were tables set up with pamphlets and Party publications that were free. Karel paged through them, keeping an eye out for someone he knew (who was he expecting to see go by? he wondered. Leda? Albert?). He kept three: a comic book called *Secret Service* with a naked girl in a waterfall on the cover and two pamphlets called *Investigations into Science: The Nomad Race* and *Torture: Why Not?*

Wissinger arrived in a car hooded in black cloth with its headlights painted over with blue calcimine. He saluted some children before he mounted the stage. He introduced a huge man by the car as Freddy the Crusher, his bodyguard. The crowd applauded.

He announced this would become an annual event of the Party. He added as if it followed that the Praetor was angry at the disturbances in the cities, the results of delinquents.

He promised that those involved or thinking of becoming involved would feel the nation's anger when the war was settled. The crowd applauded again. Karel started threading his way out, thinking he'd go by Leda's on the way home. Somebody bumped him, and he felt protectively for the pamphlets in his back pocket. The Praetor, Wissinger said, like his nation, knew the emotion of anger, of being insulted. The teenage boys closest to the stage roared. Karel took a lemon from one of the calves' mouths on the way out of the square, and had it checked carefully by a young soldier taking no chances when he passed through the cordon.

When Karel left for the zoo that morning Kehr asked him where he was going. He looked at Karel soberly over his coffee like an attentive father. He was wearing his full uniform. Karel tried to indicate by his tone that where he went was his decision. Kehr said, "The zoo is a good idea." Stasik opened the door and held it.

Albert hadn't left any instructions, and it took a while to track him down. When Karel found him in Maintenance, Albert handed him a flat rock and continued rinsing out a rag in a pail. Karel hefted the rock and told Albert he had news for him.

Albert nodded. It wasn't clear he heard or cared. He had by his feet in a deep dish covered with a warped piece of screen a pair of flat-bodied lizards. He was cleaning and rearranging the emptied cage. In the dish one of the lizards placed a leg on the back of the other, gently indenting the pliable skin.

"These are granite night lizards," Albert said.

Karel knew that. Albert had apparently given up testing him.

He was aligning the granite slabs so that the spaces between them made corridors facing the front of the cage. They liked to hide in some pretty tight crevices, he told Karel, which was fine, except then nobody saw them. Which was a bad situation for a zoo. The trick, he said, was to expose them without making them feel exposed.

Karel was interested despite himself, and got angry. He had big news. He needed advice. He could wait until he dropped for Albert to ask how he was doing.

"I still haven't been paid for my last weeks," he finally said irritably. Albert looked at him. "I mean, you know, the stuff I did a while ago," he said.

Albert said, "I don't think your heart is in this work anymore. I think you've got other interests."

Sure, you do this, too, Karel thought. He was surprised at his bitterness.

"Did you hear what I said?" Albert asked.

"How would you know?" Karel said. "You ever asked me?"

Albert looked at him again and continued to shift the rocks. He leaned more into the cage. Good-sized pieces of flat rock, preferably granite, he said. Slanted and supported so the spaces were a half inch with the openings facing the front, and gravel as ground media. When you had decent gravel. The lizards stirred in the dish as if in appreciative interest.

"It's like I'm not even talking," Karel said. "I might as well not be here."

Albert stopped what he was doing. "I'm *trying* to teach you something," he said. "I've been trying since you came to me." They were looking at each other, and Karel had the uncomfortable feeling that Albert suspected him of something. After a minute Albert went on about the lizards.

Karel shrugged. It's my life, he thought. Why should you care about it?

"I've got the Civil Guard at my house," he said. "A man named Special Assistant Kehr. They moved in."

Albert set the granite down and continued to gaze at it. "What do you mean, 'moved in'?" he asked. He sounded as if it had been Karel's idea.

Karel gave him another shrug but Albert was looking into the cage. Did Karel mean they were searching his house?

"I don't think so," Karel said.

They were billeted there?

"That's it," Karel said. "Kehr took my father's room."

Albert was quiet, and disturbed, he could see. It gave him some satisfaction. What had they talked about? Albert wanted to know. Had they asked a lot of questions?

Not really, Karel said. They hadn't done much of anything, as far as he could tell. He didn't know whether to tell about his father. He was going to get some version of I-told-you-so if he opened his mouth, he knew.

"My father joined the Civil Guard," he said.

Albert put the heel of his hand on his forehead and rubbed it as if erasing something. "Who told you that?" he asked. "Kehr?"

The question shocked Karel. "You mean you think he might not have?" he said.

"What bureau?" the old man said. "Did he say?"

"The Fifth, I think. I got a letter from him."

"A jailer," Albert said. "Perfect."

"You think it's not true? You think somebody made him write the letter?" Karel asked. "*What?* Nobody ever *talks* to me."

"I don't know," Albert said. "I don't know your father. I don't know what Kehr's up to."

"*Up* to?" Karel said. "What's he care about us?"

Albert lifted the bowl to the open enclosure and tipped the two lizards onto the gravel. They fell on their bellies together with a quiet plop. "He probably did," he said. "Your father, I mean. Why wouldn't he?"

"If he did it's not my fault," Karel said.

Albert finished up with the cage.

"I don't like staying there right now," Karel said. Albert nodded and turned and led him down the hall through one of the outbuildings to the quarantine station. Karel was uncomfortable the whole time, his hint hanging unacknowledged, and he wished there were a way to take it back. At the quarantine station Perren was working alone, humming to something slightly syncopated on the radio. He was guiding a dead mouse into a bushmaster's mouth with a pair of forceps. On the table opposite there was a metal basin the size of a bathtub.

Albert peered over into it and made whispery clicking noises with his tongue. A black-and-red Gila was asleep inside. It was on its back with its legs in the air in the relaxed and oblivious manner of a puppy. Some egg yolk was drying in an anchored dish near its head. Albert remarked sadly that no one was eating lately, and Karel understood he was being asked to leave.

Albert mentioned Seelie, who was refusing even eggs. His bringing up the Komodos at this point hurt Karel in ways he couldn't explain. He couldn't quit. "Do you think I should stay somewhere else?" he finally said.

Sure, stay with me, Albert could say. You can't live with those people. It's not like you don't have anywhere else to go.

Albert seemed to be aware of Perren at the other table. "I don't see why," he said. "It's your house, too."

Karel fought the humiliation and disappointment the way he'd fought surf at the beach. His face burned with it.

It wasn't like it was a real problem, anyway, he told Albert. They got along. Kehr wasn't like the others. And he was starting to show him things.

"I'll bet he is," Albert said. Perren turned off the radio. Albert said, "Maybe you'd better not come back here for a while."

Karel closed his eyes. He felt pitiful and hated it.

"There's no work now, anyway," Albert said. "And you have all this to deal with. We haven't paid you for your old work."

"You're not letting me back here," Karel said. "Because of all this."

Perren made a clacking noise with the forceps, and Karel had the impression he was being made fun of. Albert reached in and lifted the sleeping Gila like a red-and-black baby and didn't say anything else, and Karel turned and ran out of the room and out of the zoo.

At home he found Stasik in his T-shirt and uniform pants playing with a ringtail while Kehr watched. The ringtail was on the floor in the kitchen and they were flanking it with chairs. Kehr was on the field telephone, listening, for the most part. Whoever had installed it had punched a hole through the kitchen wall.

The ringtail was curled in a crouch and jittery. They had the doorways to the other rooms blocked off with empty cartons, and it was giving each carton the once-over. It was a few feet long and had the weird amalgamated look of all ringtails, as if assembled by committee: a cat's body, a fox's head with huge, pale eyes, a raccoon's fat bushy tail banded in black and white. While he watched it lifted a pink paw to him as if in greeting.

He'd always heard from his father that they could give a nasty bite, but Kehr and Stasik seemed unfazed, and Stasik was feeding it crickets. He had the crickets in a paper bag. He set them down one by one, and the ringtail would back off, its fat tail curling and undulating warily. It ignored the crickets' first tentative hop and pounced after the second, coming down on them with both paws and stuffing them in its cheek.

Kehr cupped his hand over the receiver and introduced it to Karel as their new friend. Stasik had found it in the shed with the chickens. The ringtail backed coolly under the kitchen table at Karel's approach and refused to come out. It cheeped when he passed through heading for his bedroom, and when he stepped over the boxes it negotiated its way along the wall in the opposite direction. Near the sink it defecated.

In his room he shut the door and lay on his bed. Why was he worrying about the house like he was caretaker? Who else cared about it? What was he looking out for? Boxes of family things he didn't recognize? You don't have a family, he thought. Get that through your head. What did he care about this town, this zoo, Albert, his father? Why hadn't he run away already?

He heard someone come up the stairs and stop outside the door.

"I know somebody's there," he said.

There was a cough and a knock. "What?" he said. "What? What do you want from me?"

Kehr opened the door. He had a folder in his hands. He sat on the bed, and Karel moved his legs to make room.

"Our ringtail was having an energetic discussion with the chickens when Stasik found him," he said.

"What're you doing here?" Karel said. "All you do is hang around the house. They pay you to hang around the house?"

Kehr smiled. His skin was completely smooth, and he seemed at ease. If I looked like that Leda would love me, Karel found himself thinking. He shook it off. Kehr said, "I haven't started working yet. I'm engaged in what we call the preliminary stages."

Karel wasn't even going to ask, and give him the satisfaction. He reached over and switched on the radio. Kehr opened the folder and looked inside it as if waiting for something. The radio went on about sectors in the rear being scoured of trouble, and Karel reached over and shut it off.

Kehr said, "I have something for you." He held out the folder.

Inside was a photograph of a woman's face. She had large eyes and dark hair under a big hat. She was looking at him with a serious expression. Her mouth was slightly pursed.

He blinked. He could feel pressure in his throat, like the impulse to swallow. "Is this my mother?" he asked.

Kehr nodded. He had had it sent, he said. It had been in one of the old files.

Karel held it before him, trying to overlay the image on his blurred and incomplete memory. Kehr put a hand on Karel's shin and then took it away. The face was so concrete and open to study that it was disorienting and made him suspicious, even as he recognized how moved he was by its revelatory power: *this is her, this is what she looked like.*

"This is my mother," he said, to himself, and while he continued to look Kehr stood up and left the room, closing the door behind him.

He stood the photo against the wall and turned off the light. The face gazed down at him whitely from the darkness. It was as if he had somebody else now to think about, his father, Albert, Leda, his mother from the tiled floor, and now this woman. When he slept that night they all mixed together in ways his dreams didn't make clear.

The next morning he heard a banging in the kitchen and went downstairs. Kehr was on his back under the sink with a huge range of tools. The others were out. The ringtail was cowering under the kitchen table from the noise.

"Good morning," Kehr said. "Time to fix the plumbing. I made some coffee."

Karel poured himself a cup and sat down. The ringtail scrabbled away at his approach.

Kehr clanked and banged away unseen. Karel sipped his coffee. This was better than the stuff he made. Someone had cleaned the pot. "Time to put a little work into this house," Kehr said.

Karel rubbed his eyes, disoriented by the attempted domesticity. "Don't you have people who could do that?" he asked.

"Give me a hand," Kehr said. "Hand me the wrench." His hand waved and flopped around outside the cabinet to indicate its search.

Karel took another sip and then got up and brought the mug with him. He knelt on the floor by Kehr's legs. He could smell urine from the ringtail somewhere when he got this low. He surveyed the tools in front of him and picked up something plausible. "Is this it?" he asked.

Kehr leaned his chin on his chest from inside the cabinet to look. "That's it," he said. "You know your tools." He took it and went back to clanging. Why specific tools were important if he was just going to bang away, Karel didn't know.

Nobody'd done anything about this plumbing for a while, Kehr remarked.

"My father always said he was going to," Karel said.

Kehr didn't answer. There was the high metallic wrenching sound of the threading on the pipes going.

"You're going to have to hold the catch basin here a minute," Kehr said. He guided Karel's hand to the piece and showed him where to support it. Karel braced his other arm on the floor. The ringtail had curled around a kitchen chair in the far corner of the room and was working on one of the legs with its fine, saw-edged teeth.

"We'll handle this," Kehr said. "The two of us will straighten this out."

"I wanted to thank you for the picture," Karel said. He got a better angle under the catch basin. "Do you have anything else like that?"

Kehr made an appreciative noise and shifted around on his back. "Look at this," he said. "Come in here a little farther."

Karel shifted hands on the basin and edged into the darkness under the cabinet. He was stretching over Kehr in the tiny space. He waited for his eyes to adjust.

Kehr pointed with a hand near his cheek at the part of the wall laid open for the feeder pipe. Karel waited and then could make out coiled movement inside. He looked closer.

It was a thin black snake with a long head. It opened its mouth at them, and Karel could see the pale eggs it encircled.

"Whip snake," Kehr said. "A striped whip snake."

"That's right," Karel said. "How'd you know that?"

Kehr snorted. "Zoology is a school for precise feeling," he said. " 'The eye of the naturalist is as penetrating and as scrupulous as the eye of the sniper.' "

Karel made a puzzled face for his own benefit in the darkness. He asked what that meant.

"That means there's a lot to be gained by doing what you do, by learning what you know," Kehr said.

"There is?" Karel said.

"There is," Kehr said. He was unwrapping old joint-sealing tape from an S-shaped piece he wanted to extract. "I'm always interested in people who take the time and effort to study what's around them. They're practicing seeing with clarity and precision."

"I guess that's true," Karel said.

It was true, Kehr said. It was both a gift and a discipline. There was a thump and a light clatter, and then a tiny lapping sound: the ringtail had turned over the dish of water and was drinking off the floor. It was what his country required of him, Kehr said. And it was what his country needed: more people who could do that.

"How'd you know I knew about stuff like that?" Karel asked.

"Abilities like that are hard to hide," Kehr said, and Karel felt flattered. Then it occurred to him that there were nine thousand books and study sheets on reptiles up in his room.

"I grew up almost completely alone," Kehr said.

"You did?" Karel said. As close as he was in the darkness he couldn't see Kehr's eyes.

"I did," Kehr said. "Nature for me was something I could learn about and lose myself in, something that demonstrated order and reason: comparative study, classification, the relations of the total design."

"I don't know," Karel said uncomfortably. "I think I just think reptiles are great."

"And so they are," Kehr said. "Look. Look at the way her head scales are edged in white. Little crescents." The whip snake raised its head farther, watching them with sidelong intent.

Karel saw. Kehr was not quizzing him and not judging him. "See the way she tries to distract you from the nest?" he said.

Kehr murmured he did. They were still close in the darkness under the cabinet, and Karel began to register the heat and stillness. His arm ached. He was still supporting the catch basin.

"Let's finish this and leave Mother alone," Kehr said.

The threads on the pipe section that was the problem were now stripped and had to be refiled. Kehr had him let the catch basin down, and they climbed out from under the cabinet. He gave Karel a part of the filing job and showed him how to use the reamer and how to smooth and clear the diagonal grooves.

"Do you work with animals?" Karel said.

"Not technically," Kehr said. "I work with people. But the training with one helps me with the other."

"How?" Karel said.

"I'll tell you sometime," he said. "What I do is a lot of questioning." He hesitated before the word. He nodded toward the door. "If you and I walked into your shed, we could see certain things in some of the rabbits, couldn't we? Which ones were like this, which ones were like that."

"I guess," Karel said. "You mean like who's most scared and stuff."

"That's what I mean," Kehr said. "And when you pick one out for dinner, you don't do it randomly, do you?"

"No," Karel said, realizing that fully for the first time. While Kehr worked he thought about that.

"So you had no interest in joining the Party," Kehr said, as if summarizing an old story. He was absorbed in the pipe. "Did you ever consider joining the partisans?"

Karel was immediately alert. "No," he said. "Nobody asked me. I don't know any partisans."

Kehr arched his eyebrows. "I don't have much against the partisans," he finally said. "They're simply activists, like me. They act. If I weren't doing what I am doing I'd probably be doing what they're doing. If their fathers hadn't been Republicans they'd probably all be in the Civil Guard right now."

"Aren't they killing people and sabotaging things?" Karel asked cautiously.

"They're frustrated," Kehr said. "It's natural. They want to act. They want more of a voice. They feel all the exchange with their government's one-way. It's like the son who wants to get his father's attention so he can explain himself. Do you see what I mean?"

"Umm-hmm," Karel said. He put his section of pipe down and stood up. The ringtail was on the stove, its tail curled down the front like a potholder, and its mouth open in some sort of silent communication.

• • •

That night Kehr brought some tea up to Karel once Karel was already in bed, and they sat in the dark. Karel was under the covers with his back against the wall. Kehr sat at the desk. The photograph of Karel's mother was on the table between them, illuminated by the light from the window. Karel thanked him for the tea. Downstairs in the spare room Stasik and Schay were moving things around. Here he was in his bedroom with a stranger from the Civil Guard and a picture of his mother and there was something comforting to him about even this ghost of a family. Kehr told snake stories in a quiet voice as if they'd had plenty of talks like this before. Karel cupped his tea in his hands and listened to the occasional shooting in the distance sounding like the popping of grilled corn and was glad somebody was in his house. Kehr told a story about a constrictor that had swallowed a rolled-up rug because it had been used by a dog for a bed. He talked about the Party and the way it was like something out of nature, always growing, organic. Had Karel seen all the building going on around town? It was like that all over, and in all different ways—the whole idea was to keep doing, keep growing, so that the movement itself was always changing and becoming more radical, leaving even its own members psychologically one step behind it. Could Karel recognize that kind of excitement?

Karel said he could, after a pause in which he realized he was expected to reply. He wasn't listening well, he realized, flattered that Kehr was talking to him as an adult.

Was there anything Karel was devoted to? Anything that gave him a reason for being? What was Karel doing? What was he here for?

There were the reptiles, Karel thought. But what would that come to now? There was Leda. He imagined Kehr's response, and winced.

"I see these people's lives," Kehr said, his voice coming out of the dark, "and I just don't understand it. Their lives just go on, like lights left on in rooms when everyone's gone."

Karel slid down in the bed, imagining himself like that. He was saddened and angered by his own mediocrity. He focused on Leda. She was crouching on the talus slope with him, intent on his nooser. Kehr was still talking. The photograph of his mother was up there somewhere in the dark. He put his hands over his eyes and wished for another world. Kehr finished and got up and gave his leg a pat and then went downstairs. Karel heard him talking with the others in a low voice, and then they all went to bed.

School was now closed indefinitely. Leda asked to meet him somewhere other than either of their houses, so he chose the zoo. He didn't want to go back there, but the café reminded him of Kehr and the zoo was all he could subsequently think of. Another walk south of town was out because of all the activity around there, and he was worried that if he hesitated too long she'd suggest Nicholas's hospital. He showed up early and regretted his choice even more: he had to pay to enter. He walked around as just part of the crowd. It felt like the confirmation of his new outsider's status.

He trailed his hand on the railings fronting the enclosures and thought about the work going on behind them. The anoles and whiptails seemed miles away. It was early and the constrictors were still not out, and neither was the tortoise. He wondered if it was having problems again.

He ended up in front of Seelie and Herman. There was a shank of something dark brown and covered with flies near the glass. He guessed that she was still giving them trouble with her eating and they were letting the meat go to see if it would tempt her.

He watched her while he waited. She was drooped along a granite lounging area on the far left of the enclosure. It was the way she got when she was unhappy or irritable. Herman was lying on his side on the opposite end, his eye fixed on the wall. It was like an illustration of reptile divorce or estrangement. He imagined the two of them in their blank matter-of-fact way having given up on each other, having registered, the way Karel imagined people did, that it had come to this.

When Leda arrived they went to the restaurant. Karel showed his work card to the waiter and asked if he still got a discount and the waiter said no.

Leda said, "My mother's at home and we couldn't talk at your house because of that guy."

"So," Karel said. He folded and unfolded his arms at the table. He was unhappy and beginning to get a little worried. "What's up?"

"I want to get out of here," Leda said.

Karel made his I-know-that face.

Soon, because of Nicholas, she said. She pursed and unpursed her lips in a small, affecting way.

"Your cousin again, in the Civil Guard?" Karel asked.

She nodded. Had that guy said anything about anything going on at the hospital?

"I think he's in another bureau," Karel said. She looked at him skeptically.

"I want to have it all set up," she said. She began drawing lines and then boxes on the table between them with her index finger. "Then I'll tell my mother. If she wants to go, fine."

"It's going to be real hard to travel now," Karel said. She looked off, and he knew he was losing her when he said things like this, fulfilling her worst image of him. He hadn't done much at all to find out about getting out, as she'd asked him to. Kehr he figured would know things like that, but he didn't know if he should bring it up around Kehr, however obliquely.

"Also David says he wants to join the Kestrels," she said morosely.

He found himself trying to trace the outline of the invisible box she'd drawn. "Can't you say no?" he asked.

"My mother says it looks bad. And that they're not so horrible in the first place. It's getting so the only other kids who haven't joined are off with Nicholas."

There was an older couple beside them who hadn't said anything in a while. Karel had the impression they were listening.

Here was the thing, Leda said. She wanted to know if he wanted to come, if he wanted to help. It was going to be hard, taking care of Nicholas and David and her mother.

And getting travel passes, Karel said.

And getting travel passes, she said. She looked at him and he felt nasty and cynical. Five was a lot, she said, and it would be easier if two different families tried to get them. Plus maybe his friend Albert from here could help. Leda said, "You told me they have to travel to get specimens and stuff."

Karel said he didn't think Albert would help. He was feeling again that she just wanted something from him, and he was fighting that feeling. She ran her fingertips tenderly over her eyes and then pulled sideways at the skin on her temples, accentuating her eyes' slant. He had a momentary and clear sense of how much all of this was hurting her, how much the planning and worry were taking out of her. "But maybe this guy in my house can," he added.

She looked at him cautiously. "Him then," she said. She sounded as if she hadn't had much faith to start in this meeting and had just lost most of that. "But we have to do something soon. I'm taking Nicholas for a walk on Saturday and I'm not bringing him back. My cousin says there's going to be something over there again on Saturday night, Sunday at the latest. He says to get him out of there. When I don't bring him back they're going to send somebody, and when they do we can't be home."

"So you're going to go by this Sunday?" Karol asked incredulously.

"Yes," Leda said. "Yes."

"What if I can't get any stuff by then?" he said, panicked. "Information?"

"Then I'm going anyway," she said.

"But they'll pick you up," he said. "How will you get anywhere?"

"Do you understand what's going to happen to Nicholas?" she said.

The metal table rang with the question. They shifted in their chairs, and noticed the quiet. The older couple listened in for a minute more, and then the man cleared his throat.

"I better go talk to this guy," Karel said. "I better go now."

"Why do you call him 'this guy'?" Leda said. She was looking at him suspiciously. "What's his name again?"

"Kehr," he said. "What's the matter?"

She continued to look. "Nothing," she said finally. Then she said she didn't want to call and they should meet back here tomorrow.

"I need more time, I think," he said.

"Tomorrow afternoon," she said, getting up. "Just find out what you can. If you're not going I have to start figuring out what I'm going to do."

She waved, once, from across the street. The waiter came and asked if he was ready to order. The older couple at the next table chuckled together. They were sharing a piece of honey cake. He got up while the waiter waited and pushed in his chair before he left the table, to make up in a small way for his not having bought anything.

He had two days. On top of that he had to meet with her tomorrow, too. No one was home when he returned. The spare room was locked. He sat at the kitchen table with his head in his hands and looked at two spoons crossed and balanced over a coffee cup as if the configuration meant something and had been arranged for him to find. The ringtail tracked by in a jaunty trot.

It was what he wanted, to run away with her. But now he was confused and frightened, as if he'd been asked to do something terrible. He owed Kehr something. He owed his father something. He had the impression they were both out there somewhere waiting for him to make a disastrous mistake. But he remembered too Leda's face at the restaurant: she was equally convinced he'd fail in the opposite way.

He snorted, his hands over his mouth. Was there anybody anywhere who thought he might do the *right* thing? The ringtail sat on its hind legs near the door and licked its paws.

What was this Kehr stuff? What *about* Kehr? There was

nothing there. Who knew what the man wanted? But the idea of him stayed with Karel, like the idea of his father coming back. It was as if Kehr had demonstrated how even lives like his could have developed assurance and focus.

He went upstairs and dug out his father's letter. He kept it hidden; he wasn't sure why. He brought it downstairs and reread it.

If he loved Leda there wouldn't be any hesitation, he thought.

That was true. And here he was hesitating. He was the King of Hesitation, he thought bitterly. That's what he should do for his country: hesitate. He slapped his cheek in disgust, and the ringtail looked over with interest.

Kehr had cleared the table of his papers. Someone had set a dish of plums out, recently enough that they were still beaded with condensation. Against the wall there was a copy of the book he'd seen before: *Psychological Operations in Partisan War.* He picked it up. He had the sense the table had been arranged for him, like someone setting out milk and cookies. Outside the window something was startled into flight, the concussion of wings frightening him.

He tried to guess the idea behind the holes in the heads on the cover: bullet holes? The place the information went in? On the first page it said:

> Partisan warfare is essentially a political war. Therefore its area of operations exceeds the statutory and territorial limits of conventional warfare, to penetrate the political entity itself, the political animal. In effect, the human being should be considered the primary objective in a partisan war. And conceived of as a military target, the human being has his most critical point in his mind.

He closed and opened his eyes and read the sentence again. He got frustrated after a third try and kept going.

> Once the mind has been reached the political animal has been defeated, without necessarily receiving bullets.
>
> This book is a manual for the training of low-level counterinsurgency and antipartisan units in psychological operations, with specific application in the concrete case of the current national struggle with partisan groups and undesirables, both within and outside our present boundaries. Welcome!

Stasik came in, causing the ringtail to circle on itself and show its teeth. Karel put the book back against the wall. Stasik ignored him. Karel stretched and asked about Kehr, and Stasik had no idea when he was coming back.

Kehr never did. Karel waited up, lying on top of his sheets in the darkness, listening.

The next morning Karel found him back at the kitchen table, which was again covered with papers. Someone had made hard-boiled eggs and there was more coffee.

Karel sat at the table in his shorts, and Kehr said something without looking up about the laziness of cooks and teenagers. He finally stopped what he was doing. "Can I help you?" he said.

Karel nodded, and Kehr waited.

"I had a question about traveling," Karel said.

Kehr looked at him with stone eyes. "Are you going somewhere?" he said.

"No, not me," Karel said. "Well, I was thinking about it. I have a friend who wants to go somewhere. To the capital. I know travel passes are hard to get right now." This, he thought, was a real big mistake.

"I thought you were going to continue to work at the zoo," Kehr said quietly. "I thought you liked to work at the zoo."

"I did," Karel said. His stomach felt as it did when he finished pots of coffee himself. "But Albert over there told me he didn't need me for a while. Albert Delp. We had sort of a fight. Or something."

Kehr's expression didn't change. Karel thought of the rabbits in his shed before dinner, watching him all the way from the door to whatever cage he stopped at. Kehr said, "Nobody's going anywhere right now that's not official business. Nobody's getting travel passes. Unless somebody like me arranges it, as a special favor." He took out a small pass card, with an antipartisan symbol printed on it, and held it up for Karel to see. Then he pocketed it, and looked back down at his work.

Stasik touched Karel on the shoulder to signal it was time to go. Karel stood up.

"A friend?" Kehr asked, his attention on his work.

"Yes," Karel said. He waited, but Kehr didn't ask. Stasik led him out.

He told Leda at the restaurant, and she nodded quickly and told him she'd talk to him and left. They hadn't even sat down. She hadn't asked if he wanted to go. He was convinced he'd lost her and broke broom-handle-size sticks on tree trunks all the way home.

He stopped by the Reptile House in desperation, but Albert was out, or wouldn't see him.

He paced his room and haunted Leda's street the next day, unable to approach Kehr to try again or Leda to tell her he was going. He sat in his room that night and thought, I should be packing. Saturday morning he helped Stasik and Schay unload boxes and odd folding frameworks of wood and metal that neither of them would comment on, and then made their lunch. In the afternoon they sent him to the market. At one point while dragging his baskets from vendor to vendor he held up a melon and thought, She's doing it right now. He imagined her leading Nicholas through the gates, Nicholas looking over his shoulder at that place for the last time. He hand-washed Stasik's uniform cap, which had a thin looping arc of a bloodstain across the brim. He made dinner. He cleaned up with water and ammonia some hard-to-reach messes the ringtail had left. Finally he got away in the early evening, and ran all the way to her hedge. Lounging soldiers watched him go by and tried to lead him with pebbles, arguing over whose came closest.

The neighbors were standing around her house under the streetlight, discussing something. There was an overturned red wagon on the sidewalk. He recognized it as David's. Most of the lights were on in the house, including in Leda's room. Their front door was open. He began running again.

The collected neighbors watched him go by and into the house as if this were one of the expected developments.

The hall light was still on. Moths looped and staggered beneath it. One drawer of a small chest in the hallway was pulled out. One of the family photos atop the chest was tipped over and lying on its face. A corner of the rug was turned up.

He shouted for her and felt cold and terrified and ran from room to room. There was a half-filled suitcase on the kitchen floor. There were folded and unfolded blankets heaped on the table. He recognized empty spaces in the living and dining rooms, marked by faint outlines on the floor, and realized furniture was missing. On the dining-room table a black-and-gray spider the size of a child's hand had centered itself on one of the dinner plates.

In her room he couldn't tell how much was gone. Some drawers were empty and the dresser top looked bare. Her bed was unmade and the folds in the bedclothes formed a face. On the floor by the dressing table he found an abandoned blouse that kept the shape of her shoulders.

Outside one of the neighbors folded her arms and told him they were gone.

"Did they say where they were going?" Karel asked. He scanned the yard: a dishtowel hung from the prickly pear along the walk.

"No," the woman said. "And neither did the police."

"The police took them?" Karel asked. His throat felt closed.

They certainly did, the woman said. The whole bunch. Her companions murmured. He could see in her expression the beginnings of the notion that maybe this kid who was so interested was wanted, too.

He ran to the police station. He had to stop four different times, swaying and bent low, hands on his thighs, gasping for breath. Sweat stung his eyes.

There was an open-backed truck filled with darkness in front of the station. When he stopped to wipe the sweat from his eyes with both hands an upright piano skidded from the back of it and fell the four feet to the street. It landed with a tremendous noise and sprang open like a trick box. Two soldiers appeared where it had been in the back and threw out a full-length mirror. It pitched aerodynamically onto the piano and shattered with a spray of flashing glass. These were Leda's family's, he recognized them, and he rushed to the back of the truck and caught the leg of a soldier emerging from the darkness with an end table. The soldier kicked his hand away like a vine or rope and Karel grabbed for it again, idiotically, and the soldier holding the table looked down at him and he recognized then that the soldier could kill him and that that would be the end of it. He stood there, dumb with the knowledge, and while he did he could see the soldier formulate the decision not to. He understood from his expression that the decision represented what Albert used to call, when deciding which individual to choose when gathering specimens, a whim.

Someone put a hand on his shoulder and turned him around, and Kehr was standing there in full uniform. "Let's leave our friend here alone," he said. The soldier set the table down on the truck bed and saluted. Kehr nodded and turned Karel away, leading him with a hand on the back of the neck.

Very dangerous, very foolish, he said. He shook his head as if Karel had been caught climbing the roof of his house. Karel was still both astonished and relieved and was trying to formulate a question.

"Regular troops, recruited to help out," Kehr said, leading him into the station. "Working under the assumption that the taking of souvenirs was allowed whenever they assisted in a mousetrap."

"A mousetrap?" Karel said.

Kehr looked as if he'd been insufficiently discreet. A technical term, he said. Anyway, as Karel could see, they'd taken the news that the furniture was still the property of the state badly.

"Aren't they going to return it?" Karel said.

"In some areas it's wise not to push these types too far," Kehr said. He signaled the sergeant on duty at the desk, and the sergeant opened the swinging gate to the rooms in the back. They were blocked by a woman with thin arms and sunken eyes who was trying to regain the sergeant's attention. She asked him to check again on her little boy. Kehr excused himself, and when she stepped aside he brushed by her. Karel followed. The sergeant told her that there were no children here and that this was not a kindergarten.

At a blank door Kehr paused and looked down the hall at a corporal seated on a child's chair and reading a magazine. Kehr waited for his attention and then pointed interrogatively at the door, raising his eyebrows. The corporal saluted, and nodded yes, that was the one. Karel could hear voices behind it.

Kehr mimed an "oh" and nodded thanks and then delicately turned the handle. He held the door open and gestured Karel through. He said he'd give him a few minutes. When Karel hesitated, Kehr reassured him with a puzzled look, as if to suggest he had no idea why Karel might hesitate. Once Karel was through he shut the door behind him with exaggerated politeness.

The Schieles were all in the room, with three suitcases and a bundle made from a bedsheet tied with rope. Two of the suitcases were open, and Stasik and another member of the Civil Guard Karel didn't know were going through them, holding shirts and pants up, giving each a gentle shake at eye level and dropping it on the floor. Leda was standing against the wall. David and Nicholas were sitting beside her on a bench. Their mother was in a folding chair nearby. Leda caught his eye but didn't change her expression, and he didn't cross the room to her. Mrs. Schiele was looking at her suitcases as if someone were spitting in them or filling them with animal parts.

Stasik nudged the other Civil Guardsman and pointed out Karel, and they left everything where it was, and waited for him to get out of the way so they could leave the room.

Mrs. Schiele thanked God once the door closed. She'd been crying. She seemed to believe things had been turned around by his presence. "I told Leda your friend would help straighten this out," she said gratefully. "I told her."

"Be quiet, Mother," Leda said. David waved a hello. He had a paper cup on the floor next to him, and a toy boat, and he was shaking iridescent water from the boat.

"What happened?" Karel said. He was talking to Leda. She was looking at him closely, and he was chilled by her expression.

"You tell me," she said. "I took Nicholas for the walk and when I got him home your friend Kehr was already there. They had David and my mother and were loading the piano into the back of the truck."

"More and more people kept getting into the truck after we did," David said. "We kept having to move over."

"That piano is an antique," Mrs. Schiele said. "Do you think they'd just *take* it like that?"

"How'd they know so soon?" Karel said.

"What a good question," Leda said.

"I didn't do anything!" Karel protested. "I didn't tell anybody!" He took a step toward her. Nicholas looked at him intently and then returned his attention to David.

Leda turned her head a little and kept her eyes on him. He couldn't tell whether she believed him or not.

"Now I'm accused of kidnapping," Leda said. She

seemed fiercely calm. "And they say they found other things, publications, in my room."

"You mean those newspapers? Those pamphlets?" Karel said, and realized from her face that she thought someone was listening.

"I told them people come and go from my house all the time," Mrs. Schiele said. "With all the work I do for the Women's League it's a shock if I'm home at all. With membership drives and contribution collections they absolutely run us ragged. Who knows what's where? Who knows how things get in your house?" She shifted in her folding chair, and Karel understood that even she realized they were being listened to.

He crossed to where Leda was standing. She was giving David and Nicholas hard candy from her pockets and they were filling their cheeks like squirrels. Nicholas had figs in one hand as well, and David had between his legs a hat-sized bag with most of his smaller toys in it. It was as if in a modest way she was spoiling them in anticipation of disaster.

While they were working on the candies she showed him a folded piece of paper by lifting it slightly above the top of her breast pocket and tapping it down again. She took him aside. "This is what convinced Mother," she whispered. "They sent us notification of Nicholas's death today. A day early. The date's for Monday. He was on his way home with me when it arrived."

"You say to yourself, be patient, act responsibly, and one of these days things'll be quiet again," Mrs. Schiele said. "And then—one piece of bad luck like this." She eyed the half-empty suitcase, clearly wondering if she dared repack her things. David was reading a small book from the bag between his legs: *Dr. Catchfly: Fantastic Adventures in the World of Insects.* "I'm so confused," she finally added. She seemed to be getting angrier. "You don't know what to do. After a while you only think of the children. You think, what'll become of the children?"

"We're not the first family to be brought here," Leda said.

"We're the first family *I* know," Mrs. Schiele said. "We didn't *know* the other families in those cases."

Leda turned away.

Karel put his hand on her wrist. Mrs. Schiele sat by herself on the folding chair away from them all and touched her eyes and hair and clothes in small repetitious cycles. He had a momentary sense of how put-upon and abandoned she felt. She'd always been frightened of most things, and now her fear was more comprehensive.

"Nicholas, I need to talk to David a minute," Leda said quietly. "Can I do that?" She nodded to encourage him. Nicholas stood and walked to the other side of the room. Once there he put his hand on the wall and seemed to be studying its texture.

"David, they're going to talk to us soon, one by one," Leda said, her voice low. "And they're going to want to know about my books. The books I kept in the special place. Now, Nicholas doesn't know about them and Mom already knows what to say. What are *you* going to say if they ask?" She was holding him by both arms.

"The books?" David said. He was clinging to his toy boat.

"You know, the books, the secret books," Leda said. She was keeping her voice calm, but Karel could hear the desperation in it. "Now everything depends on you. Remember what I whispered to you in the truck? What are you going to say?"

"In the truck?" David said.

"David!" she said, and shook him hard, once. He began to cry.

"David, don't cry, don't cry," she said, near despair. Across the room Karel could see Nicholas looking over, unsure what was going on and sad that he had so little he could contribute.

"What will you say, honey?" Leda persisted.

"The man brought them in when you were out," David half-wailed. She hugged him tightly.

"That's it, that's it, honey," she said. "Did I know him?"

"No," he wailed.

"Did any of us know him?" she said. She was looking up at Karel.

"No," David said. He pulled away and rubbed his eyes.

She let him go. He sat down and focused on his boat with fierce concentration. She put her hands over her face and remained where she was, kneeling.

Karel crouched beside her. "They're going to interrogate you?" he asked. She didn't respond. She brought her hands down from her face. "Are you scared?" he said.

"Yes I am," she said, without shame. "Very."

Kehr opened the door and signaled. Karel leaned forward impulsively and kissed Leda on the cheek. "I'll get him to help," he whispered. "It'll be okay."

She made her mouth into a tight line and nodded. Mrs. Schiele stood up and gave him a hug. Kehr waited at the door with an easygoing patience.

Outside in the hall he raised a hand when Karel was about to speak. He shut the door and led Karel in silence to a small room a few doors down. The corporal was gone. The room was dark, and Kehr sat him in front of a pane of glass and then left, shutting the door behind him.

The pane glowed with light and Karel realized he was gazing in on another room. There was a bare black table centered in it with a hard-backed chair on either side. It was absolutely quiet.

Kehr interrogated them alone. They came into the room one by one. Karel could hear nothing.

Mrs. Schiele was first. Karel sat in the dark and watched her and heard nothing. She gestured and swung her arms around, leaned back as if to physically avoid certain questions, leaned forward to seem confidential. He imagined her chatter: defenses of Leda mixed in with scraps of old fights and resentments, protests against the injustice of all this, assurances that someone somewhere had made a comic mistake. Toward the end she gave Kehr a sly look and Karel figured she was attempting some sort of maneuver. Kehr looked bored.

Nicholas was next. He was there only a few minutes. He gripped the edge of the table and sat upright, making a visible effort to be alert. When Kehr stood up and dismissed him, Karel could see in his face his sense that he'd failed again to provide something that somebody wanted or would approve of.

Leda followed. He sat right up on top of the glass and he still couldn't hear anything. She faced Kehr with the same calmness Karel knew and loved from the afternoons in her garden, that expression that was at once open and placid and intelligent. She was questioned a longer time than the first two, but when she got up he knew she was still safe.

He shook with excitement and fear waiting for David. There was some delay. He put his fingertips to the glass and they trembled across it like something dropped into hot oil. When David finally came in, Kehr acted differently, sitting on the floor in the corner as if too shy to confront him. David had his boat and sailed it back and forth across the table.

Karel waited in something that was getting to be like agony. Kehr was still in the corner, and now David was talking to him. He stayed in the corner but finally put his elbows on his knees and his chin on his fists and said something, and the boy instantly looked warier. They talked some more. Kehr stood, still shy, and approached the table. He had his hands in his pockets. He took them out. He swung both down on the table so hard the concussion made David jump and the boat flew into the air. He shouted something, and the boy started crying. Karel was up on his feet, helpless. Kehr shouted again, banged the table again. He shouted. David started to wail, though Karel could still hear nothing. Kehr lifted his end of the table and crashed it down, intent on David. He shouted. David put his hands over his ears and began shouting back.

Karel lunged for the mirror. "Don't tell him! Don't *tell* him!" he called, pounding on the glass with open palms, but he knew he already had.

"Here's the situation," Kehr said to him later, the two of them alone in the room. Karel was moving back and forth in agitation as if tied to a perpetually restless little animal. "She kidnapped her brother from a state institution. She's in possession of subversive literature concerned with the overthrow of the state. There's evidence she's part of a group helping to produce such literature."

"What?" Karel said.

Kehr held his hands up, as if to say he wasn't enjoying this either. "We found ink, we found blank paper, we found boxes for the paper. And the younger brother told us strange men drop packages at the house."

Karel's mouth dropped open. "None of that's true," he said.

"She's confused," Kehr said, as if that were the end of the subject. "The state isn't in the business of trying to fill its prisons. I'm not in that business. You help me, I'll help her."

"What? What do you want me to do?" Karel asked.

Someone in this town was running the partisan cell for the area, Kehr said. He thought Karel knew who it was.

"Is *that* what you're doing here?" Karel said.

Kehr didn't answer. Then he said, "All I want from you is a confirmation of what I already believe."

"I told you I don't know any partisans," Karel said. "I don't *know* any."

Kehr shrugged, as if he had all the time in the world.

"What'll happen to her?" Karel asked.

"There are people in our prison system who are absolutely reprehensible," Kehr said. "I could tell you stories."

Karel was breathing through his mouth. Sweat appeared on his back and forehead like magic.

The sort of people who believed any scruple could be overcome by a good beating, Kehr said.

"Oh, God," Karel said. "Oh God."

"We use the law as far as it serves us," Kehr said. "Then we move to other methods."

Karel stood and paced. He pulled at his hair. "I don't know anybody who's a partisan," he said.

Kehr grabbed him by the shirt collar, so quickly it terrified him. They were face to face. Karel could smell mint.

"Listen," Kehr said. "Leave your hair alone and try to concentrate. You've been getting by without decisions. With inertia decorated with sentiment. *That's over.*" He let go, calmer. Now, he said. Mistakes became errors only when persisted in. He smoothed the front of his jacket with his spread palm. He needed Karel's decision.

Karel sat, blinking back tears of frustration and fear.

"You just want to be left alone, with this girl and your reptiles," Kehr said. Karel nodded, after a moment. "Well, even the little man with no ambitions needs help just to be left alone. Like men joining hands in the surf against the waves." He leaned forward when Karel didn't respond. "Am I *clear?*" he shouted. "Am I coming through to you?"

Karel nodded, swallowing. He was looking straight ahead, at the glass. There was no one in the other room.

"I need your answer now," Kehr said. He straightened up and went to the door. He put his hand on the handle.

"Albert Delp," Karel said. As he said it he felt the earth open and himself fall into it.

Kehr sat back down. Karel felt hyperaware, as if his fingertips had gone to sleep. His head tingled. He blinked often and tried to focus. Kehr quizzed him on details. Karel told him as if he'd gotten on a slide and it was now much too steep to stop about the tea cozy, the mysterious visitor, the secret space under the false bottom of the kitchen cabinet. Kehr, after rechecking, looked him over from head to toe and then stood and congratulated him quietly. He shook his hand. He left the room.

Karel sat where he was left, not moving.

At some point Stasik came back in and helped him up and led him down the hall and into the room where the Schieles had been. They were waiting there.

Mrs. Schiele hugged him immediately, and Leda looked

grateful but wary. He still felt numb. Mrs. Schiele talked about repaying him and having known Karel would help, and Nicholas told him they had train tickets to go to the capital that night. They were all hugging him goodbye. Leda hugged him and he could feel her relief and happiness and smell her damp hair and he believed as he hugged her back that everything else in his life was some sort of vanity except his love for her.

Stasik led them all outside to a car that was to take them two towns over to the train station. Karel wasn't going. Kehr was nowhere to be seen. While they loaded the car's trunk, David was the only one who was able to stay calm, which was only right, he said, since he was a future Kestrel. He asked if he could sit near the window on the train as he got into the car.

Stasik took the portable radio out of Nicholas's hands as he climbed in and dropped it on the pavement and stamped on it. "No radios," he explained.

Leda was the last one in. She turned to Karel.

"Why didn't you tell me you were making pamphlets?" he blurted.

She looked at him in surprise and shot a look at Stasik, who was obliviously jamming the trunk shut.

"What did you tell them? What did you do for them?" she demanded. "Why are they letting us go?"

"Get in the car," he said. Stasik had come around and stood behind them. He was suddenly terrified that it all might collapse. "Get in the car."

"What'd you do? What'd you tell them?" she said.

"Ask them," he said.

"You are not them. They are not you," Leda said.

"All right, lovebirds," Stasik said. He loaded Leda into

the car like a particularly awkward plant and shut the door. He banged on the hood and the driver put the car in gear and drove away.

Karel stood where he was, watching her disappear. Stasik chuckled and went into the station, energetically cleaning an ear with his little finger. When he came back out he asked if Karel wanted a ride home. Karel didn't. He went home instead by a shortcut he knew. He moved as if asleep and appreciated with an aesthetic detachment a far-off yellow streetlamp over the black twist of a path. Farther on he caught at a deserted intersection his own reflection sliding along the darkened glass of a passing staff car.

At home he dreamed about an old teacher taken from his house and dragged down steps covered with fruit and vegetable rinds, thrown into a snake pit (the snakes Karel couldn't identify, and they limited themselves to disinterested coiling and the first stages of courtship). The sequence ended with a strange hybrid of anole and skink sitting on the teacher's head and applauding with its forepaws.

When he didn't get out of bed in the morning Kehr came up to his room and pushed open the door and sat heavily on the patched coverlet like a dad whose patience was pretty much exhausted. He tossed Karel a nectarine and said, "I suppose we're in official mourning now over our loss of innocence."

Karel said, "I don't feel good." He set the nectarine on the mattress beside him, and it wobbled when he shifted his weight. He kept the top of his sheet where it was, below his eyes.

"This is a tragedy," Kehr said. "It really is. Here's a man who's doing everything he can to bury this country and poor you had to help turn him in."

"What happened to him?" Karel asked. "Where is he?"

Kehr looked at his watch. "I imagine he's at the zoo," he said. "Most people have been out of bed and busy for hours."

"You mean you haven't done anything to him? He wasn't arrested?" Karel asked.

"You sound disappointed," Kehr said. "Did you think we would hurt him?"

Karel blinked. "Yeah," he said. "I did."

Kehr shook his head briefly at the fancies of children and stood up. "We'd like lunch, at some point, at your convenience," he said. "And our friend the ringtail's been leaving exploratory turds in various places. I can smell them."

"You're not going to do anything to him?" Karel asked.

Kehr paused at the door. "As I told you, he is the head of the partisan cell in the area," he said. "Who he meets, who he has contact with, is of some interest to us."

"Aren't you afraid he'll get away?" Karel said.

"The only people who leave are people we want to leave," Kehr said tiredly, going down the stairs. "How many times do you have to be told that?"

He checked. He got dressed and said he was going to the market and went to the zoo instead. He slipped in the back gate and found Albert making his rounds. He stayed out of sight. Everything seemed fine. At the gate on the way out, Perren appeared behind him. He was not surprised at seeing Karel. He said, "This area's closed to visitors," and demonstrated by shutting the gate and giving it a rattle.

So why did he feel the way he did? They'd known about

Albert before him and everything was the same. And maybe Albert was doing something he shouldn't've been. But he couldn't sustain the righteousness because the image of himself terrified and selfish and saying the old man's name rose up in front of his eyes while he walked, to renew his self-disgust.

He felt sorry for himself and moped and felt disgusted about that and so moped some more. He wished he'd never gone to the station, blamed Leda, blamed Nicholas, blamed Albert, blamed Kehr, blamed himself. None of it helped. He passed mirrors and scowled, as if no one should have to face what he'd seen.

Days he spent alone. Kehr and his assistants almost always now worked late. At night he lay in bed and Kehr talked. He felt lost and hopeless and didn't protest. Kehr wore his full uniform and explained the stripes and bars and pins signifying the honors and theaters of service and the distinction displayed in training. He left a replica of the antipartisan badge he wore on the lamp table beneath the photo of Karel's mother. He gave Karel a replica of the small ceremonial dagger he wore, with the antipartisan symbol flanking the Party letters on the hilt. He talked with patience and attentiveness while Karel toyed with the dagger or tossed and turned or lay on his stomach with his chin on the pillow and his eyes on the wall.

He talked about some of the unfortunate lapses of discipline Karel had witnessed and suggested that soldiers in such cases were unsuited to their roles, and who after all could blame wolves set to guard sheep?

Karel at one point interrupted to wonder aloud if the Party had done all it wanted to do and was ready to stop.

There was no answer in the darkness. Then Kehr said in

a low voice that all they'd done so far was impose the illusion of order, as though they'd laid a slab of glass over a whirlpool.

The people, he went on after a short silence, were always more malleable than expected. They were now habituated to government by surprise, to believing the situation too complicated for the average citizen to comprehend and too dangerous to talk about. They worked hard to live by the rules, and the Party changed the rules, slightly but enough to continue to make obedience compelling work. The appropriate image, he suggested, might be the blind man who continually had to negotiate his way past rearranged furniture.

Of course, some complained, Kehr told him. Most remained where they were: removed from politics.

What about the partisans? Karel asked. He knew who Kehr was talking about: his neighbors, his father, himself, before his naming of Albert. The partisans, Kehr said, believed, as did the Civil Guard, that there was more latent opposition to the Party out there than anyone might think, ready to be agitated into motion.

The partisans understood violence, Kehr said. They understood a central point: that violence was the only way to create a hearing for moderation. And, of course, they didn't accept the consequences of their actions unless they were caught: they didn't stay around to take the punishment.

Within everyone there was a little man claiming Common Sense and Common Decency, Kehr said, but there came a point when people became used to even the unnecessary brutalities. Did Karel ever wonder at what point people would say, of the steps the Party felt compelled to take toward national solidarity, "No, not that"? Did Karel know that all around him people demonstrated that there was nothing they would not stand for? Karel pulled the pillow over his head. Did Karel know that feeling Kehr remembered from long ago, the feeling he'd never forgotten, when he first understood that all sorts of things that had been supposedly forbidden, impossible, and criminal seemed more and more natural, more and more possible, to this new version of himself?

Karel was standing at the stove preparing some simple pastries Kehr had shown him how to make called Prisoners' Fingers while Kehr worked at the kitchen table, every so often taking a break to continue what he called "our discussions." Karel rolled the dough with dirty hands and didn't retain much of what was being said. He thought about Leda and how much she suspected. He'd asked if he could write to her, and Kehr had said that right then the mail in their area wasn't moving in any direction.

Kehr talked about violence and aesthetic standards, and when Karel's interest was flagging completely he asked what Karel thought should be done with Leda's journals.

Karel turned so quickly one of the pastries made a cricketlike hop and stuck to the wall before rolling off. Kehr was incompletely successful in hiding his pleasure. He repeated the question.

"You have her journals?" Karel asked stupidly.

"We do," Kehr said. "A search of the house turned them up. We'll save them for her, naturally. I just thought you'd be interested."

In the other room the ringtail was tapping on something with his claws as if working on a typewriter. "I am," Karel said.

They were going to be going over there this afternoon, Kehr said. Karel was welcome to come.

All the way there Karel felt guilty and nervous. The house was double-padlocked BY ORDER OF THE NATION AND THE CIVIL GUARD and Kehr had the keys. While he got to work with them Karel waited on the front steps. Neighbors peeked from behind blinds and curtains.

Kehr opened the door and went in. He moved some packing boxes from the hall and led Karel to Leda's room and hefted a shallow box off the desk and put it in Karel's arms. Then he left the room.

This was wrong. Karel knew it. The dresser had been dragged over and the floor molding behind it pulled out. He could see the hole where she'd kept the journals. These were things she had a right to keep to herself, things she could have shared with him if she'd wanted to. But he was excited at having secret access: Leda herself answering all his questions. How did she feel about him? How much did she think about him? Was there anybody else?

And suppose this was his only chance? She was gone. Suppose this was the only Leda he'd ever get again?

Kehr seemed to be bumping around innocuously downstairs. It wasn't clear to Karel what he was doing.

There was still time. He could leave it all, let Kehr know he knew he had no right to do this. But what if she'd gotten herself into trouble with what she'd written here? If Kehr or somebody had read it? He'd need to warn her then, or plead her case. He hefted the box higher and said, "That's true," as if saying it would make it so, and left the room and headed downstairs.

He spread everything in front of him on his desk and then with suppressed excitement limited himself to the first of the three spiral-bound notebooks. It was filled with pencil drawings. She had titled some of them: *Nicholas, Nicholas and David, Nicholas Asleep, Sad Crow and Rabbit, Dog,* and then, filling him with hope and joy, *K's Hands.* That one featured three sets of hands orbiting a lizard's foreleg and claw: one with the right hand curled inside the left (washing?), another hefting a rock, and the third operating a nooser. The design puzzled and bothered him. Was she comparing his hands to the lizard's? Did she think of him in terms of the Reptile House? She'd done the foreleg from life: the toes ending in the sharp curve of claw, the keeled scales. He tried to push ahead but found himself flipping back to that page, unable to stop looking.

He left a piece of paper there as a bookmark and paged quickly along looking for other parts of his body. He came across an old man with Albert's hair and tired expression, dressed in a zoo smock. He was holding a bird in one hand and a gun in the other. His legs ended at the ankles. Whether he was supposed to be standing in something or Leda couldn't draw feet Karel couldn't tell. It looked like Albert, and the connection disturbed him. More and more he was having the queasy feeling that his whole world was interconnected behind his back. The bird had a leafed branch in its beak. There were lines radiating out from the man's head. Holiness? A thought? A headache? A vulture or other huge bird sat in space above him. She'd drawn *NUP* on its breast, the letters curved to fit.

He shut the notebook. He'd look at the drawings more later. He wanted more of her voice and thoughts.

On the first page of the second notebook it said, *This is my letter to the world that never wrote to me.—Leda Schiele.* A sheaf of pages following that had been torn out. The first entry remaining had no date but was numbered *17,* at the top of the page.

Elsie was right: I hurt her feelings, and where did I get the right to do that? I'm never happy with anyone else but where do I get the idea I'm so great? From the bottom up I need to work on myself. I say I want to be an artist but what do I do to prove it? I hardly draw anymore and I have zero patience for my books. We learned to draw pretty well in school even though our art mistress was mediocre and very young, and what've I done with what I learned? At least I've stopped turning out complete trash like I did with Mr. G. Sometimes the other thing that cheers me up is that I think I'm learning, and that's the main thing. The rest should come by itself.

It's not a game anymore. My ambition should be to perceive things clearly and calmly. I'm surrounded by false information and false people. For my sake and my family's I have to figure out the truth and act on it. And how is the truth discernible? The truth is discernible first by means of logic and second by the precise investigation of things. Nicholas's treatment an ex.

She sounds like Kehr, Karel thought. What wasn't a game anymore?

Why do I let what other kids think about me affect me? Don't listen or care so much about what others say. You retain your independence when you don't rely on what other people can take away.

Do not do yourself what you dislike in others.

Develop yourself. Develop yourself.

I have to find friends I can trust. I never feel completely happy or relaxed around people. It's like every word I have to examine from every angle, and I always have to watch myself. I hate it. I should not close myself off. I should develop for what's coming a hard head and a soft heart. Too many people around here have the opposite!

Every day someone I thought was half all right turns out to be an idiot. The little idiots support the big idiots. Today the radio was going on as usual about things I can't even talk about, they make me so angry. Nearly everyone's lost their minds. Everything runs on lies, everything generates lies, everything is so tangled and mixed up it's getting so I can't imagine it any other way.

My pessimism is getting worse. I feel like skepticism and cynicism are poisoning my soul. I want to save it by running away, but where to? Instead, I create a wall around me and keep adding to it. Who will climb it? Why do I want anyone to?

God, listen to me.

I have to see clearly and be stronger. For all my big talk about self-improvement I'm still working at the same old pace. I get childishly pleased with every bit of progress I make, but every day I see how far I have to go.

There was a poem entitled "Anxiety." Most of it had been furiously crossed out. He could decipher only *perhaps I will learn/perhaps I will draw them,* and in the final long stanza, two phrases: *never-ending,* and *leaves me tethered.*

A mimeographed note was folded into the next page: *I hereby permit my daughter Leda Schiele to use the outdoor and indoor swimming pools.* ____________ *: Father's Signature.* Someone had drawn a line through *Father's* and had written *Mother's.*

There was an short entry in a code, nonsense words repeating themselves in various patterns, followed by:

can't remember
possibly
not sure
oh

There was another.

> Man was CREATED to have these doubts and terrors and miseries of self-examination. I believe that. So he can't just vegetate, like a plant or a lizard, because his mind won't leave him alone. What the mind tells the soul we say to the state: WE WILL NOT BE SILENT. WE ARE YOUR BAD CONSCIENCE. (save)

He shut the journal and put it down. He stacked the other two on it and put all three in his bottom drawer. Then he went downstairs and outside, past Kehr, who kept an eye on him as he went by. Out away from the house he cleaned the shed in the company of the rabbits for the rest of the afternoon.

He managed to stay away from the journals for another day. He sat and watched one hundred and forty-one trucks roll through the square at noon heading for the front. The cloud of dust they raised stayed level and thick. The trucks were coated with it. His eyes watered. The canvas flaps on the trucks were tied down on the sides and back. When they were gone the dust took its time settling. It moved unhurriedly past the buildings like wandering cumuli. He thumped his clothes to produce his own clouds and tried to loiter in the square afterward, but his dread of running into Albert finally drove him home.

He thought about going over to Leda's and worried: suppose the neighbors saw him. Suppose the police or Civil Guard were watching the house. He was passing through the kitchen in distraction when Kehr asked if he'd been listening to the radio recently.

Stasik was leaning on the stove, looking at nothing. Kehr had a file open on the table, and Karel wondered if that was all he ever did, sit at the kitchen table and look at papers. The top page was divided into three columns: names, addresses, and something he couldn't decipher in the third column.

Here was a hypothetical for Karel, Kehr said. A partisan near the capital had thrown a bomb into the backseat of a Security Service car carrying a Special Investigator. A group of kids Karel's age had deliberately gotten in the way of the Civil Guardsmen in pursuit. The partisan had escaped. The question was this: what would Karel have done with the kids?

Karel got a glass from the cupboard and poured himself a drink from the faucet. The plumbing still made noise. Was the Security Service man killed? he wanted to know.

"Blinded in one eye," Kehr said. "Otherwise fine. Laid up for a while."

Karel guessed he would have given them some sort of work detail, or something. Stasik snorted and told him they'd been flogged and given prison terms. Of course, before this they'd been good boys, he said bitterly. That was supposed to make a difference.

"My junior officer has an endearing faith in corporal punishment," Kehr said. Karel imagined Stasik years earlier, in a place like this, standing where Karel was standing, an actor wearing Karel's clothes.

Karel said he had other things to worry about.

Kehr smiled. "Your father," he said. "How he's doing, no doubt."

Karel shook his head, a tight little shake.

Kehr continued to smile, and drew a straight, easy line through two of the names on the list. "Seems to me our friend Leda was happy to leave," he said.

It wasn't that, Karel said.

"It's interesting," Kehr said after a pause. "I had business at the station the night she left. Her train was delayed. I stopped to visit and she wanted to know, out of nowhere, if you'd assisted us in any way. I assured her you'd been as unhelpful as you'd ever been. In fact, I told her that even though we were letting you go we were not at all pleased with your performance." He cast down the list, touching the pencil point to each name, and made rapid question marks beside a few of them. "I don't believe in not telling the truth," he said. "But every so often a little fit overcomes me."

Karel thought, My head's made of glass. I might as well just walk around with signs. "What'd you say when she asked why you were letting her leave?" he said. He tried not to look as though the news had affected him.

Kehr stood the file on its edge and straightened the pages with short thumps on the tabletop. He set it down and clasped his hands over it. "Her friend Albert arranged it. Travel passes. At your request.

"She was, if I'm any judge of emotion, quite moved," he added.

"You lied to her," Karel said. But he was relieved. He felt better. He realized he'd now be doing things to keep people from finding out about things he'd already done. He imagined her on the train thinking of him, and his face heated with guilt at his excitement and pleasure. He *had* saved her, hadn't he? He had a flashing sexual fantasy of her gratitude.

Kehr and Stasik returned their attention to what they'd been doing, in Stasik's case, apparently, brooding. Karel got up to go, anticipating the illicit feeling of being alone with her journals again, but Kehr reminded him about dinner and pointed out the recipe on the counter for Flat Lamb Pie.

"I want you to do me a favor," Kehr said later while they ate. The ringtail sat on its haunches by his chair and begged with its forepaws up like a dog. "After dinner I want you to pick up some packages for me. At Albert Delp's."

Stasik smiled and then put his hand to his mouth.

"I don't want to go there," Karel said, astounded Kehr had to be told that.

Kehr looked at him. "I'm asking you a favor," he said.

"I can't," Karel said.

Kehr shook his head at his lamb. He sawed gently at it with his knife. He said Albert had no idea about what had happened the other day. They'd done nothing to him. As far as he knew this was a routine search. It was being handled by a member of the Security Service and they were directed to share what they found with the Civil Guard.

Karel put his hands on his cheeks and rubbed them and looked over at Stasik, who was interested only in his food.

"Which considering the imbecile in charge won't be much," Kehr said. "But you never know."

"Why can't you pick it up?" Karel said. "Isn't it top secret or something?"

"This is not a discussion," Kehr said. "And we aren't errand boys."

"I don't want to go there," Karel said. "I don't want to face him."

Kehr nodded as if he understood completely. "A favor," he said.

The Security Service officer who came to the door at Albert's house was Holter.

"Look who it is," Holter announced. "Karel Roeder."

Karel stared, open-mouthed.

"It's Karel Roeder," Holter called over his shoulder, as if a good party were now getting better. He held the door open. "It's Karel Roeder, and he can't close his mouth," he added.

Karel came in. "I tried to find you at the parade," he said. "Didn't you see me? You're in the Security Service now?" He wasn't sure he was making any sense.

"However my country can use me," Holter said. He wasn't wearing a uniform.

"I have to pick up the stuff for Officer Kehr," Karel explained, dazed. He was standing in the hall, not wanting to go any farther. The tea cozy was off the phone and the magazine racks in the living room were empty.

Holter made a series of affirmative noises and led Karel into the kitchen. Albert was at the table. The kitchen cabinets were untouched.

Karel stood where he was, awkwardly.

"You know each other, of course," Holter said.

Albert scratched the bristle on his Adam's apple with his fingernail.

Karel couldn't tell, but thought Kehr was right: Albert didn't know.

He turned to Holter. "My father," he said. "Did you see him? Did he join the Civil Guard?"

Of course, Holter said. What a question.

"The messenger arrives," Albert said.

Karel's face burned. He said hello.

Holter suggested Karel sit. His group would be finished in a minute.

Karel could hear people upstairs. Albert seemed tired and disgusted, but Karel could see he was listening, too.

"So," Holter said. "Feel free to engage in zoo talk. Pretend I'm not here."

"I'm allowing my house to be searched," Albert said. "Like a good citizen. Do I have to submit to this as well?"

Holter shrugged theatrically. Karel looked away. There was banging upstairs. Holter drummed his fingers on the tabletop.

Karel stole occasional fearful looks at Albert, who seemed to be contemplating something disappointing. Holter studied his fingers. He had large moist-looking fingernails that were closely bitten down. He wandered the room and then sat on the table edge between them with a leg dangling and a foot on the floor in an imitation-jaunty pose that irritated them both. "Have you been listening to the radio?" he asked Karel conversationally.

"Now don't *you* start," Karel said.

Holter knitted his eyebrows and gave up. His complexion made Karel wonder if blood could back up and pool. He said he'd been going to ask if Karel had heard about the assassination in Naklo. Subsecretary Wissinger, who maybe Karel had just heard right here in town. He'd been giving a speech about the Old Guard—what else did he ever talk about?—and asking that those executed for assassinations during the days of the Republic be commemorated from here on in as war dead. Apparently he'd been waiting for applause on that suggestion when he'd been shot.

Albert snorted, and Holter shot him a look so penetrating it frightened Karel.

It was sad what was happening, Holter said, after a pause. Everywhere it was the same. Where was the respect? Where was the order? The more they worked, the more there seemed to do.

"I need to be at the zoo before nine o'clock," Albert said. "Some of the nocturnals need special care."

Holter looked at him. "People don't realize that police have a hard time of it in a police state," he said. "And what is it, really, that we want? We're not asking our citizens to love us, or even love one another. Just to do their duty."

When no one answered he swung his leg down and walked to the window. He peered at his reflection. He pushed tenderly on his cheek with two fingers. "It's always the same tooth," he said sadly. He made a sideways squeaking noise and opened and closed his jaw. He looked over at Karel as if testing his eyesight.

"But what you got is what you got," he said. "Life is work. In bad times you work for nothing. In good you get a little something out of it."

They could hear the others coming down the stairs. Two young men tramped into the room. They were also in street clothes. All that was left was the crawl space, one of them said. Holter nodded, and they left. After a pause Karel could feel them bumping around beneath his feet.

A lot of false travel papers had been turning up, Holter said to Albert apologetically. Duplicate birth certificates, fraudulent work papers. He crossed the room to the kitchen cabinets and turned, his back to them. Albert didn't have anything like that to worry about, did he?

Albert didn't answer.

"Rude question," Holter said. "Of course not."

"Yesterday one of my assistants' house was set on fire," Albert said. "Now he and his family are out on the street. The neighbors said the men wore Party pins."

"That sort of arson is really planned and executed by big-city types," Holter said. "We're fairly helpless in cases like that. It's pointless, but who can tell them that? Or maybe they were partisans seeking to blame us. Who knows?"

He turned to Karel. "Do you?" he asked.

"No," Karel said, startled.

Albert shook his head, and Holter looked over at him with amusement. "I don't understand why a citizen who respects the law would support the partisans," he said. "I mean, everyone has his passion for reform in the early going, but most of us realize we're just wasting time and energy better spent in other directions. And who are the partisans trying to reform? Did you hear the joke about our countrymen who wanted to seize the train stations but couldn't because they hadn't bought tickets?"

"Couldn't you be helping them with whatever they're doing?" Albert asked. "Do you have to torment me?"

"One more story, not from the radio," Holter said. He pulled a chair out and swung it around and sat on it backward.

Karel found Albert looking at him and had to look away, at his feet, at the table. What was happening here? Why had he been sent here? He understood something sadistic was going on but didn't know what or why.

"For months we knew a lot of people who'd gotten away from here were in hiding in the capital, in bunkers and mazes built out of subbasements, wine cellars, storm drains, everything. Informers told us that much and showed us one or two. Big question: how would we find the rest? Kuding, Lenz, Kruse—remember them?—they were all down there somewhere."

Albert looked away, agitated. "It's eight-thirty," he said.

"Well," Holter said. "Finally, we hit on it. Bang: the electric bills of the businesses above! Get it? All those sites would be siphoning off electricity. Right away we found a central cell, maybe forty people. We've identified most of the bodies."

Albert paled. He ran his hand up the back of his neck and let it drop.

"Kuding's actually alive," Holter said. "Though he won't be a problem. As our Justice Minister says, show me a man and I'll show you a case."

Albert put his hands over his eyes. He was trembling.

Karel stood up, abruptly, and had no explanation when Holter looked at him in surprise. The young men returned from the crawl space dirty and empty-handed and saved him. One had cobwebs hanging from his hair.

"I'm supposed to be back," Karel said. He couldn't take any more of this.

Holter lifted two boxes from the hall and brought them to Karel. "Children need two things, don't you think?" he said, addressing Albert. Karel put his arms out and he loaded the boxes on them, tilting the weight back against Karel's chest. "If they don't get them, the result is unhappy children. Routine and discipline: the child who doesn't get them will have all kinds of trouble."

Karel said goodbye to Albert over the boxes and left. He

had to wait at the door for one of the young men to open it. Holter called after him as he went down the steps that what he recommended was that children be given plenty of little tasks, and then be made to do them regularly.

> Today we tried to read the future by dropping melted wax and lead into bowls of water. E asked, Will Leda marry Karel? and everybody thought that was funny. Sometimes I feel so excluded from their company! and I just want to sit outside under the sky and feel sorry for myself, like mother says.
>
> Poor K! Always around, so sure he's in love. I'm amazed how my feelings for him have grown. Because of what? He's very maddening and almost always strange. That time with N an example. Mom and David like him a lot. Only Nicholas seems skittish around him. I kissed him, but would he ever kiss me? I think about him often, but what does that mean? Sometimes I think it's like I don't love him but the world in him.
>
> K: 1 Political?
> 2 Kind, thoughtful
> 3 Attractive
> 4 Good?
> 5 Emotions not good or bad—just up and down
> 6 So self-consc.—never just does something. I think that bothers him.

The People's Voice announced that the conversion of the Retention Hospital to museum space was now fully under way. A large number of patients had been moved to unspecified centers around the region, and others had been unfortunately lost in an outbreak of typhus the hospital had surpressed to prevent panic. Those families involved in the loss of loved ones had each received an urn, a certificate, and a bill. In rare cases there had been inevitable bureaucratic errors involving notifications, and these were deeply regretted.

Karel took long walks, wanting to get out of the house. It was hot. He passed an old man walking a dog on a lead. The dog stopped endlessly, and the old man conceded the dog that right, as if any kind of delay he experienced because of it made no difference in a world like this.

He sat in the shade and read the posters on a kiosk: nomads had formed teams of stranglers that roamed the countryside at night. Victims had been found with their ankles broken and eyes put out, according, it was thought, to a secret nomad tradition: the eyes so the dead wouldn't recognize their murderers, and the ankles so they couldn't follow them and indicate to everyone their guilt.

In the square a band was playing, sweating in the heat. The music was nervous and worn out and the band members played number after number with their eyes on the ground, their fingers working the stops. The heat staggered drifting mongrels and cats. In a cleared field he saw hawks and sparrows panting and standing beside each other in the shadows of fenceposts, on a truce because of the heat. Their wings slanted downward and trembled in the dirt. Beyond them through a window in the cool shade of a whitewashed room a woman with Leda's hair and eyes served something from a shallow bowl with the smooth silence of a painting come to life.

He worried that he'd gotten no letters from her and asked about the mail situation at the post office. The clerk informed him in a harassed voice that he wouldn't predict that anything got anywhere in any amount of time. He asked Kehr if he'd heard anything and Kehr said no and added that he was not holding his breath waiting for a note of thanks from the Schieles.

He tried to ration his time with the journals. He discovered with a shock that he had a rival:

> Where is your smoothness? Why have you left? Now, when others pass their hands through my hair I resent it. Dark boy, I'm hypnotized by your black eyes. So much is happening all at once! You're four years older, four years smarter, four years better, four years worse, four years more experienced. Am I aiming too high? Oh, I want you to be happy.

The next three passages said nothing more on the subject, as if he'd hallucinated it. He was flipping frantically ahead when Kehr appeared in his room and announced that they needed the journals right away for a while, he'd get them back, there was no need to get all excited, he was going to have to call Stasik if Karel continued to make a fuss, and no, it couldn't wait.

Karel came downstairs early the next morning and moped around the kitchen inefficiently gathering what he needed to start breakfast. Kehr eyed him from his chair. Karel asked if he was finished with the journals yet and Kehr said as if he hadn't heard, "Do you think you'd like to do what I do someday?"

"I don't even know what you do," Karel said. He scooped the coffee with extra vehemence and it slopped onto the floor.

Kehr shrugged. "Fair enough," he said. "Today you come with me."

Kehr drove. Stasik stayed at the house. They went out of town by the southern route. Karel saw where he and Leda had walked, where she'd leaned close to see the horned lizard. The morning was already hot. He rode with his hands on his thighs, watching the sun pinwheel off the metal on the dashboard. He was rarely in cars and enjoyed the speed, though he thought this one's ride was bumpy.

They drove through stands of creosote and shadscale that seemed like brittle clouds of thin branches lining the road. He tried not to think about the dark boy in Leda's journal and got angrier and more frustrated as he did.

They were going to a Prisoner Assessment Center. In the Guard you called them PACs. This one was a converted animal hospital.

It was a low white building with corrugated tin roofing and a central metal gate leading to a courtyard. The front had been a circular drive with a rock garden, and all that was left was a single exhausted desert sage and a small saltbush. Cars and trucks were parked everywhere.

They were checked through the gate by a slovenly guard in an army uniform who gave all his attention to a cat leashed to a ring on the wall. The inner courtyard was being hosed down.

Kehr gave a little tour. On the first floor there were offices, a dining room, staff lounge, kitchen, and bathrooms. On the lower floors, prisoner assessment rooms, the infirmary, and holding cells. These centers were new and were all a little makeshift but were being modernized. They'd been mandated and funded by the Statute for the Process of National Reorganization. The statute turned over responsibility in the cases of actual and potential enemies of the state to the intelligence-gathering services. Both the Civil Guard and the Security Service operated within these centers, and not always harmoniously.

But first they'd eat. Kehr took him to the dining room, set up cafeteria-style, and they sat under an overhead fan and ate Skewered Variety Meats, mostly lamb hearts and kidneys. A few officers waved hello or exchanged a little banter. No one seemed surprised at Karel's presence.

They'd be talking today with a young man who'd been caught painting slogans over Party posters. He was probably no partisan but his activities were worth looking into. People like him thought, Kehr said, that the partisans and all opponents of the current government were like a runaway horse, leading its rider back home. His only question to such people, he said, was, where is home? Who in this country wanted a return to the old days of the Republic?

Balls clacked in the next room, and Karel could see a billiard table. A woman passed it hooded and wearing shackles on her wrists and ankles. Two men were leading her. They were wearing shorts and bright yellow shirts.

"Lot of people being talked to today," Kehr said. He quartered a piece of kidney on his plate. "Very busy."

He asked if Karel wanted the dessert, a rice pudding with currants. Karel didn't and Kehr said that that was on the whole a good move. They bused their trays and went down a corridor that turned every so often at right angles until Karel understood they were circling the first courtyard. They stopped at a staircase, and Kehr opened the door with a small key and headed down. The stairs were lit by a yellow light high on the wall, and they had to step over a coiled fire hose on the landing.

Kehr asked him to wait opposite a holding cell and with another key went into the next room over. A small square peephole on the center of the door had been covered with black masking tape. Under the peephole there was a pale green poster entitled. "Regulations: Group Holding Cells, Prisoner Assessment Centers." Karel read around in it waiting for Kehr to reappear.

> 1: Individuals who discuss politics for the purposes of inciting rebellion, or make inflammatory speeches, or meet with others for that purpose, or form cliques, or loiter about, or collect true and untrue anecdotes for the purposes of spreading propaganda, or receive such anecdotes in writing, secrete them, pass them onto others, or attempt to smuggle them out of the cell and so the Prisoner Assessment Center, etc., by any means, or draft secret documents, will be considered to have committed an act of violence against the state and will be dealt with according to that consideration.
>
> 2: Individuals who attack or insult a guard, who refuse to obey or incite others to do the same, who hoot, shout, taunt, spit, or make speeches, will be considered to have committed an act of violence against the state and will be dealt with according to that consideration.

The door of the next room opened and Kehr signaled him in.

A young man maybe ten years older than Karel was sitting at a bare metal table. His arms were tied tightly behind his back, and one side of his jaw was swollen as if he'd filled his cheek with nuts. He was blindfolded, and he turned his head slightly at Karel's entrance.

Kehr put his finger to his lips. "This is a colleague," he said to the young man. "He'll be sitting in."

The young man's expression didn't change.

Kehr motioned for Karel to sit in the available chair. There was nothing on the walls, and the floor was smooth concrete. There was no other furniture.

"Where's my sister?" the young man asked. He had dark hair and a dark complexion.

Kehr seemed to enjoy shifting slightly in his seat so that the young man's blindfolded head would tip and turn experimentally to try to keep a fix on him. He told the young man his sister was being assessed in another part of the center and was doing quite well so far. The young man struggled and rocked in place and quieted down.

Kehr asked a series of questions, sometimes repeating himself. He asked the young man where he'd gotten the paint, where he'd heard the slogans, who had originally given him the idea. The young man didn't know, didn't remember, had nothing to do with those things, and finally stopped talking altogether.

Kehr after a moment said they could go on to the next step, if that was what the young man preferred. The young man didn't answer. Kehr leaned forward and slapped him hard on his swollen side. Karel recoiled. "Would you like to go on to the next step?" Kehr said. "Would you like to go on to the next step?" He slapped the young man again, back and forth, twice. Saliva sprayed out the second time. "Would you like to go on to the next step?" he said. "Would you like to go on to the next step?" He held his hand close to the young man's cheek, so that the fingertips were just touching it. The young man shied away, turned his head violently.

Kehr looked over at Karel, who was frozen in his chair. He expelled a breath through his nose and stood up. The young man's face hung forward, ready for more blows.

"Tomorrow we'll go on to the next step," Kehr said. "That may jog loose the occasional forgotten detail."

The young man swallowed, his face red, his expression intent and blank at the same time. Karel imagined him as Leda's dark boy. Kehr indicated the door, as if being silent out of deference to the young man's feelings, and followed Karel out.

On the ride home Kehr explained to him the best methods of interrogation, which he said were no secret. The interrogator should repeat the same question many times, at unpredictable moments, and always as though it had never been asked before. Then it was just a matter of carefully clarifying the variations in the replies, and pointing out to the subject the apparent contradictions. Until the right reply, or the one suspected to exist, surfaced, he said. Everything else, including the use of force, was at least partially theater. The collared lizard lifting itself onto its hind legs, the horned lizard squirting blood from the corner of its eye, the basilisk spreading its hood. Did Karel follow what he meant?

Karel rode home through the creosote feeling hot and cold together at the slapping, and his reaction to it, and said he did.

Kehr brought an envelope upstairs to his room after dinner and flipped it to him on the bed. "Mail call," he said.

The envelope had Karel's name and address on it, in Leda's handwriting. There were no postmarks or stamps.

"Hand-delivered," Kehr said. "Some of our men shuttle between here and the capital and one of them was kind enough to do me a favor." He smiled helpfully and nodded at the letter, as though Karel probably wanted to get at it. He left the room and shut the door behind him.

The letter was in her handwriting as well.

Dear Karel,

How are you? How is the Reptile House? Have you heard anything from your father?

I'm writing to thank you for your help in getting my family here: your house guest told me about your persistence with Albert concerning the travel passes. I didn't believe him at first but he showed me the passes. Why didn't you tell me? Why did you act so strange?

It dawned on me (well, my mother helped it dawn on me) how mean I'd been to you that night, considering. What kind of impression could I have left you with? I can be so nasty and sure of myself sometimes. I hereby apologize. Do you accept a long-distance kiss and hug?

We're staying here with my aunt. We've got the whole third floor of her apartment and we need it!—Nicholas and David are in one room, Mother and I in another, and we have a little sitting room piled with boxes to go get away from people in. She's happy enough to see us though Mother's concerned about becoming independent as soon as possible and so am I. She's hoping for a position as a housekeeper and is wearing out all my aunt's friends looking for useful connections to wealthy families. I meanwhile was immediately signed up in the youth work study program in a nursery care center for mothers working in vital industries, which doesn't pay much but allows discounts on food. I'm hopeful, but I don't know what to expect from our boss, who has the brain of a chicken and considers herself a beauty. I start Monday.

Otherwise, life in the city isn't so much right now. You can smell the sea everywhere, though, and that is wonderful.

Everyone seems meek and willing to go about their business. Nicholas and I have a game on streetcars where I try to make men blush by staring at them, because he said once that girls blush if men look at them long enough. I used to play a game like that with Elsie.

People here follow the war news more closely than they do at home. You see little crowds around the kiosks all the time after announcements are posted. Even though there's nothing new there, either.

What else? All the big shots show off like idiots driving around in their requisitioned cars and occasionally bang into each other in the process. I think there are as many casualties here as on the front. Mostly we stand in line for everything (yesterday for a piece of cheese the size of your finger). Two days in a row the same married couple stood behind us and asked us where our Party pins were. We couldn't stand them. When the wife got sick on the second day and started throwing up right there in line we started pinching each other so we wouldn't burst out laughing.

You'll have to forgive me if this rambles. I've lost my journals so you're in some ways standing in for them.

Have you seen the new language rules for writing letters? You get them handed to you when you go to buy stamps. Euphemisms, and launderings of less pleasant and more precise words. All correspondence is supposed to be subject to them. Have you noticed there are no unpleasant words in this letter? Mother insisted, and I suppose she makes sense. Still, I worry daily that I'm becoming too sensible. . . .

Do you miss me? I miss you. Though sometimes I think it's good we're apart, because I couldn't take one person's company for too long. Don't misunderstand, but I think sometimes if you spend a lot of time with one person he or she might exert too great an influence on you. Have you ever felt like cutting adrift from everyone? I think I get very touchy when someone makes a lot of demands on me. As you must know yourself, there are hours of solitude that make up for the days you spend pining for someone.

Anyway sometimes I think if we keep in touch it could be nice this way, with two people keeping each other company w/o promising to meet up at such and such a place or stay together forever. They travel the way they're going together for a while, and then if their routes diverge they understand. But I suppose that's mostly wishful thinking on my part. A lot of times everything takes a less pleasant and rational course, and there's a lot of sadness and tiredness and inertia and hurt. . . .

This whole letter will probably strike you as odd in the extreme. Maybe you're sitting there thinking, Who is this person? Do you think about me? If you do, don't just think about me as I am—think about me as I'd like to be. We don't know each other well enough, I think, and I'm a lot to blame. Do you know what I'm thinking? Do you know what I'm thinking about? Will you write?

Leda

The next day they went through another set of double doors past the holding cells and interrogation room. They were going to what Kehr called a prisoner assessment room. On the way he showed Karel the punishment cells they called "the tubes." He showed him the infirmary. He showed him some of the converted kennels. They passed a grating covering a small set of stairs leading to a subbasement. Somebody had taped a paper handwritten sign next to it that read *Juvenile.*

The prisoner assessment room was a white room like the interrogation room, with cement floors and walls and a wooden lattice screen with small desks behind it. The overhead lights flickered and buzzed. The desk and chairs were undersized, as if they'd been taken from a grammar school. There was a long unpainted metal table with two chairs. There was a metal bedframe with shackles on its four corners, hooked up improbably to a field telephone. There was a mop and pail in the corner. There was a big wooden box like a toy chest beside it filled with instruments. There were no windows.

"This is a torture room," Karel said. He felt the way he had when giving Albert's name, hyperaware, and he could feel his insides racing.

"Torture is what we do here, yes," Kehr said.

Karel backed up a step. This was like a blank wall. He'd imagined when he'd imagined anything at all dungeons and chains, fire and darkness. This was dirty, it was empty, it was ordinary. "I don't want to be here," he said. "I don't want to see this. What are you going to do?"

"It's the next step for our young man from yesterday," Kehr said. "It's the next step for you."

"What're you going to do?" Karel asked.

Kehr sat in one of the chairs. His jacket bunched and creased, and he sat forward and straightened it. Karel put his hands behind his back and leaned his shoulders against the wall and did not look around, his stomach feeling emptied and urgent. He looked at the far wall near the ceiling, at a short row of iron grappling hooks. Below them there were fanlike patterns of scratchmarks on the concrete.

The door opened. The young man from the day before came in escorted by two others. The young man was naked except for his underwear, which bagged in an oversized way like a diaper. He looked rapidly around the room and didn't recognize Karel, but then, Karel remembered, he'd been blindfolded. Each of the other men had one of his arms.

They brought him to the bedframe and made him lie on his stomach. The springs in the frame creaked and jangled. No one said anything, and Karel had the surreal sense that he was watching the reenactment of a horrible crime.

The two men manacled the young man and shook the manacles to test them, and left. Kehr was still in his chair. He rubbed his eye with a fingertip and blinked. The young man lay spread-eagled where he was, gazing at a spot on the wall. The weight of his head was all on his chin, and he ground his molars. His jaw was still swollen. His toes curled and uncurled against the frame.

Two other men came in. One was short with heavy glasses and wore a white apron. The apron had OP printed on its upper left corner.

"This is someone we call Mr. Birthday," Kehr said. The man in the apron smiled in acknowledgment. The other man was filthy and unshaven and looked like a prisoner himself and apparently didn't rate an introduction.

"This is Karel Roeder," Kehr said.

"I don't want to be here," Karel said. He was still against the wall. The man in the apron smiled sympathetically and crouched near the bedframe to examine wires that ran to the field telephone. The unshaven man crossed the room stiffly to the lattice screen and sat behind it at one of the desks. The shadows made patterns across his face and clothes. The desk was too small for him and it looked as if he were being made the object of a joke.

"Mr. Birthday is one of our up-and-coming experts in public safety training and civic action," Kehr said. The man in the apron gave the wires an expert tug and nodded modestly.

The unshaven man behind the latticework had taken out a small writing pad and a pencil.

"What you're interested in is over here," Kehr said, inclining his head toward the bedframe. "Not behind the screen."

The unshaven man hadn't looked up and was concentrating fiercely on his writing pad. Kehr remarked that the prisoners here did their part to run the system; that way the customers served themselves, as they liked to say.

"It teaches them responsibility," he added.

"I think we're about ready here," the man in the apron said. He was bending over the toy box with his hands on his thighs. He reached in and extracted a silver rod a foot long and a narrow length of cheesecloth. The cheesecloth he folded and refolded and then wrapped around the tip of the rod and lashed it with string from his pocket. Karel recognized the knot from camp. The bedframe made a creaking and shifting sound.

"Sit down," Kehr said to Karel. Karel was looking at the rod. "I would suggest it," he warned. The man in the apron indicated the chair with the rod, as if offering an open seat on a bus. Karel sat down.

"What happens is this," Kehr said, and he took hold of the crank handle on the field telephone. "The field telephone is battery-operated and generates a current when the handle is turned. The voltage produced depends on the speed at which it's turned."

He turned the crank at an easy pace, the way he might grind coffee. The man in the apron reached over and flipped the switch beside the crank and the young man howled and shot from the metal frame all at once, a rigid board, a magic act. He came back down and bounced and screamed and then twisted and thrashed. Kehr stopped.

Karel pressed against the back of his chair as if he wanted to push through it. Kehr reached over and took his hand and put it on the crank over his, and Karel tore it away, trembling. Kehr turned the crank and flipped the switch as if introducing Karel to an uncomplicated but soothing craft. The young man shrieked and tore upward at his manacles, and the bedframe jumped an inch across the floor.

Kehr relinquished the crank to the man in the apron.

The man in the apron cranked at various speeds and thumbed the switch intermittently. The young man shrieked and cried and jabbered in between the shrieks. The manacles were making raw red lines on his wrists and ankles and he'd bitten his tongue.

"What're you doing?" Karel asked. "Why aren't you asking him questions?" He was trying to turn his head away, but he was too close and Kehr was restraining him from getting out of his chair. *"Why aren't you asking him questions?"* He looked wildly at Kehr, and Kehr put his finger to his lips.

The man in the apron unhooked the wires from the bedframe and wound them through an eye at the base of the rod. He cranked the field telephone again and touched the cheesecloth tip of the rod lightly to various parts of the young man's back. The young man screamed even louder than before. The rod made coin-sized burn marks. Karel could smell it. The man in the apron shut off the switch and adjusted the cheesecloth.

Karel had his hands over his ears and was trying to keep his eyes shut. "Why aren't you asking him *questions?*" he asked. His voice rebounded around the cement walls.

Kehr gave his arm a pat and then pulled it down, freeing an ear. He said, "Is it so hard to figure this out? What we do is administer fear in small doses, which we then gradually increase. Education. We're teaching him a story with two themes: ultimate brutality and absolute caprice."

"I can't watch this," Karel said. He was starting to sob.

"In fact you can," Kehr said. "You're not up pounding on the door. You're not retching. You're not doing anything to stop us."

"No no no no," Karel shouted. The man in the apron walked the rod tip down the bumps of the young man's vertebrae and the young man started screaming the same thing. He drowned them all out.

Kehr said it was like Karel's herpetology and that Karel should've recognized that already. The man in the apron described a grid pattern with his prod across the young man's back and legs. The young man screamed as if someone were pulling his throat out. That sort of study created an identity for the object being studied, provided an essence. He was talking about a kind of power over the natural world. This was about power, the power to see clearly what one was designed for. What he was talking about, he said, was the *audacity* he had, the audacity Karel had—he shook Karel, hard, to focus his attention, and the man in the apron poured a small bottle of mineral water onto the young man's back and touched the rod to it—the audacity they had, to circle, as it were, like birds of prey over inarticulate suffering.

Karel was crying. Kehr was unbothered by it. After waiting for Karel to stop he got up and led him to the door and opened it for him. He said something in a low voice to the man in the apron. Out in the hall he shut the door with a clang on the young man's shrieks and smoothed his hair and reminded Karel that *he* had gotten up to leave, not Karel. This was nothing, he said. This was not torture. This was a long way from what it could be. This was exercise.

Karel,

Mother says the light here will ruin my eyes and here I am writing to you anyway. I'm in bed already, and I've even been to sleep and had a dream. Now I can't sleep, so I'm writing you, though I'm not sure you'll ever write back or that you got my other letter or that you'll even get this.

In my dream we were hiking. (I almost always dream I'm going somewhere.) We came to a big lake. It was night and there was a moon. You wanted me to swim the lake and I told you I wanted to eat first. That's all I remember, though later you kissed me. They say dreams depend on the noises you hear in your sleep. Maybe it's true. I always feel the same in dreams: like I live in this peculiar world where I'll never be entirely happy, but still . . . It's strange. It always makes me melancholy. Am I getting really sentimental?

I've been thinking of you more often than usual. Maybe because I'm always tired with work and everything. I tell myself: you're looking for a crutch. You know you can depend on him, how he feels about you. (Leda being presumptuous.) But then I find myself thinking about you anyway. I think, What do you know about him? And I find myself going over all the good things and remembering things like our walks. Karel!

If I ever get completely sappy, promise to shoot me, like a horse.

After all my talk about self-sufficiency. I do really believe what I'm saying, but how many times am I able to act that way?

Well, if you didn't answer me before you'll never answer me now.

Work at the center is endless and all I do is complain about it. David and Mother try to stay away from me at night, and even Nicholas starts to yawn and blink after a while. I work with ten other girls and we're responsible for sixty-six children. (!) We waste a lot of time standing around waiting for our supervisor, etc. Even that's tiring. The worst times are the lunch breaks when we either monitor the children (who throw everything and trade food and fight about it nonstop until the period runs out) or eat with the other girls on the staff. The children wear me out so quickly: it's tiring having to think myself into their world and stay detached from it at the same time. And the girls on the staff are worse: I have to close my ears to their chatter. Sometimes I actually start humming to myself while they talk. Every time I join in it seems like a big concession and I immediately regret it. They come in every morning thrilled with the NUP and the war and go home just as blinkered. I usually manage to stay in the background, because of my shyness. I wish I could keep it up, but I catch myself showing off in little ways, trying to teach them. It's awful, this craving I have to be noticed. And look: even as I write that I'm wondering how it looks on paper. Where do I get ideas like that? Who am I to think I'm too good for these people? What arrogance! Where did I get it from?

They fired off some live ammunition near the center this afternoon. My ears are still buzzing. . . .

Will you write? You never tell me about yourself, though I suppose I don't ask as much as I could. I often wonder who you're with at some point in the day, and who you're friendly with in general. You never talked about that. Who you like best, for instance. Have you met anyone new? Are you mostly alone? Are all those questions stupid at this point?

Leda

The image of the young man would not go away from Karel. He saw the young man's face on the window glass during the whole trip back to the Assessment Center. He didn't speak to Kehr until they'd arrived and gone inside. The heat had let up a little and they sat in the patio off the dining room. The patio was littered with broken red and white ceramic tiles that crunched and skittered when they moved their feet.

"Thanks for the letter," Karel said.

"It came while we were gone," Kehr said. He looked at his watch.

"Lucky the people you know going back and forth are willing to carry those letters," Karel said.

"Yes it is," Kehr said. "Luck follows me around."

Gnats had settled into Karel's drink. "I couldn't sleep last night," he said. "Thinking about that guy."

"Weakness is kicked in the teeth in this world," Kehr said. "Which is a shame."

Two men at the next table were explaining a long-handled metal instrument to a third man, who had trouble catching on.

"What'd he do?" Karel asked. "Did he do anything? Aren't things like the bedframe against the law?"

The laws were iron, Kehr said. And some people were outside the law's protection.

In the far corner of the courtyard two children were sitting on a square of cloth on the pavement and playing with rubber balls and a toy lizard. A haggard man in a prisoner's shirt was watching them.

"Some of our officers occasionally have to bring their children," Kehr explained. "I've seen days when it was like a school around here."

"There are no rules?" Karel asked faintly. "Anybody can do anything? Downstairs?"

Not at all, Kehr said. In fact, they were cleaning up the system. That had been a big source of tension. He looked over at the children. The prisoner was pointing out to one a ball that had rolled away. Karel should have seen the conditions and methods at the Ministry of Social Welfare: Kehr had thought he could not watch such things. Much different from the sort of things Karel had seen. Another order of intensity altogether.

He saw Karel's expression and tried to explain. By "excesses" he meant for the most part acts carried out individually, for personal goals. There'd been for example what they'd considered too much individual initiative on the part of operatives at night in the prisoners' cells. Especially the women's cells. This for the most part had had to stop. This was why: no one really minded what was being done as long as it was continually clear that it was being done at the instructions of the state. Because once people were clear on that, it was just a matter of finding out the rules and playing by them.

Karel looked shocked.

Please, Kehr said. This wasn't news. Everybody knew. He surveyed his glass, which was also dotted with gnats. He said there was an argument that those who restrained their cruelty did so only because theirs was weak enough to be restrained, but that, he thought, oversimplified the situation. The political man at arms had to be a model of correctness in dress, deportment, and behavior. Otherwise where was his authority in ideological reorientation? Those who understood that had nothing but distaste for the rabid types who behaved as if they were dressed in horns and pelts. The good torturer lacked the capacity for hatred. Pain was administered the way power was to be exercised: dispassionately, from on high.

They left the patio and headed to the prisoner assessment room again. Kehr said that one could get to the point where what he did made extraordinary wine or fragrances possible, made contemplation possible, made sleep possible.

The young man was carried onto the bedframe. The man in the apron returned and did not seem to be in as pleasant a mood this time. Two prisoners set up bright lights on tripods and a third took photographs. The man in the apron introduced innovations: a horseshoe-shaped electric prod applied simultaneously to the ears and teeth that they called "the telephone," and a small electrified metal rectangle with legs that sparked and hopped erratically around the young man's back and that they called "the spider." While they worked the lights created a double image behind them of their shadows gigantified on the walls.

Afterward the young man passed out and nothing could be done with him. He was carried to the infirmary.

Kehr sat Karel down behind the lattice screen and told him it was time they examined what had been going on here. He asked if Karel had any questions. Karel asked again despite himself why they hadn't asked the young man any.

He was not ready to speak, Kehr said. With experience

you understood that. Softening up was required before it was even worth the bother.

Karel wanted to know how they knew someone was telling the truth. Kehr explained that a specific tone appeared in the voice in that situation, and that again, training and experience allowed one to recognize that tone. Subjects under that sort of stress invented the most farfetched things. One woman he'd been associated with had sent over fifty people to prison, and none of them as far as he knew had provided anything yet, or seemed likely to.

The special methods were indispensable to the cause of truth; with each application another layer of deceit was stripped away, until the last truth was told, finally, in the last extremity.

Why was he here? Karel wanted to know. What did they want from him?

It was becoming clearer and clearer to the Civil Guard, Kehr said, that to do its job with maximum efficiency it would need to recruit more heavily among nonmembers of the Party, to systematically build a core of people who were not Party members or known supporters. They'd allow for greater flexibility in operations. That would do two things: it would create a more omniscient intelligence service, and it would create the impression of a more omniscient intelligence service.

And they wanted to Karel to do that?

Among other things, Kehr said. An example: there was a certain protest organization, of families that had had family members disappear. It had been particularly hard to penetrate. Kehr had proposed months ago that one of their female operatives be accompanied to the meetings by a young boy posing as her son to give her greater credibility. It could even be arranged to have the son save the day during a faked police intervention and thereby cement his position within the group.

There'd also be paperwork around the centers, more routine activities—release orders, transfer orders, final disposal orders—all such things that needed to be done and that there was always so little time for.

Karel sat upright. "I wouldn't do that," he said. "I couldn't do that."

Kehr nodded. He seemed undisturbed. "That I think is a common reaction," he said. "But it's a little more complicated in your case. Take for example the prisoner who was sitting here yesterday recording the session. What he intuited some time ago was that there was nothing a man wouldn't do to save himself, and having saved himself, there was nothing he wouldn't do for increasingly trivial reasons, and that eventually he finds himself doing these things out of duty, out of habit, out of pleasure, or for no reason at all."

Karel shuddered.

"Strange but true," Kehr said.

"Are you going to torture me to make me do it?" Karel asked.

"I suppose I should be more frank with you," Kehr said. "There is in my business what we call Involuntary Recruitment. This is carried out through private consultations between the operative and the subject, during which the subject is introduced to compromising actions and situations. At some point the recruit is asked to join the struggle. Should the recruit refuse, which is likely considering the reasons for which the recruit was chosen in the first place, it is then pointed out to the recruit that he or she is already inside the movement, and that he or she will be exposed to his or her friends—as well as the partisans, who unfailingly act very badly in such situations—if he or she does not cooperate."

Karel was thunderstruck.

"But of course you have time to think about it," Kehr said. "We should be going. I think someone will soon be using the room."

Karel followed him on his rounds, in shock and feeling he had nowhere else to go. They dropped in on a woman who was being released as soon as she recovered fully, and Kehr asked if she'd write down for him her full name and address. "I like to keep in touch with my girls," he said. He told Karel after they left the cell that he'd drop her a card every so often to see how she was doing. In the courtyard they passed a file of prisoners with sticks tied to their legs who were being taught to march. The partisans would not go away and this contrary political activity would not go away, Kehr remarked as they left the center. But we're not here to adjust to this world, he said. We're here to adjust *it.*

THE REPTILE HOUSE

THE NEXT NIGHT, WHILE KEHR AND STASIK WERE out, he heard a noise downstairs. He was in bed. The noise was weight somewhere on the floorboards; it was too large and too heavy for the ringtail. He went down the stairs expecting nearly anything. He passed the bathroom and could smell the ringtail's droppings on the tile. The house was still dark. Something moved over the bathroom sink, and he looked closer. There was a cough and a face bloomed in the dark mirror as he fumbled and scrabbled for the light switch. He got it and flipped it on and his father was behind him, reflected in the mirror, wearing the uniform of the Civil Guard.

"Surprise," his father said.

"You," Karel said. "You."

"They have an animal living in the house?"

his father said. He gave Karel a dubious look and sniffed around.

"How'd you get here?" Karel asked. "How long have you been here?" His father was exploring the living room, turning on lights. Karel was trembling. He asked if his father wanted something to eat or something.

His father told him not to bother, that he had eaten at the center before coming over. He sat on the sofa, still sniffing.

"How long can you stay?" Karel asked.

His father straightened the service cap on his belt. He had fewer stripes than Kehr and no antipartisan badge. Until tomorrow night, he said. They'd put a lot of work into the house, hadn't they? It looked good.

Yes, they had, Karel said. He sat in a chair across the room.

Had he helped? his father asked.

Karel nodded. Something skittered along the wallboard behind the couch.

"Is that the animal?" his father said.

They were both sitting in the chairs the same way, feet together, knees apart. Karel didn't say anything.

"They told me about it," his father said.

Karel had his hands between his thighs. He was not going to cry in front of him.

"What a guy like him wants with a filthy little pack rat I don't know," his father said. "Don't ask me." He was uncomfortable around Karel but even so seemed more relaxed than usual, and happier with himself.

"What happened?" Karel said, his voice a little hoarse. "What happened to you?"

"Fell in with the wrong crowd?" his father tried, and then looked apologetic. He explained that that had been a joke. He concentrated. He'd been picked up by the Security Service. Remember he'd told Karel that morning that he might've gotten in trouble? He'd been shooting his mouth off. He'd been frustrated, he didn't have a pot to piss in, it was natural. Someone nearby, it'd turned out, worked for the Service. They'd had some talks with him, nothing rough, and then referred him to Kehr, who it turned out had been very interested in his abilities.

"Kehr was?" Karel asked. He didn't know who to believe anymore. "Why didn't you call or write?"

"I did," his father said.

"You know what I mean!" Karel wailed.

"Okay, okay," his father said. "I wanted to. I couldn't."

"Why not?" Karel said. He was crying.

"They just thought it was better that way," he said.

"I looked everywhere," Karel said, sick. "You told me you'd never just leave like that."

"I didn't," his father said. "They took me away."

Karel shook his head. He wiped his face with his hands. "And you joined the Civil Guard," he said.

"I was told you knew all that," his father said.

"I didn't hear it from *you,*" Karel said. The ringtail nibbled at the back of the couch. It sounded like someone scratching burlap.

"You think it's such a terrible thing?" his father said, peeved. "You remember what it was like before?"

Karel put his forefinger and thumb to his mouth and looked at the floor and said nothing.

"What should I be doing?" his father said. "You tell me. What should I be doing? Nothing? Should I be doing what you're doing?"

Karel put his hands over his eyes. "Kehr took me to the center," he said. It was half lament, half accusation.

"I know that," his father said, and Karel looked up. "I

know what you've been doing. And let me fill you in on a little something, since you're so ashamed of your father: I never took part in any prisoner assessment sessions. The first time they asked *me* I refused."

Karel gaped at him for a moment and then broke down.

He could see a blurry father sitting back on the couch, unimpressed. "Here I come back after how long and all you can do is blubber," his father said.

"Why didn't you call me or write me?" Karel asked. "Why couldn't you have let me know you were there? Why couldn't you have looked out for me?"

His father fumed. He said grimly, "So now this is Dad's fault, too."

"That's not what I meant," Karel protested. "That's not what I meant."

"Let me tell you something," his father said. "I didn't tell you because that was the way it had to operate. I didn't tell you because Kehr told me not to. That was the way we worked it. You think all of this is *coincidence?* You think all of this just *happened?*" He spread his hands, and then gave up on Karel and looked away.

Karel could see himself sitting there, open-mouthed. "You *let* them do all that?" he said, with as much force as he could get into his voice.

"Please," his father said. He raised his rear up and felt behind the sofa cushions. Karel got out of his chair and went upstairs and slammed his door.

"Very adult," his father called after him. "Very impressive."

Karel could hear him banging around in the kitchen. The faucet over the sink went on two or three times and he knew he was testing the plumbing.

He lay on his back in the dark and listened but there were

no more sounds. He couldn't concentrate. His shirt was humid and smelled. He thought how stupid and alone he'd been. The thought of Kehr and his father having done this together made him want to split his head open on the floor.

He'd run away. He'd find Leda. He lay on the floor and starting flexing his knee impatiently, as if leaving in minutes.

Later he heard Kehr come back. Karel's father suggested they sit on the front steps; the house was like an oven. Ice tinkled in a glass. It was quiet.

He got up and went to the windowsill and peered over. They were just around the corner; he could see their legs.

"How'd our friend handle the reunion?" he heard Kehr say. He couldn't make out his father's response.

"Where is he now?" Kehr asked. His father said he was upstairs, asleep.

His father started explaining to Kehr his position, and Karel couldn't tell if Kehr was listening or not. His father asked in a low voice what people expected him to do. The situation was the situation; was he supposed to change it? The thing to do was to try to protect yourself, keep your mouth shut and do the best you could. Karel listened with his back against the wall and his head beneath the windowsill, drained of energy, a marionette.

His father said he'd even figured at the beginning that he could help the Party change for the better, become a little more reasonable, a little more, you know, reasonable. Kehr said something quietly, and Karel's father answered that his group had had nothing to do with that; it'd been a Security Service deal top to bottom, and whoever said otherwise was lying through his teeth. That was the way it was, anyway, his father added: his group got the dirty jobs, the kind where you got decorated if everything fell right and strung up by your thumbs if it didn't.

He could hear the ice when his father took a drink. The kid's mother had left him holding the bag, his father said, and did Kehr think the kid blamed his mother for that? Here she was out working for her Republic without another thought for the kid, and he, Dad, the guy who had stuck around, was the one that was supposed to be worthless. Figure that.

"You have only the most glancing idea of what you're talking about," Kehr said, distinctly enough that Karel heard every word.

His father was quiet. He had a way of exchanging a quick smile with someone who'd insulted him, and Karel imagined it now. If he lived long enough, he thought, would he begin to be like that? Would people see through him as easily?

His father said something apologetic, and Karel reflected on his cowardice and the way he saved his courage and bad humor for Karel. There was a long silence and then his father started talking about knots. He told Kehr he'd learned them during his days on the seashore and he liked to trot one out every so often to see if he still had the knack. Karel remembered each of them—the bowline, the pistol grip, the monkey's tail—and got even sadder, remembering how much being able to pull them off had pleased his father, remembering the way in which in their elaborateness they'd always seemed to him his father's way of attempting to make his world safer, more controllable.

"Write your father off," Kehr said. It was the next morning, Karel's father was gone for the day, and Karel was sullenly cleaning the coffeepot with an abrasive cleanser he hoped would make the coffee taste like paint. He didn't respond.

Karel shouldn't allow himself to be so swayed by his father's example, discouraging as it was, Kehr said. He was not limited by his father's limitations. Kehr could tell that much even now. Did Karel think his father could've handled all this the way he had?

Karel rinsed out the slick residue and stacked the metal pieces to dry.

This was not an opinion, Kehr said. He was not wrong about human behavior.

Karel wiped his hands and left the room.

"I have another letter for you," Kehr called after him. He followed Karel into the living room.

Karel was sitting where his father had been on the couch. "Where is it?" he asked.

"I'm not finished," Kehr said. He sat where Karel had sat. Some notes were on the table between them. On top of one was a short sentence: *Roeder proposes fire.* Kehr collected everything into the folder and closed it. He said, "He has petty ambitions and no real feelings for you. He believes in his own sentimentalities the way third-rate executioners do. He's denounced two of his colleagues to the intelligence services and he no more firmly believes in what we're trying to accomplish than your mother did." Karel looked at him. "He has no family feeling, no loyalties. You should learn from him and move on. He is going under even as he prefers to believe he's not. You owe yourself a certain ruthlessness in this case."

"Can I have the letter or not?" Karel asked.

Kehr stood, surveying him, and took it from his jacket. He held it out. "I was told this would be the last one for a while," he said.

"Why? Has something happened? What's happened?" Karel asked.

"That's what I was told," Kehr said. "This was a favor. I'm sure the girl's as safe as you are. Try to remember what I've been saying." He left the room, and then after a minute or two the house.

Karel read the letter where he was. The ringtail perched on the arm of the chair Kehr had vacated and cleaned its pinkish paws and blinked at him.

> Karel,
>
> Don't go getting conceited if I write to you again so soon, but I'm bored stiff. Got your short note, which was strange and didn't help much.

Short note? Who had written her? Kehr?

> I'm writing in bed again. Praetor (our cat) is sitting on my stomach. She sits on my head in the middle of the night. Mother hates our name for her and won't allow us to let her out for that reason.
>
> What's new around here? Almost nothing. We played so many practical jokes on our old boss that she's being replaced, and our new one's a real 150-percenter, so I guess we're getting what we deserve. (It's amazing to me how much I like bamboozling superiors.)
>
> This will probably be a short letter. It's getting harder and harder to keep our spirits up. There's a lot of the usual whispering about horrible things. We're no closer to getting enough money together to move into our own apartment. Four people downstairs were dragged off two nights ago and Mother still hasn't recovered. She's obsessed with the idea of our family being separated. She watches David all the time and

won't let him outside, either. All he has now is Praetor. At the market I was approached by a small smelly man from the Price Control Board who said I'd just been swindled at a fruit stand and asked if I'd act as a decoy for the police the next time around.

I'm less and less relaxed or patient enough to deal with the children. It's like everything else: I'm getting too tired or lazy to take all the stupidities in stride. I'm still arguing with Mother, of course. We're taught that you're supposed to back your family regardless of the situation. Personally, I can't raise that much family feeling. I think a person's relationship to his parents is like the one with his country: respect and obedience, fine, but what if they're doing wrong?

I'm always arguing with Mom about that, and I feel strongly about it. I never just argue for argument's sake. (You're probably rolling your eyes as you read that.) She seems to think I can just drop the issue, like we were talking about tastes in food. Do you? I can't imagine two people living together and believing different things along those lines. Do we have the right to always be ambivalent just because everything else seems to be? How are things supposed to turn out right if nobody's willing to work to make that happen?

I'm a fine one to talk. My thoughts are always flying off on tangents, and how often do I do something I really think is brave or right?

See. I always come back to myself.

Who's done this? Who's made us different?

I think about what we might do if you came. I'm too tired to make plans, but I do anyway. I had a daydream this morning that made me happy: we were going for a walk near the sea and had the whole day to ourselves.

I get so discouraged! Have I been any use to anyone?

You once told me you thought that because of me you knew a little better what you were supposed to do, supposed to try to be. I think about that a lot. If that were true I'd think it was the greatest thing in our friendship, and the one thing I was proudest of.

Here this was supposed to be a short letter. Now look at it.

Love,
Leda

Perren found him loitering around the turtle enclosures and asked him if he'd forgotten something. He said Albert wasn't there. He didn't answer when Karel asked if he'd be in later.

"He's on his break," someone Karel hadn't seen before said. Workers in the area laughed in a muffled and discreet way.

Two soldiers were inside the tortoise enclosure rooting around under the straw and rotting lettuce. One tortoise was hunkered down on top of some dog food soaked in water and sprinkled with bone meal. The other followed their progress inquisitively. At another cage a soldier lifted up the albino mud turtle and inspected it closely. It hung in the air looking miserable.

At the Komodo enclosure two soldiers were tantalizing Seelie through the feeding grate. Herman was quiet against the wall, content to be uninvolved.

Karel told them to stop, and they turned to him the way they'd turn to a yapping dog and told him to move on.

Searches were underway in every section, and the animals were getting anywhere from skittish to traumatized. The anoles were wedged under rocks, and the Nile crocodile stood warily in the center of her enclosure with one of her hatchlings standing in her open mouth and the other two burrowed headfirst under her side.

The snakes were nervous. He could see mites on the hog-nose, around the eyes. Did Albert know about this? Beside the cobra cages someone had left the rolling tray of mice cubes, small mice frozen in water to prevent dehydration. They were half thawed. Soldiers were gathered apprecia-tively around a spitting cobra close to the glass, which raised and spread its hood carefully as if searching for in-formation. Perren remarked to them that no one was ever interested in the nonpoisonous ones, and that his old boss had told him once that the wax museums in the capital charged extra for the murderers but the missionaries and reformers and statesmen you could see for nothing.

He had two soldiers lead Karel out, past the mambas, thin and graceful and gliding so swiftly through their stand of field grass they seemed to be swimming, and then past the puff adder, satisfied with its quiet life and few rats. Karel asked if he could stay, and the soldiers said no. A Civil Guardsman shut and locked the gate behind him.

He walked south to the barren hillside he'd visited with Leda. There were still mangy dogs around the refuse dump. He climbed until he reached a place he thought he remembered and then sat in the sun on the scree and looked back at the town and the Reptile House in the dis-tance.

It was already late and he stayed where he was until after dark, watching clouds red from the sunset roll toward the town. He saw a small convoy of six transport trucks parked in an orderly line to the east. The heat from their running exhausts made them flex and wobble. When it was fully dark he could hear cicadas and night feeders starting to move around on the shale, and the convoy started moving, stringing through town like a necklace. Single points of headlights broke off onto each street leading to the zoo and crawled to a stop at the dead ends. When each stopped it went dark. There was about a half hour of silence, and then when Karel got up to go a gathering wail of sirens, and floodlights were trained on the zoo from out of the darkness, and as he ran down the slope half out of control on the loose rock there was the cracking and popping of guns.

The neighborhood around the zoo was completely changed. Soldiers and police and Civil Guardsmen manned roadblocks of oil drums and sawhorses and herded people back into their houses. Karel was turned away at three different points, one teenaged soldier hoisting a rifle butt and shaking it at him to indicate what he was capable of, and finally got through by climbing over the hoods of some transport trucks guarded by two drivers playing dice.

The zoo was on fire everywhere. He tried to shout or call—what? who?—but everything was lost in the roar and wind of the fire's updraft and the cacophony of the animals. At the inner gate soldiers were coming and going hurriedly while Civil Guardsmen stood in groups discussing the chaos with equanimity. He could smell their coffee. He followed the wall a few hundred feet and scrambled over to get inside. The smoke choked and blinded him and was filled with diesel exhaust and burning rubber. Something collapsed with a crash nearby. There was a whirl of sparks upward and he got a clear view of the fire for the first time, and then the smoke curtained together again and the sparks showered down around him in a golden rain, bouncing and staying lit where they fell. He saw heavy black smoke pouring from the basement windows of the monkey house and saw the intensities of the separated fires and the soldiers still rolling drums away and realized that they had set this, that they were destroying the zoo.

He ran to one and began pulling at his arms and the soldier released his drum with one hand and caught Karel in the temple and ear and the ground swept up and hit him. He got his cheek off the dirt and felt around with his open palms and thought, *Seelie and Herman.* The side of his mouth was swelling and his jaw throbbed. He staggered to his feet. Something flashed by with a squawk and he registered it as a parrot. High above him a heron flapped into the smoke, glowing red in the reflected light. There were no firemen at work and it seemed as if everyone was on his own: one group was clubbing down flamingoes and another had herded together the wild sheep to protect them. The sheep were bleating in terror and turning in a circle like a storm cloud.

At the Reptile House he didn't see any of the workers. The doors and windows had been shattered and the fire was mostly inside. As he ran in he was knocked aside by a soldier rushing out, squeamishly carrying at arm's length an untroubled iguana.

The hall was empty and the fires were spreading along the walls. Equipment was smashed and scattered. Near the turtle tiers benches and tables had been piled around the tortoise enclosure and the fire there was already unapproachable. He could see the geckos and anoles pressed belly first to the front glass of their enclosures, already dying from the heat. He hefted a shovel he found on the floor and started breaking the glass, just swinging and sobbing, but when it shattered and rained around him like spray the freed lizards stayed where they fell, limp and unobtrusive in the debris. He tried to work closer to the turtles but the heat drove him back, burning his face so that he thought his skin was on fire, and he could see their dark shapes and hear their shells hissing like iron cooling in water. The hall to the iguanas was blocked too now and he could hear the teakettle hissing and whistling of their agonies.

He ran outside and around the building to get to the snake enclosures, dragging the shovel and just avoiding a sweep of fire that billowed out a side window. The cages and enclosures were smashed and everything that wasn't dead was out; part of the wall had collapsed and taken down the front restraining grates. Soldiers everywhere were shrieking and shooting and swinging axes and shovels. The hognose fled over his foot and the bushmaster passed along the inner side of an ankle, freezing him. It was brown and six inches wide and longer than he was, and he could see the rhomboids like black felt on its back. It glided for cover under a jumble of oil drums. A second wall collapsed with a shower of sparks and embers and knocked a Civil Guardsman to his knees, spilling a king cobra in front of him. The cobra reared up to face him and the Civil Guardsman groped around with his hand at the cobra's base and Karel understood he was looking for his glasses. The cobra's fangs backlit were like lancets of curved glass.

He heard a voice cursing the snakes and cursing the idiots who had started the outer wall before the inner one had really taken and he knew it was his father. He turned, his body moving erratically after the double shock of that and the bushmaster, and followed the voice, and was knocked sprawling by soldiers running in the opposite direction.

He got up and kept moving, and there was Holter, out of the smoke, his face black with soot and sweaty, supervising something around a tree that was already starting to smolder. Holter was here, he thought, but it was as if he'd lost his capacity for surprise, and he kept on after his father's voice.

A Civil Guardsman stopped him by grabbing his arm and swinging him around, and asked by shouting in his ear what he was doing there, and it was as if he had no words for such unprecedented things, so he didn't answer, and while the Guardsman still had his arm and was hurting it he saw through the trucks and men and debris a huge gray shape, one of the Komodos, Seelie, rumble down an incline trying to get to the unfinished moat, scattering Civil Guardsmen and dragging a soldier who'd tried to collar her with a rope along behind her, and what looked like an army of uniformed bystanders plunged after her, firing, and while Karel screamed and struggled she rose into sight again on the opposite side of the ditch and he could see the bullets impacting frenetically along her side and back and she lurched sideways, a foreclaw up, and tumbled back down the embankment. He realized he still had the shovel in his hand and swung it and hit only the man's legs with the handle, and the man clubbed him to the ground and hit him twice more, on the top of the head and the collarbone.

He awoke outside the barricades, where he'd been dragged. He was off the street near a hedge. The house was shuttered and dark.

It was quiet and the fire seemed largely out. The night was paling and he knew it must be close to morning. He could smell the charred wood and general sootiness in the air.

His head was sore in a kind of corona, and when he tried to lift it he groaned. He was aware of his collarbone, too, and he had to keep his arm still and close to his ribs. A tiger beetle perched on his calf, its antennae curled downward, like feelers, and he shook it off. He became aware that for some reason ants had filled one of his shoes.

A dog was barking a few streets away and was finally quiet. He sat up and dragged his shoe off. He'd stepped in something. He shook the shoe out, blinking fiercely to shake his grogginess. The ants tickled his foot and rained onto the ground with an audible patter. At the barricade one sleepy soldier sat with his rifle across his lap and his back to the sawhorse.

When it was lighter he got up. The soldier was asleep. He passed through the barricade, holding the shoulder with the injured collarbone lower, the pain in his head coming in gentle waves.

People were coming out. Nearer the zoo he found a small boy playing on a blackened playground. The soles of his feet and his hands were black.

Beside the playground the bakery was still standing, and still had power, and the baker was putting breakfast rolls into the ovens in the back. He was working under a single light bulb and wearing slippers and trousers and an apron but no shirt. The apron needed changing.

Closer to the zoo some houses had burned down. A girl Karel's age was standing outside the ruins, which were still hot, and picking at what she could, dusting it off and throwing it away. Some neighbors had gathered to watch. She ignored Karel but the neighbors nodded when he stopped.

They disagreed about the fire. Two women thought the whole thing was terrible and what they were looking at unforgivable, but someone else argued that the zoo had been a staging area for insurgents, that soldiers had told them it had been destroyed by a spontaneous people's response.

Obviously no one wanted property destroyed, but law-abiding people had a right to be protected. The girl Karel's age was writing on a blackened wall with chalk, and they all read it as she wrote: *Where are you? I will be at Etz's. —Sisi.*

Most of the zoo was still too hot to explore. The soldiers were gone. He found Albert's office, standing alone like a separate building erected in the rubble, untouched by the fire. It had been ransacked and was ankle-deep in debris. A small iguana gasped on the wall. The only undisturbed area was atop one of the file cabinets. He could see tiny mice prints in the dust. Beyond them there was a folded map of the region with holes from use worn in the corners. He took it. He groped his way back through the destruction, remembering walls and spaces that were no longer there. It was as if he'd become his own ghost.

By what had been the snake enclosures he found the bushmaster, dead, and the king cobra, though not where he'd seen it, and the boa, and the granite night lizard, and the coachwhip. The gopher snake and the lyre snake and the leafnose. Herman was still inside his enclosure, half buried and on his side, and Seelie he found at the bottom of the ditch, and he went down to her and put his hand inside her slack jaw and cried. Somebody passing by stopped and peered more closely before moving on.

At home even the ringtail seemed to be gone. The house was completely quiet. In the kitchen he hunted through the papers on the table and found nothing useful. Kehr's leather briefcase was under the table, open and unlocked. In it he found one of the pass cards with the antipartisan symbol. Above the symbol it said, *Civil Guard: Civic Action—Intelligence;* below in smaller print that the bearer should not in any way be detained or otherwise identified. He sat at the table and painstakingly and hurriedly copied Kehr's signature at the bottom, using as a model a directive on the table, and printed his own name at the top, and then took the card up to his room.

He shut the door behind him and packed what he needed or had into a canvas beltpack: the pass, his father's money, Albert's map, a lozenge-shaped canteen, a change of shoes, another shirt, a floppy sunhat. He added some thin rope and a clasp knife, and matches in a tin. He took the picture of his mother Kehr had given him off the wall, considered it, and hid it in the bottom drawer of his desk. He took all three of Leda's letters.

He returned to the kitchen and filled a paper bag with a round loaf of white bread and some figs and dates and two plums. He topped off his canteen. He found some very old salt tablets in the odds-and-ends drawer. On the way out he heard a noise in the spare room. He waited, and then eased himself out the door and broke into a sprint as soon as he could.

It was still very early. He was chilly and the sun was barely up. He intended to skirt the busier streets and then head east on the national road. He passed a barefooted man sitting on a crate and reading *The People's Voice.* Inside the house Karel could see a thin girl working a pump in the kitchen and could hear the sound the water made in her bucket. After that he saw no one, and he was struck by the emptiness of the roads.

The checkpoint was a sawhorse next to a shack of corrugated metal. A teenage soldier was manning it alone. Karel recognized him as the one with the swollen eye who'd harassed them before. He fought his despair and fear and kept walking toward him.

The soldier's face and cap were coated with dirt. He leaned against the sawhorse and didn't raise his rifle at Karel's approach. What was this? he asked, when Karel stopped in front of him. Running away from home?

Karel took his pass card and held it out. His arm was trembling and he tried to make it stop.

The soldier did not take the card. His eye looked worse. He nudged Karel's paper bag with the barrel of his rifle, and Karel opened it and showed him. The soldier took one of the plums.

"I know you from somewhere," the soldier said. He peered at Karel with his good eye.

Karel held the pass out stubbornly.

The soldier took it and examined it as if he'd never seen such a thing before. "This means I'm supposed to let you pass?" he finally said.

Karel nodded. The soldier exhaled with exasperation and knitted his eyebrows and thought about it and then waved Karel through. Karel passed around the sawhorse and held his hand out for the card, and for a long terrifying moment the soldier pocketed it and clasped a hand over the pocket. Then he gave Karel a slow smile and took out the card and returned it.

When it felt as if he'd walked forever he had lunch. He was well out of town and there was nothing on either side of him but bunchgrass and creosote. He ate the figs and a piece of bread he sawed off with his clasp knife and looked back at the town. A convoy passed. There were seven or eight open-backed trucks filled with ordinary people of all ages. They were heading away from town. The trucks had wire mesh over their headlights and windshields, and the people in the back looked disturbed or thoughtful. Some of them waved or pointed at Karel.

He kept walking. He was headed for the nearest train station, at Naklo. It was too far away to walk to, he knew, but a bus from the south passed a junction that was only maybe two days' walk by a shortcut trail, and that he could get to. From Naklo he'd take the train to the capital.

At the point the road turned north, he paused at the start of the trail, which continued east. It was a white gravelly track between spiny shrubs, and it cut across what looked like an endless number of deep washes.

It was quiet. Brush mice darted across open spaces and then sat motionless in the creosote, watching him. He was apprehensive about the desert but reassured by the map and filled with instructions, mostly from Albert when they'd traveled for the zoo. He should rest in the shade for ten minutes every hour. He shouldn't remove his shirt because it would speed dehydration, and he needed to watch at all times for the symptoms. At night he should stay out of the washes and gullies, and watch what he picked up or handled. If he left the trail for some reason he could tell directions from the areas of plant growth along the culverts and inclines: south faces were bare, north mostly covered. There was usually water below the surface near bunchgrass, but when in doubt he should trust the rabbit and prairie dog and mouse tracks, even if they seemed wrong, because those animals weren't guessing; they knew. He should watch coyotes at night, too, where they pawed and snuffed the ground. He could eat a lot of the berries, and some beans if they were pounded up. The oneleaf pines had edible cone-kernels. He should look for tender green shoots of other plants inside the prickle bushes and prickly pear.

On his map the trail crossed a stream and skirted a dead lake to the south like the one Leda had told him about and then climbed northeast across a low range and descended to the junction. It looked fairly simple. He remembered the stories about the northern mountains.

The sun was over his head for a long time, then behind him. The only sounds he heard were his shoes on the gravel and the swish of his shorts. His head still hurt but his collarbone felt better. As he walked he turned over memories of his father in his head the way he'd examine puzzle pieces, in search of a pattern.

He could see scavenger birds black in the distance against the treeless hills. The sunlight was so blindingly intense it seemed to be splitting the stones. The air was like breathing hot cotton wool. He walked as far as he could and finally found a fair-sized boojum tree and sank to a sitting position in its shade, stunned by the sun. Two sparrows with their beaks parted edged over in the shadow to make room for him, unwilling to be frightened in this heat. His head was buzzing and spinning, and he took some water and salt.

He woke with the colder air at night and the patter of sand against his cheek. He could feel the heat coming off him, still trapped in his clothes. When he stirred a large insect stalked a few feet away and then paused to see if it was being pursued. He stood up, sore and chilly, wrapping his arms around himself, spooked, and then continued walking, the slightly more trampled area of the trail whiter in the moonlight. He was not sleepy.

He walked all night. He passed skeletal silhouettes of dead bitter condalia trees and catclaws, and a dead lagoon that apparently had once fed the dead lake. It was filled with reeds that were gray in the moonlight and brittle to the touch. He passed more brush mice and a ground squirrel, and heard bats. In an uneven and rocky gully he found the trail alive with tarantulas moving like dull, sinister flowers.

In the morning he thought he might have seen a bicyclist off on the horizon, a small dark figure against the stillness, but he recognized that he could've been mistaken. He was dizzy. He walked as far as possible while it was still relatively cool and then finally lay down to rest again on the side of a steep wash overhung with peppergrass. The stream on the map was nearby, and he refilled his canteen and washed his face and eyes. He had more water and bread and ate the other plum and fell asleep with his head on his beltpack, his muscles twitchy from the endless walking, and his hands between his thighs.

He woke up terrified of the vague darkness and chill, his mind washed blank of its sense of where he was and what he was doing there. He drank some water in a wary crouch, surprised at how long he had slept, and ate the last of the bread.

The dead lake had been only a few hundred yards away. It was a huge wasteland flat, cratered and broken by traverse cracks so that it looked like an endless horrible cobblestone plain in the moonlight, with things moving distantly across it in various directions.

He changed his shoes and shirt and walked as fast as he could around it while keeping his mind on Leda, until the trail began to climb, and when he crested the ridge and looked back once more at the lake it stretched black and even and still in all directions below him.

He saw a house and a few outbuildings a short way off the trail to the south, silhouetted on another ridgeline, and after some hesitation decided to head for them. There were no lights showing.

He approached from a low draw to stay out of sight, every so often craning his head up to look for movement or danger. When he was very close he crouched low and waited. The front door had been kicked in and a piece of it swung on the lower hinge in a forlorn diagonal. There was no sound from inside, though a shutter clapped gently against its sill every so often. He threw a rock through the open door and ducked down. He got closer and threw a bigger one, and it made a disconcerting crash inside and he lay flat in mortification, but still nothing happened. Finally he got up, brushing off his shorts, and crossed to the door and looked inside.

He could see only as far as the moonlight penetrated, but the house had clearly been ransacked. The smell was horrible. He lost all interest in food, or in spending the night.

He circled around to the back. When he turned the second corner a goat standing against the wall startled him. It moved a short way away and continued grazing, relieved it was not going to be bothered.

He found himself on a rough terrace, flooded with moonlight. Beneath his foot there was a rusty old key, and on the brick wall a hanging twist of wire. He could see off to the east a slope and lights undulating slowly along its base: the national road again. He'd be there by tomorrow, he thought, and let out a small whoop in gratitude and relief.

The smell was still bad, worse than anything he'd smelled. He'd entertained ideas of hunting for food but couldn't bring himself to and thought now he couldn't even sleep here, either. He left the terrace to continue his circuit and kicked the body of a woman covered with flies. They rose up in a small agitated cloud. She was lying on her back and her arm was resting on the stone of the terrace as if she'd made herself comfortable. Her hair was over her face in a black sticky wing. There was another body behind her in the darkness with its legs folded and neck back at a severe angle. He ran blindly away from the house back toward the trail, sending the goat clattering in panic out of his way. The smell and the image stayed with him all the way back to where he'd turned off and longer, and he cried and swung his arms and cursed and felt revolted and horrified, and sorry for himself for ever having seen such a thing.

The bus driver waved him on without even looking at his pass card. He didn't see any soldiers or Civil Guardsmen among the passengers. They looked at him strangely as he came down the aisle. When he settled into his seat a cricket sprang from his pocket.

His head throbbed and he was thirsty and wanted to empty the sand from his shoes. As they crested the hill in long winding turns he kept his face to the window, looking back at the dark green patterns like underwater vegetation on the desert floor below.

At Naklo the bus let him off across the street from the train station. He stood in line to buy his ticket behind a woman who held her baby up against her chest and continually apologized to it. When it was his turn he pushed his money under the slot and held his card up to the glass and again there was no trouble. He bought a pineapple drink from a sidewalk vendor while he waited for the train and drank it slowly, the cup cool in his hand.

Nothing was on schedule, but the noon train ran in the afternoon and the afternoon train at night, so that every so often a train came in right on time because it was the previous train six hours late.

The train came as the sun was setting. They passed a small factory in a narrow valley just outside of town and some small farms before he stopped looking out the window and tried to sleep. A fat man opposite him caused an epic amount of trouble endlessly getting in and out of his seat and finally disappeared before the ticket taker arrived. The ticket taker checked Karel's ticket and pass card and left with them and returned a few minutes later with another official while Karel pretended to doze, his heart thumping. The ticket taker prodded him and returned the card and ticket and passed on.

He slept. There were creakings, snores, conversations, jolts. He woke every now and then at the water stops, hearing the trainmen murmuring. When he woke again they were stopped at a quiet station and nothing seemed to be happening. He saw moths around the light illuminating the station sign. A discarded timetable stirred and fluttered on the platform. Somebody coughed. He could make out part of a loopy painted slogan on the side wall: ——STAYS. Another train passed with a noisy rush and reflected his window and he saw himself spying out of a fluctuating plane of lights and then he was gone. Their train started again, giving all the passengers' heads a lazy shake, and he watched the station and its water tower diminish around a curve with the rails crossing ties and spinning into the darkness and then he was dozing again, more exhausted than he'd realized, thinking about Leda and relaxing himself as much as he could with the steady clicking and rocking that were taking him away.

He felt the humidity and salt air in the closed compartment before he saw the sea. They came in along the high ridge of the cove, and he gazed down on the warehouses and storage tanks around the docks and the harbor glittering beyond them. There were boats, more than he remembered. The train let him out at the top of the city, and he swung his beltpack around so it rested on his hips and began his way down a road so steep the houses along it could only be entered from the top floors. He kept his eyes on the harbor.

He had Leda's address, but it was too early, and he was hungry besides. As he got lower, shops appeared on both sides of the street. He passed garages, a butcher's shop, a fabric store, a dealer in military antiques. At a welder's three men were beating on a metal object with hammers and cursing. The noise stayed with him for blocks. He could smell the salt in the air and the humidity after the desert was wonderful. He passed a bakery and then a café and stepped inside.

He ate back near the kitchen and it was narrow and cluttered. A black iron stovepipe went up to the slanted ceiling and while they made his breakfast he gazed blankly out of a triangular skylight. Above the stove on racks were spices he could smell in small wooden boxes, and a dirty dishtowel hung on a peg over his table. Flies wove past him and disappeared.

For breakfast he had coffee and shredded nut pastries and then asked if it was too early to make some cuttlefish with spinach and lemon. He'd been away a long time, he explained. While he ate he watched a beautiful blond woman in a Women's Auxiliary uniform who waved her spread hands like a fan over her tea, letting the cherry polish on her fingernails dry.

Back on the street he passed blocks he'd never seen before, and odd sights—a dwarf stopping to give some coins to a blind couple jointly playing the accordion, a pigeon perched just above a sleeping cat—but it seemed that every street, every simple corner of a house, retained a shiver of something from his past, some old tremor of feeling. He was here, he thought as he walked. He was here.

He showed a passerby Leda's address and asked directions. He passed small trees growing out of square open areas in the sidewalks and tightly fenced gardens. Dogs occasionally raced or clawed along the fences, eager to get at him.

The Schieles turned out to live in yet another part of the city that was unfamiliar to him, and he was beginning to feel discomfited at the continued undermining of his nostalgia.

He found himself in front of a shabby and narrow house facing a courtyard where buses were apparently stored. There was a fish store on the ground floor. Their apartment, a helpful neighbor said, was the small dark place on the third floor. The house was very old and had in its keystone arch a fierce mythical lizard of some sort with a fish in its mouth. The second-floor landing was dark and filled with junk: a bicycle wheel, some sodden cardboard boxes, stacked metal pails, a tangle of rusted and broken knives.

He smoothed his hair and knocked and thought belatedly about cleaning himself up.

Leda opened the door and surprised him completely by not being surprised.

"You're here," she said, and her expression was so beautiful he knew he loved her completely. Her hair was lighter and finer and pinned up on the sides. She hugged him, and stood back from him, smiling. She tilted her head and smoothed her hair on one side by bringing her opposite hand all the way over the top of her head. "Come in," she said.

Their apartment was just as she had described it. Everyone was gone.

Mother had taken Nicholas and David to the beach, she

explained. Aunt was working. She'd waited here for him.

"You knew I was coming?" Karel said.

Leda looked puzzled. "Didn't you send me this?" she asked. She showed him a printed note: *Coming soon should arrive Thurs or Fri. Love, Karel.*

Karel stared at it, dumbfounded. Something told him he should lie, that if he told the truth Leda would be less happy to see him.

"I forgot," he said. She looked at him strangely.

"So how did you get here? What happened?" she said. "Are you hungry? Are you okay?"

She got him iced tea with mint while he told her about his father's return and the destruction of the zoo. He told her about the desert and the bodies in the abandoned farmhouse. He did not tell her about the prisoner assessment room. She put her hand over her mouth. He regretted having upset her, though he appreciated her concern for what he'd been through, and he sipped his tea, aware all at once of how filthy he was.

She shouldn't grill him like this, she said. She put a hand on his cheek. She'd been going to suggest they go to the beach and find everybody, but she didn't think that was such a good idea anymore.

He shook his head.

He was probably tired, she said. And he probably wanted to wash up. She took the glass from his hands and set it down and tenderly helped him up, leading him to the bathroom door. She took off his beltpack and he raised his arms dumbly but she didn't take off anything else. She disappeared and came back with a towel and a scrub brush that looked as if it was used for pots and pans. She told him to let her know when he was finished. She gave him some of Nicholas's shorts to sleep in.

He washed himself in a small claw-footed tub. Was she in danger? Why had Kehr send the note? It had to have been Kehr. What was happening? What was Karel doing to her and her family by lying to them?

The water when he got out was gray. It left a ring, and he knelt and tried to wash it away with his hands. When he came out she looked pleased and the air in the living room was cool.

Now a nap, she said, and he was thrilled at the idea of her lying next to him, her family gone, his having braved great dangers to be at her side.

But she kissed him once on the mouth and pulled herself away from his hands, and told him it was wonderful to see him, and hugged him again. She shut the door behind her as she left.

He was disappointed but the plainness of the bedsheets in the sheer white morning light seemed paradisical. He sat on the mattress with his hands on his knees, gazing unsurprised at the extent of his own exhaustion. He lay back and thought it was possible to have kinds of homecomings without home, and fell asleep.

He woke to voices through the walls, the next apartment, and listened for a while before deciphering that the people were refugees and they were arguing over whose situation was worse. He heard other voices, too, and realized the rest of the Schieles were home.

They were all happy to see him. Nicholas pointed out that Karel was wearing his shorts and that Leda was much happier now, and the insight made him radiant. He sat across the room still wearing his bathing suit and smiled as if he knew each of Karel's secrets.

David stood with both hands on the arm of Karel's chair and asked about the desert and did Karel see any nomads or scorpions and said he had plenty of things to show Karel in the city. His mother hushed him and made Karel relate everything he'd already told Leda, stopping him to shake her head and then nod every so often. He knew she'd retell some of what he told her as part of her store of catastrophe tales, all of which featured her in a prophetic role, unheeded by the foolish ("I had a *feeling* something was going on at that zoo . . .").

There was news for him. The war was as usual but there were reports of troubles inside the army and there'd been in the city alone in the last month nine explosions, set by God knew who. There had been two bombs left at municipal offices in bookbags, and in one of the markets a donkey had exploded; down by the waterfront a blond boy had walked into a hotel foyer and had blown up. They were now in a special state of emergency, which Leda's mother confessed she thought they'd *been* in, though officially the explanation was still that these were not partisans but delinquents.

The hotel explosion had destroyed the front of the building housing the nursery center, so now Leda was out of a job.

When he looked at her she arched her eyebrows and shrugged.

Which didn't help financially, but still, her mother said.

Did he have a place to stay? she added.

"Can't he stay with us?" Leda asked. "After all he's done for us?"

Karel looked away in genuine embarrassment. "Of course," Leda's mother said. "I was just curious. I'll fix it somehow."

"I can get a place," Karel said. "I've got money."

"Plenty of time for that," her mother said. "For now you're our guest."

They were all awkward and silent and then Karel said that what he wanted most was to have some real seafood again, and would they let him take them out for dinner? Leda's mother graciously vetoed the idea, to his relief, over the protests of David and Nicholas. She suggested slyly that the two of them go. Leda colored when he asked and said she'd love to.

In the street she took his hand. She was wearing the red linen dress and he considered it a good sign. She'd glossed her lips with something even though he'd heard her complaining to her mother when getting ready in the bedroom that there was no lipstick or anything else she could use anywhere.

She said she knew a restaurant and led the way. She asked if he was sure he could afford it, if maybe this was irresponsible of them, considering. Then she squeezed his arm and said she thought celebrating his being here was not going to hurt anything, really.

They passed cinnamon and cypress trees that made the air fresh and fragrant. Down a side street people were being made to scour slogans off a wall with wire brushes while soldiers looked on. Leda didn't notice them and Karel didn't point them out. They passed wide yards of washing, and ahead of them on the street from the backseat of a car a woman's hand stretched to caress a man on the sidewalk who leaned toward her. Karel began to recognize where he was. Leda crouched and spread a finger and thumb around a cricket, but it shot ahead and disappeared into a hedge. Everything seemed suddenly touching to him, his return, the city, Leda, the shadows of the leaves on the streets, and he felt the need to stop and put his hand on his heart and look around. As they turned a corner he imagined himself imprisoned or stranded on a far-off island and remembering the ordinariness of this walk with her as the perfect walk and the perfect happiness.

The restaurant was the Sea's Trade.

They sat in the open-air section, furnished now with new wire café-style chairs and smaller tables. They could see down into the harbor and the sun flashed off the water around the boats. The gulls he remembered still circled and settled endlessly.

"This is so nice," Leda said.

They ordered wine and melon. Karel told her he loved her letters and quoted passages from them, and she was pleased. She apologized for always being so mopey and pessimistic in them and he said not at all, they were wonderful, and she was even more pleased. She asked him if he was getting taller and he sat up straight and said he thought he was. She asked if he was okay considering everything, and he looked away, guilty, and said he was, though he was worried he wouldn't see her enough even here in the city.

Was that a major worry? She wished she had his problems, she said, but she smiled to indicate she was flattered.

How about her? he wanted to know. Was she okay?

Much better now, she said. The menu was on a chalkboard, and the waiter brought it by. She ordered ocean catfish with dates and turmeric and he got fried brislings or sprats, tiny and plump fish he hadn't seen since he was six or seven.

It was hard, though, she said when the waiter went away. He could see she was delighted at the sophistication of eating out, of the two of them here alone. Today he had perked everyone up, but it wasn't always like that. It seemed as if everyone had lost his enthusiasm for everything, which was understandable. She put her hands down and touched her silverware and plate with appreciation. It had been hard on her mother especially. Not all the girls where Leda had worked had been let go, and her mother was convinced Leda's attitude had had something to do with it. She smiled at him. She said, "Nicholas meanwhile has gotten completely quiet, and David I really worry about—he's getting like the dog from across the street, Eski, full of all these terrors that just come and go. He's always waking us up, and he sits there during the day saying these little wild things to himself. But maybe the scariest thing is that I can feel it wearing *me* down. I'm getting slower mentally. I can feel it. Sometimes when I'm reading I have to go back and read the words aloud, and still they just lie there and it's like I don't absorb them or something."

Karel stroked the top of her hand sympathetically.

"It's scary," she said.

They were quiet, though they smiled at each other occasionally to show they were half sorry the conversation had gone in that direction.

She asked if it had been harder than he thought seeing his father, and he was surprised by how sad it made him even now. He told her that over and over again he thought he understood how little he meant to his father, and over and over again he found out he meant even less.

"He just doesn't like me," Karel said. He shrugged helplessly.

He told her how much his father had always mistrusted him—him! What was he going to do? Who was he going to betray his father *to?*—and the way he'd always been amazed that all that suspicion had never seemed a burden for his father to carry. He gave her examples, and the food arrived. She said quietly that in the case of her and her mother she was beginning to realize how much alike they were. "My aunt says I'm turning into her," she said.

The notion bothered him and he thought she was leading him to something, that she thought it was true in his case. Maybe she was right: if things were bad between him and his father, did he really think it was all his father's fault? He remembered the way even as a small child when he watched his father doing something wrong he would think, I'll always be able to use this against him. He had collected and exaggerated his father's faults. They were always reacting to each other, and that had something to do, he realized, with their helplessness together.

Leda saw his sadness and leaned forward and whispered something he didn't hear. He was grateful and reminded of an early memory of one of his mother's quiet counter-demonstrations of sympathy on his behalf.

Over dessert she didn't seem bothered by his suggestion that his father had changed. Her mother said if you lay down with dogs you got up with fleas, she said. The comment stung him. He imagined her discovering where he'd been with Kehr.

They walked home in step behind a drunk who seemed perpetually ready to topple over. They balked for a while at the riskiness of passing him and finally slipped by when he collapsed against a fence rail. When they looked back again he'd slid to a sitting position.

It was quiet and the lights were out when they got home, and Leda took off Karel's shoes and settled him into some blankets on the floor. He realized he had drunk too much and he felt vague and slightly paralyzed. She kissed him goodnight and disappeared, and he lay back while the ceiling wavered above him in the dark. He listened to David's breathing and Nicholas's slight snore. He felt with some sadness that even loving Leda as he did he hadn't succeeded in adjusting himself here, to these people, either, and that even in this city that he'd dreamed of coming back to he was still an outsider.

The next morning they went to the beach. He still hadn't met Leda's aunt and was nervous about that. She was out when he got up. They took Nicholas and David, and Mrs. Schiele left with them to look for work. Leda would have to as well in a few days, she warned before they split up. She told Karel in an aside that he should keep an eye on David's cough. Leda told him as they waved goodbye that her mother was becoming obsessed with everybody's health. She speculated that it was her way of dealing with her powerlessness in everything else.

It was a hot day. The breeze off the water made him wonder just what his favorite smell was, if it wasn't this. Leda seemed very happy, and he wondered if in some situations thoughtlessness was justified.

The beach was a startling bone color, and in the shallows offshore the water was an electric blue. Both were crowded. They crossed a paved area to the sand and spread their blanket in the shadow of an upside-down white dory with a shattered keel. Leda warned David about splinters and he and Nicholas whooped-hooped their way across the hot sand to the water's edge.

Leda lay on her back facing the sun. Karel lay beside her, propped up on his elbows. She took his hand. She was wearing a pale gray bathing suit, and he looked down at the water and told her she looked beautiful. Her toes waved in his line of sight, acknowledging the compliment.

The sand was powdery and made him think of hot ash. He dug around with his heels and unearthed a green wine bottle choked with sand. Adults on other blankets were bobbing their forefingers, counting children crouched over tide pools. He closed his eyes. Leda murmured something beside him. They could live here with every day the same as the day before. He'd provide for them all and they'd make him happy and drive Kehr and the image of himself in the cellars of the Civil Guard out of his mind.

They went down to the water to swim. Sandpipers milled around nervously in the glaze of the wave's retreat, and he thought he could hear the suction of their feet on the wet sand. On the reef he could see the shadow of a sea bass lunging at nothing, and at their feet a jellyfish had washed up onto the sand. It trembled in the wind and David poked at it and dropped rocks on it. Karel dove in, and when he surfaced and looked back Leda had her arms out but instead of emulating his dive sat down suddenly at the water's edge and began to splash herself. Her brothers surprised her from behind and threw her in.

He opened his eyes in the underwater silence while she swam to him. Below them in the hazy green light they could see scraps of a fishing net rotting over tin cans and a whelk gripping a holster. Above them the surface rippled like the ceiling of a luminous tent, and they held hands and floated with the dreaming motion of clouds leaving the world behind.

Back on the blankets they watched her brothers and other boys splashing around a tide pool to collect crabs for a crab war. They toweled off and stared at gulls perched on the dory and the gulls looked back at them as if they knew that when these people were gone others would show up and stare at them, too. Leda lay back and settled herself comfortably with her face to the sun again. Beyond her someone was swinging a baby so that its toes skimmed the sand and the baby was screaming in terror and glee. Karel lay with his hand on his cheek and looked at the wet dark hair combed back from her forehead and the grains of sand that glittered in her ears and imagined with a kind of onrushing contentment that his life was starting now, that what he could do now, finally, was figure out the ways to be happy.

When he met Leda's aunt she told him it was nice to meet him and that he had to leave. She made him repeat the story of how he got there alone, and it was clear she thought something was suspicious about all of this and that there might be trouble in it. Leda and her mother protested and argued and claimed they couldn't believe she was acting this way, but in the end it didn't matter and Leda's mother explained to him that this was her husband's sister, and he found himself out on the street with his beltpack and a bag of food, saying goodbye to Leda while the aunt looked down at them from the upstairs window. He still didn't know her name. He was a little frightened but he had money and he told Leda he was going to stay at the Golden Angel, at least until he could find a cheaper place, and that she should look for him there.

It took him longer than he expected to find it. The same manager, the tubby man with the sunburned head, was sitting on a wooden chair in the cool shade of the entrance. He didn't remember Karel. He led him inside.

Karel stood taking deep breaths while the manager fussed with the register. The lobby was the way he recalled it, musty and fragrant with the scent of wood. He went into the common room and visited the painting of the cavalry charge. He had tears in his eyes. For what? he thought. Those days? The situation now? He turned to the manager, who was waiting. He realized he wanted to bring Leda back here and couple an old happiness with the present one, though he wasn't sure why.

It turned out that all the rooms were much too expensive. The manager repeated the price. Karel stood at the desk feeling that whatever sense he'd had that he could get along in the city alone was gone. The manager added that there *was* one room, very small and no view, it was nice enough but no luxury suite, and next to one of the service rooms besides. He could let Karel have it for less than half the standard rate.

It was fine. It looked out on a narrow street. It had an iron bedstead, a desk, a wooden armchair, and a warped chest decorated with phlox and pale trumpets in a clay pot. The bathroom was in the hall. He set his beltpack on the desk and opened it in a parody of someone settling in with his luggage, and the manager handed him his key and left.

He sat on the bed and tried to determine what to do with himself. It occurred to him that he needed long pants, that he stood out and that it would get colder here. He decided instead to see his old house.

He found it after a few minutes' walk. The new owners had put an addition over his porch, and there were flower boxes on the balcony. When he tried to get a better look a woman poked her head through the kitchen window and told him to get away from the house or he'd be explaining his sightseeing to the Security Service. He spent the rest of the day down by the waterfront, watching the loading and unloading of cargo.

He returned to the Golden Angel after dark and went up to his room and lay on the bed with his hands behind his head. The room had a small round clock on the desk and he watched its hands move. When it was past ten someone knocked. Leda came in and shut the door behind her as if there were wolves in the hallway. She was furious, she said, and ashamed and sorry, and she felt terrible for him. He got off the bed and went to her with no clear idea of what he was doing and put his arms around her and kissed her. She kissed him back, her hands on his head and arms and then his head again, and they reeled around the room, bumping things, putting a hand out every so often to steady themselves, and she was crying and he kissed her more passionately for that. He eased her onto the bed and she looked up at him, intent on his expression, whatever it was. The moment was frozen and detached from itself and from what seemed to have gone before. Their kisses were intent and noisy and her lips were glazed under his. He pulled at her clothing and she pulled at his. Her skin when he touched it was so delicate that he left pink spots that resisted fading. He had his clothes off, all but a shoe, and hers were in a tangle near them. She had her hands on the back of his neck and was still looking at him intently. She scratched herself so that the bed shook. That sense of a revelatory something about to happen returned, and she laughed, looking at him, at his expression, laughed at the suddenness of his own transition from not seeing to seeing the extent of her love for him.

Somebody came to the door and knocked a few minutes later. Leda pulled her legs up and covered herself with the bedspread in terror, and Karel rose to all fours on the bed and waited. There was some muttering and a voice outside the door said, "Whoops whoops whoops," and then they heard rapid steps heading down the corridor the opposite way.

"Oh, God," Leda said. He settled beside her and hugged her, and she shifted and got up and turned off the overhead light and switched on the little desk lamp. Then she pulled the covers back and got under them, and he followed.

She huddled against him. He was still excited but thought maybe he should just hold her. Just before, she'd been worried and careful even through her passion and had frustrated his attempts to enter her. He kissed her again, and she made a pleased sound. They were quiet for a long time and he realized she was beginning to doze. He heard the light uneven sound of rain beginning on the window, and then it accelerated, the droplets on the glass catching light against the darkness and slipping individually down the pane. He hadn't heard or felt rain for months. The window was open a crack and he could feel the dampness in the air outside the blankets. He imagined the wet terrace of a nearby café, the waiter wiping slabs of tables. He turned to Leda, determined to watch her all night, to remember everything.

It was still raining. The window curtains bellied in the wind. He brushed a damp hair from her ear and drifted a thumb across her temple. Her hair was still slightly pungent from the sun and the ocean. He ran the tip of his tongue lightly along her bottom lip and kissed the place at the outside of her eye where he imagined her tear duct to be. She murmured something in her sleep or half-sleep about his being so nice, and he had the impression that even her hidden thoughts were innocent, that she had no secrets or only virtuous ones, and he was overwhelmed with his good fortune at being here with her. He found himself considering and reconsidering her sleeping profile with the tenderness that someone going blind would have for what he still sees.

Sometime in the middle of the night she woke up, with a quiet start. She took his face in her hands and kissed him, and when he moved up against her small noises flowed out of her with a kind of thrilling ease. He understood her reticence with certain things and so wished he knew better what he was doing in terms of pleasing her, wanted his touching to be not only tender but intelligent. She pulled him closer and he wanted to be everywhere she was, imagined himself dissolving like sugar in her mouth. She stopped him again after a while and said she was sorry, and he said no, don't be sorry. She lay still after that with her mouth to his ear and then she said, "Listen. I was going to wait, but listen."

He moved back on his pillow and waited. Somewhere in the distance the rain was hitting the metal roof of a shed like far-off pebbles in a pan.

She sighed. She stroked his arm and then sighed again, with more resolve. "We keep saying we don't know what to do," she said. "And everything we hear is a little worse than the last thing we heard. Only a little worse. That's how it works; you wait for the next thing, and then the next thing, and *then* you'll do something."

Karel took a deep breath and blinked with shame.

"My mother sees how bad it is and still she says I'm an alarmist. I *am* an alarmist. Now she says it's too late and we didn't stop it, so now what?

"We have to do something," she said, when he didn't respond. "The people I talk to can't imagine changing anything. There's this—reverence, for what they assume *must've* existed at some point." He felt the intensity of her desire to understand, and her frustration. He took her hand and squeezed it.

"I want you to help me," she said.

He didn't want to hear this. "What?" he asked.

"There's no point in trying to put him in jail, or get people to overthrow him," she whispered. "Everybody's sworn allegiance to him personally."

"What are you thinking? What are you trying to do?" Karel said.

"We have to kill him," Leda said. "I don't know how yet. I don't even know if it's possible. But I think somebody's got to kill him."

Karel was staring at her. The roof was going to fall in, spilling Kehr on the bed. Holter was going to break in the door and take them away.

She turned to him and took his face in her hands again, holding it the way he held newborn rabbits. "If it isn't possible it isn't," she said. "But we should be finding out. We're not infants anymore. Maybe now that we're together there really is here somewhere a way to act, maybe all we have to do is *look* a little for it. I'm *ashamed* of myself sometimes. It's like I think I'm just here to sit and wait. I'd like to find out if I *am* all just talk."

"They'll kill us," Karel whispered. "Are you crazy?"

"It's dangerous right *now,*" Leda said. "You think all those people who disappeared did something?"

He thought of the young man in the prisoner assessment room and put his hands over his eyes.

"They'd kill everybody," he said. "They'd go crazy."

"We'd only do it if we could do it," she said. She came closer and kissed him, and then held him, his chin on her shoulder.

It was as if she held his fears a little bit, and settled them. He began to recognize a war inside him between the responsibility she was talking about and his old self, and he tried to settle back to observe it, like a spectator. He imagined himself learning to cherish what she cherished instead of just his own happiness and hers, imagined himself opening up to her, confessing his silence, his cowardice, his complicity, and being forgiven and purified. His mind wandered to the beach in the darkness and the rain, and he felt that he was unable to anticipate what was going to happen, that the future stood with its back to him.

"All the good I've tried to do I didn't just do for its own sake," Leda whispered. "I did it to look good. I did it for myself."

He told her no and held her and decided he'd help, he'd do it even though nothing about him was heroic, because she was precious to him and it meant everything to her. She said, I won't let anything happen to you, and it was her mothering voice, the moved, fearful one she used with her brothers, and he said, no, no, nothing'll happen to us, and held her and prayed that whatever would come would at least spare her.

He wasn't sure if he woke up slowly or just never slept. It was extra cold outside the blankets and the solid things in the room were darkening as the space around them paled and took on light. It was still raining and the darkness outside was blue.

He heard keys in locks and the squeak of a metal cart and imagined an old woman in black making the bed next door, smoothing wrinkled white sheets with her palm. He lay still, pondering a mysterious reflection in the mirror over the washbasin: a stripe and the corner of something wooden he couldn't identify when he looked around the room. A swallow scissored past the window.

Leda sat up, abruptly, and wrapped herself in the outer blanket against the chill and then padded barefoot to the door and went into the hall to the bathroom. He got up and put his two shirts on and wished again he had long pants. His shirts smelled. He crossed to the window and gazed down to the street. People were up already, walking quickly with light short steps because of the rain. In a men's shop through the streaked display window he could see little hats on pegs, only now becoming visible.

Leda came back in and crossed the room and hugged him, and then tried to get dressed while keeping the blanket on her shoulders. She spread her elbows and shivered, and the blanket tented out and flapped with her movements. Karel stayed by the window and thought of the kind of peace she brought for him to particular objects like the blanket or moments like this morning. Outside dew had frosted the hood of a parked car, and he registered two soldiers standing beside it, their arms folded. There was something else wrong and his mind was about to remark on it when the old metal washbasin near Leda rang softly and she said their first words of the morning: There, I'm finished, and the door banged and crashed open with such force that she seemed to be thrown backward not so much from the shock as the concussion of air.

Four men swept into the room wearing army shirts and civilian pants and two of them pulled the blanket up and over Leda's head and wrapped it tightly around her and one produced some rope. Karel rushed to her and the fourth man hit him across the face with what felt like a small flat plank and a thousand stars sprayed the room, and while he rolled on the floor arms grabbed and pinned him and they put a small paper bag over his head and locked his hands behind his back with a series of sliding bars that squeezed his wrists. He felt and heard loose grains around his head in the bag and realized it was an empty sugar bag. Leda was screaming for help, muffled under the blanket, and they told her to stop or they'd kill her. He heard the grunts as they lifted her and then they pulled him up and shoved him from behind, and led him into the hall and down the stairs and out of the building at a great rush, orienting him with twists or pulls of his neck and shoulders. They were piled into a car. Leda kept calling his name and he would say, *I'm here,* his voice harsh and trapped in the sugar bag, and then she cried out when they hit her to quiet her down. There was something wrong with the car, it wouldn't start, and eventually he had to get out and they unlocked his hands and told him to leave the bag on his head and he had to push with two other men at the back of the car until it started. They were quiet the rest of the way until Leda said, her voice still muffled, Why are you doing this? This is a mistake, and then the man beside Karel who was still breathing heavily from the pushing asked her angrily if she had any idea what was involved in an operation like this. Arms, civilian coordination, training centers, transports, intelligence gathering, paperwork: did she think all that operated in the service of mistakes? And the man in the front seat told him to shut up.

Then they were rushing along a corridor, with spaces he could feel opening out and closing suddenly behind him, as in a dream, and he felt a chill at his back from not knowing what was around him. Someone said Here, and he heard a heavy metal door swing open, and he touched his palm and fingertips to the rough wall beside him as a last gesture before they shoved him through the doorway.

He heard voices and had the impression of a large room and was pushed down to a sitting position against a stone wall, scraping his back. The sugar bag was removed and his handcuffs taken off.

Leda was beside him. She hugged him. They were in a huge dark cell with a low ceiling. The walls were lined with sitting or squatting people. Some had bundles and small overnight bags. The floor was cold with seepage and he felt it through his shorts, so he got up into a crouch. Leda was on her knees.

An officer of the Civil Guard sat at the table near the door, flanked by two soldiers. The officer said, "You new arrivals should turn your valuables in here, voluntarily. At the depot there's a lot of stealing goes on." He was addressing the group around Karel and Leda. Karel looked at the man beside him, and the man looked away timorously, like someone too shy to acknowledge an invitation. A few people got up and crossed to the table.

He could hear sobbing from around the room and realized there were a lot of women and children here. "Thank God they haven't got my family," Leda whispered, and he understood she'd noticed, too. She seemed both more frightened and more despairing, and he wondered if that meant he was courageous or ignorant.

He could smell moldy clothing. An older man on the other side of the room stared at him hopelessly. He tried another direction and a woman asked him sharply what he was looking at. He moved closer to Leda.

They stayed there for hours. New people were brought in

occasionally. Karel and Leda shoved over to make room along the wall. A boy David's age was thrown to his knees so hard he skidded on them. The soldier who did it gave him an apple afterward. They boy sat whimpering against his mother, holding the apple.

They heard rumors. What this was all about, who was about to be released. The officer at the table said No talking. There was the metallic sound across the room of someone urinating into a tin. On one wall there was an adjoining cell connected by a door, and someone from the other side was poking straw through the keyhole. Another officer came in and the first stood up and saluted him. The one who'd come in announced they were all prisoners of the Second Army Group in action. He crossed the room to Karel and regarded him with his hands on his hips. He didn't say anything. Finally he turned away. All of Karel's previous courage left him and he crouched sweating and shaking afterward. The new officer on the way out bent over a sleeping or unconscious woman near the door and asked how Madame was tonight. He saluted the officer at the table and left without waiting for an answer.

Later there was a genteel ringing the officer at the table identified as the dinner bell. Some young men in gray uniforms came in lugging pails with ladles and stacks of wooden bowls. The adults got porridge with a kind of gravy and the children something the officer called milk soup. The eating cheered up the woman who'd snapped at Karel and she said out of nowhere that they couldn't torture her. She'd confess to being a leader of the nomads if they tortured her.

He couldn't eat and neither could Leda. Other people took their food. While the young men in gray were collecting the bowls the officer who'd stared at Karel returned and said something to the officer at the table. Then he turned and gestured to Karel, whose stomach jumped and heaved. Karel pointed to his chest and the officer nodded and indicated with two spread fingers the both of them.

He took them out of the room and down a corridor, walking ahead of them. Leda held Karel's hand and said this was some kind of mistake, but the officer didn't respond.

He led them through one hallway after another and then across an enclosed courtyard that haggard men were sweeping with switch brooms. They passed through more hallways and then another courtyard, this one muddy and strewn with empty suitcases and a rotting mattress. Karel thought this prison went on forever and remembered what Albert had once told him: now we have prisons for people who've done things, prisons for people who haven't, prisons for people who might, prisons for people who might not, prisons for everybody because everybody is somebody who could go to prison.

The officer turned them over to a sad man in civilian clothes at the end of another long corridor. There was one yellow light over the man's table, and the corridor was very dark. Two cell doors on either side of him stood open. The sad man watched the officer leave and then turned to them. He had a patchy gray stubble on his cheeks and bleary eyes, and he appraised them as if they were an acquisition for the zoo while Leda asked him questions he didn't answer. When she was finished he dug into his shirt pocket and pulled out a sugar lump for each of them. Then he put them in separate cells.

On the floor of his cell Karel remembered sharply the look of tenderness Leda had given him as they'd trooped along behind the officer, as if she'd already figured out (and *he* hadn't, being an idiot) that this could be their last private moment together. He made a small noise of surprise and pain and then howled with the thought, the room echoing the sound, and then was silent.

There was one small window very high up, and the peephole on the door was shut. He called and called to Leda but he didn't hear any answer. He strained to listen and thought he heard hammering, and distant singing. He sat there and sat there while the sky turned dark outside his window and the terror of his position poured in on him like black water: all of what had felt to him at first like a frightening misunderstanding now gaped before him like a canyon. He fought the realization that he was abandoned and lost to the world: what would happen to him now? And if something bad happened, who would know?

In the middle of the night there was a clatter of keys at the door and it opened, throwing yellow light across the wall. Two men entered in silhouette carrying a small folding table and chair and set them up and then left. Then Kehr came in, with a lantern, and set the lantern on the floor.

"Why am I here? What are you doing with us?" Karel shouted, and when he got off the floor and tried to get to Kehr, Kehr hit him in the face first with his open palm and then with his closed fist, and Karel experienced a blackredness behind his eyes and a bloom of something that turned into fiery pain. He swallowed blood. He thought: I've been dealt with. I've been guilty and now I've been dealt with. He'd fallen on his arm. He got off the stone floor and rose from his knees as if on a trampoline, and swayed a little in front of Kehr's table. Kehr sat down.

"This is a turn of events," he said. "In the future when you address me pay particular attention to your tone." He laid out a pad of paper and a pencil and brought the lantern up from the floor. He sharpened the pencil with a clasp knife. Karel sat down, holding his nose and mouth. Both were swelling, and he swallowed the blood intermittently in small amounts.

"We didn't do anything," he finally said. He sounded defiant and whiny.

Kehr shrugged. "We not only punish action," he said. "We also prevent it. If we looked only to the politically active to fill these prisons, who knows where we'd be."

"What are we doing here?" Karel said.

"Why should you understand this?" Kehr asked. "How intelligent are you? How intelligent have you been?"

Karel snuffled and held his nose and mouth with his hand. Pain branched out from his nostrils and he wondered if his nose was broken.

What they were doing here were things that imaginations had outlined but never realized, Kehr said. He cleaned his ear with his little finger and ran a palm along his jawline. One could say no category covered their activities; that they were beyond categories, conducting an experimental inquiry into what was possible. And learning centers like these were their laboratories.

"I don't want to know," Karel said. "I don't care about that."

Kehr smiled. "See what I mean?"

He lifted the pencil with a slightly mocking anticipation. "Now," he said. "I have some questions for you."

"I have questions for you," Karel said.

"I would limit myself to comments that don't endanger your life if I were you," Kehr said.

Karel was quiet, his attention focused on avoiding another blow.

"I need names," Kehr said. "Albert's associates. You were close to him; you know who I mean. It's the fault of those people the zoo was destroyed."

"The Civil Guard destroyed the zoo," Karel said. "I saw it."

"After a while one's patience runs out," Kehr said. "I understand the men's feelings. If Albert's friends had turned themselves in, the zoo would be standing today."

Karel sat lower against the wall and looked at the blood on his hands.

"The names," Kehr said.

"I don't know any names," Karel said.

"What did I tell you about tone?" Kehr said with a softness in his voice, and Karel was frozen with fear. They were quiet for several minutes. Karel could feel his heart. Kehr breathed out exaggeratedly and said, "What have these people ever done for you? Have you asked yourself that?"

"At least they left me alone," Karel said, despite himself, and he waited in terror for Kehr's reaction.

Kehr sat back in his chair and put his chin in his hand and gazed at Karel. "Let me give you an idea," he said, "of what you're playing with here, playing the hero: your friend next door. And her family."

"You have her family?" Karel asked.

"My subordinate when interviewing the older brother asked him his rank in the organization," Kehr said, shaking his head at the memory. "I said, 'Organization? Mr. Stasik, he was in an institution, a home.' On the other hand, it had been considered by many to be a possible staging ground, and that was never disproved. So on the whole the entire family would be safer outside of Mr. Stasik's custody."

"I don't *know* anything," Karel said. "If I knew I'd tell you. But I don't know anything."

"Your friend wouldn't even have to know her family'd been taken," Kehr said. "They could be back on the street that fast. As could she. As could you."

"I don't *know,*" Karel cried miserably.

Kehr seemed to be pondering him. Finally he arched his eyebrows, as if he'd come to some conclusion. "The reasonable man adapts himself to the world," he said, standing up. "The unreasonable man adapts the world to himself. Therefore, all progress depends on unreasonable men." He crossed to the front of the table and leaned close to where Karel was sitting on the floor, and took Karel's chin in his hand. Karel shrank back. "Later on, if you haven't changed your mind, I'll kill your friend, while you're listening," he said. "And then I'll come here." He drew his finger delicately across Karel's belly. "I'll open your stomach and play with your insides."

Karel was breathing out as if getting ready to hold his breath. He said, "You're trying to frighten me."

"Yes, I am," Kehr said. He stood up, and knocked on the door.

"Leave her alone," Karel blurted as he was leaving. "Do whatever you want with me."

That was very good, Kehr said offhandedly, on the way out. Those were admirable sentiments. He signaled something Karel couldn't see to the man outside and shut the door behind him.

It was cold. There was a mattress on the floor but no blanket. He ran in place and waved his arms to keep warm but only succeeded in making himself sweaty and even colder. The peephole opened with a sliding sound and an eye appeared in it, blinking, to see what he was doing.

He felt better for the company. "What am I doing here?" he asked, and the peephole slid shut.

The floor was wet. He rolled the mattress into a tight tube to keep himself off the dampness, and half sat, half lay on it, but it was damp and cold and smelled and he couldn't sleep. He stayed like that for long stretches thinking of nothing. He called and pounded on the walls but Leda didn't seem to hear him. He held imaginary conversations with her in which he told her everything he'd done and she forgave him, forgave anything. He tried to imagine them back in the Golden Angel, but it seemed to have been shattered from within.

He heard shots and listened attentively for more, and then listened to the silence. He played a game of geography with Leda's face. He began to be more aware of basic needs: to eat, to relieve himself, to sleep, to find the resting position that was the least painful. He lay on his side on the rolled mattress and resigned himself to being wet on that side. He thought about raisins with cinnamon, and the image was momentarily soothing.

He was dozing when the door rattled and opened and he jerked upright in alarm. The damaged part of his face throbbed with the movement and he felt some trouble completely closing his jaw. Someone was peering over him. He realized it was his father. He burst into tears and then stopped, angry with himself, and started rubbing his eyes. His father set the lantern down and reached over and patted his head and shoulder helplessly. "How are you?" he said. "How are they treating you?"

"They put me in prison," Karel said. He sat up farther, shivering.

His father had brought a small blanket, and laid it on Karel's lap. "What happened to your face?" he asked.

"Kehr hit me," Karel said. "The soldiers who took me hit me." He had to look away. He thought that this of everything was the worst; that before this moment maybe his father hadn't known, maybe his father would've helped.

"They hit you?" his father said.

"Will you help me? Help us?" Karel asked, though he felt himself sliding hopelessly down the sentence as he asked it, knowing the answer.

"Of course," his father said. "Kehr'll listen to me. All you have to do is your part."

"My part?" Karel wailed. *"My part?"*

His father made patting motions on the air, teetering in his crouch. "We're talking about just confirming what we already have information on," he said.

"I don't know anything," Karel cried.

His father nodded, and looked puzzled. "Kehr says you do," he said.

Karel closed his eyes tightly and wanted everything different.

"Does it hurt a lot?" his father asked.

He didn't answer.

"I can help you, but you've got to help me," his father said. "Karel."

Karel was crying silently, now, and refused to see his father anymore. He looked at the door.

"What position do you think *I'm* in?" his father asked. He got to his feet. "You think they're happy with me about this?" He waited, but Karel would not look at him. "Who are you to judge me?" he finally said. He was angry again. "You know better than all these other people? You're so sure what the right thing to do is? Which one of us is obeying the law here and which one of us isn't? *Who are you to judge me?*" he shouted.

Karel kept his face to the wall.

The peephole slid open. "Everything okay in there?" a voice asked.

Everything was fine, his father said. He waited for the peephole to close and then went over to the door. Nothing happened for a minute or two, and then he sighed, as if exhausted. "I've never known what to make of you," he said. He sounded drained, and Karel felt acutely sorry for him. "I've never known how to get any support, any . . ." He sighed again. ". . . support out of you."

Karel was quiet. He thought that all his anger at his father's failures had turned inward. I never hated you, he wanted to say; I only always wanted to talk, I never learned how to talk. Why didn't I ever inspire talk? And he thought he understood his father a little and pitied him, but was ashamed of him, and ashamed of himself. He was thinking all that when his father left.

The next day no one came to see him. He didn't get any food and his joints ached from the dampness and when he banged on the door and said he had to go to the bathroom no one answered. He relieved himself in the corner and the cell stank from it.

Some food appeared the day after that, chick peas in a bowl with water, and he realized it had been brought in while he was asleep. The eye at the peephole apologized for the day before and said they'd forgotten.

That night he had another visitor, carried in on a pallet

and left there. He couldn't see who in the darkness. He stayed near the wall at first, wary.

"Hello, there," Albert said. He raised an arm off the palette. Karel knelt beside him and Albert said, "They're trying everything."

"How are you?" Karel whispered. "Are you all right? What'd they do to you?"

"They want information," Albert said. He swallowed audibly and Karel could not look at his body.

"They think I know something," Karel said. "I keep telling them I don't."

Albert nodded as best he could. "My fault," he said. "I should have let you know what was going on." He sniffed at himself and swallowed.

"Got you mixed up in this," he added.

Karel took his hand and was shaking with fear and pity. The fingernails were destroyed and the fingers lolled and rolled back against the palm.

"They did something to my eye," Albert said. He took deeper breaths.

Karel got his father's blanket and put it behind Albert's head. He wanted to help and couldn't. He wanted to ask questions and didn't know where to begin. He was afraid of being here and afraid of being hurt and afraid for Leda, and afraid of dying as ignorant and stupid as he was. His mind raced around to no purpose and the words he had were crippled and inadequate and eluded his attempts to order them into sentences.

"I've exorcised Kehr," Albert said, and he breathed more evenly. "He's shown me the instruments and I'm still here. I've reduced him. I've made him ridiculous," he said. "I believe in miracles."

"What are you talking about?" Karel said frantically.

"That leaves you," Albert said. "I'm supposed to be here to show you what can happen, or urge you to avoid it. I forget which. But I do want to tell you: after me he'll come for you." He looked at his hand, the way he used to look at a lizard's mite infestation. "He always believed you were closer to me than you were, he wanted to recruit you, sure, but he also wanted to get at me, at the organization. After me he's got nobody. After me he's got to get it from you."

Karel felt his forehead and back chilled, and he shook Albert's pallet. "Can't you tell him I don't know anything?" he asked.

"I don't think he believes me," Albert said. He smiled, his eyes closed. "I am in amazing pain," he said.

He opened his eyes and looked up at Karel. "Are you okay?" he asked.

Karel nodded, though he wasn't sure the old man could see him.

"I am sorry," Albert said. "For everything."

Karel was crying again. "Listen," he said. "I need to tell you something."

The old man waited, his breath wheezing a little.

"I need to tell you," Karel said, in agony. "When Kehr wasn't going to let the Schieles go, when Kehr—" The old man was looking intently at him while he fumbled for the words, as if he didn't want to forget anything of what Karel was about to say. "I *identified* you," Karel finally said. "I gave them your name."

Albert lay there on the pallet and just looked at him. The moment expanded into an awful vacuum. "I thought you did," he said finally. He just looked, and nothing in his expression suggested absolution.

"Please," Karel said.

"They already knew about me," Albert said. He lifted an arm toward Karel and gave a small wave. "I'm going to try to help the girl."

"Have you seen her?" Karel asked wildly. The door opened and two soldiers came in and lifted Albert's pallet. "Have you seen her?" Karel repeated, and Albert said no and gripped Karel's hand and then they were gone.

Only a few hours later there was a noise at the door again. "I don't even know why I bother to lock this," he heard his guard grumble. More soldiers came in and grabbed him and dragged him into the hall. Kehr and Leda were waiting there, next to the open door of Leda's cell. The soldiers released Karel and she hesitated and then ran to him and they embraced in the dark stone hallway, with Kehr, three soldiers, and the sad man who guarded the table all looking on.

"Oh God," Leda whispered in his ear. He wanted to tell her about her family, tell her what he'd done, but there was no time. He covered her head with his hands. "I wish I could be more for you," she whispered, and he hugged her more closely and gave an involuntary cry. "He wants something he thinks you have," she whispered in his ear. "Listen to me: when he does what he does most people do what he wants. *But some don't.*" She had her cheek to his and her lips to his ear and he could feel her tears. "Maybe that's what we have now," she added, and tightened her hug so that he would feel the urgency in what she said. *"Maybe this is our life's work."*

"I hope you're telling him the compelling reasons he should cooperate," Kehr said. "I hope you're telling him where you're going."

Karel held her arms and separated himself from her. "Where are you going?" he asked wildly. "What's happening?"

She hugged him again despite his resistance. *"I love you,"* she whispered, and holding her then was like what he felt when his eyes were closed and still he knew the sun had come out from behind clouds, a suffusion of warmth, of tenderness, and when they pulled her away before the sad man pinioned his arms he realized as she gazed back at him that he had no words or gestures for this, nothing to convey to her the extremity of his feelings but those words and gestures he used every day for everyday things.

They held him in the hall and made him listen. She was only two or three doors down, with Kehr and one of the soldiers. She shouted she loved Karel and then something else about the regime he couldn't make out and then she screamed. He fought and tore at the arms holding him but the sad man had him around the throat and one soldier hit the side of his knee with something that made him cry out and unable to put weight on it anymore. Leda screamed again, and he could tell from her voice that she stood on the edge of something she couldn't master, and he registered that he was breathing in and out and had to continue to do so or else he would suffocate, and the screaming went on and on until there was one more that rose above the others and seemed not to come from a human being but from some sort of terrified instrument. The stone rang with it. In the silence that followed Karel was shrieking and shrieking her name, and they hauled him back into his cell and threw him across it with such force that he hit the opposite wall and bounced back toward them.

• • •

It was warmer. He found himself gazing on an astonished cloud through the high square of his window. There was blue sky behind it. He'd been up all night and he was chilly and spent. When he closed his eyes his head reeled and he tumbled through empty space. He thought with some simplicity of the things he would never have: time, happiness, Leda. He would have told them anything at that point; he would have told them anything earlier, but no one asked.

He touched the edge of his mattress. His knee was in intense pain and swollen to twice its size. He seemed surprised by the resiliency of objects.

He sat where he was for he didn't know how long, gazing up at his window. Transparent knots swam across his eye. He wanted Leda to know: he would have helped her, together they would have acted the way she'd wanted to.

He heard the door unlocked and someone pacing behind it, back and forth, as if that someone were the prisoner. Then his father came in and shut the door behind him. He looked terrible, but Karel felt his sensibilities had coagulated or stiffened inside of him and so just sat there, watching his father enter.

He knelt beside Karel and Karel looked at his face and saw his pain, saw the pain of someone who now could do nothing to protect his child, who couldn't fulfill even that responsibility, and couldn't be forgiven because of it. His father was talking to him. His father was asking for something. His father was telling him that Leda had died feeling nothing bad was happening to her, after that first part. His father was saying he had to let him help. Karel said, "I don't want anything. I don't want you. I don't want help." It occurred to him that his father had in a profound way never realized what he'd been doing; that there was an interdependence, in his father's and his own case, between thoughtlessness and evil.

His father was asking him for something, pleading, and he had nothing to give. He was helpless in the face of this suffering. There were no words left to exchange whose value he trusted. His father said, Please, Karel, and he said again that his father had to go, and Kehr came into the cell, and looked at them both, and said the same thing.

"There is, I think, in every one of us something mineral and unteachable," Kehr said. "You see it when all evidence—all the dictates of logic—suggest one course of action, and the individual persists in doing something else. It interests me," he said.

They were in the room Leda had been taken to. It was different and darker than the room in the other Prisoner Assessment Center. On the wall there was tin shelving that held instruments with silhouetted long and narrow attachments. They reminded him of the mandibles and antennae of insects. The floor was concrete and had been washed and was puddled with water. In one corner a sump pump labored on and off. There was a sign embroidered like a sampler over the door: *If You Know Something, Sing for Us. If You Don't, Suffer.* It brought back to him the calendar from his home.

He was led to a slanted iron rack painted yellow and spotted with rust. The bottom of the rack had a gutter. Two weak and bare bulbs burned above it. Kehr had two assistants, heavy men in bright yellow shirts who helped Karel off with his clothes and looked at him with the neutrality of old cows. They locked his wrists and ankles into shackles so he was spread-eagled on the rack, the iron cold everywhere against his bare skin. While they worked on him he said harshly to Kehr, "Is Leda Schiele dead?"

"Leda Schiele is not your concern right now," Kehr said. "Believe me."

"I'll kill you if I get out of here," Karel said. "I'll kill you."

"Well said," Kehr said. "Now." He shook out Karel's two shirts before him. "Who are the people we're interested in?"

Karel looked at him, breathing hard. He shook his head. *"I don't know,"* he shouted, straining and banging at his shackles. "I never knew. I would have told you. *I would have told you."*

Kehr nodded as if that was exactly what he'd suspected, and gave Karel's bare shoulder a reassuring pat. Karel shivered involuntarily. Kehr folded his clothes carefully and gave them to one of his assistants, who looked around for a moment and then dropped them on the floor.

"We're going to start with the knee, and the face," Kehr explained. "They're already—how should I put it—sensitive."

"Please," Karel pleaded. His hatred for Kehr was gone. Fear was sweeping over him like cold air after a shower. Kehr was rummaging around the shelves, and the instruments made a quiet racket on the tin.

He returned with a simple pair of pliers and an awl and a complicated something that Karel didn't recognize that looked like a plumber's helper.

"Now," Kehr repeated, with an exhalation of breath like someone sitting down comfortably to a long monotonous job, "who are the people?"

"Please please please," Karel said.

One of the assistants put a soft piece of wood in his mouth. He looked at the man's eyes in wonder and shock and felt he was watching things happen in which he only vaguely participated, that this couldn't be true, because no one would do what they were about to do, and no one would do it to him.

"Who are the people?" Kehr asked.

"Please," Karel said. One of the assistants held his leg with both hands.

Kehr put the tip of the awl under Karel's kneecap and drove it through the swelling.

Karel shrieked and jolted upward and cried out so that the sound tore his throat.

Kehr was holding the awl in place and Karel could feel it under his kneecap, probing the joint. He jiggled it. Karel howled and thrashed out of the assistant's grip, and the awl came out.

He could feel the blood and the pain and he swept his head from side to side. This was worse than anything and he would have renounced anything to stop it.

"So who are the people?" Kehr asked.

"Please," Karel cried. "I don't know, I don't know, I don't know."

"It occurred to me a while ago," Kehr remarked, "that this for me could be an intriguing test. Do you know what I mean? What would it be like, doing someone I genuinely liked? Someone I genuinely had hopes for?"

Karel writhed on the rack, feeling only a bestial, desperate terror. It paralyzed everything in him but physical reaction.

Kehr reinserted the awl and Karel felt it get purchase on something inside his knee and then Kehr levered it outward and there was a tearing and cracking sound and Karel screamed so that he brought a blackness on himself, and when it passed the pain was a disk within his skull, tilting and oscillating, and then in his knee, flexing and spiraling outward. It rolled and pulsed and there was a grate of bone and he shrieked again. Kehr took the pliers and they clamped onto the kneecap with a wet and gritty sound and then he lifted and pulled.

The room reassembled like a pattern discovered in a cloud and Kehr was putting the instruments away on the shelf. Someone was wrapping Karel's knee in a large loose gauzy bandage that was soaking through. Karel's head was down and he was bringing up slaver and his chest was wet with it. He raised his head and the light through his tears prismed in concentric and iridescent circles. He couldn't breathe and the air seemed to come back to him from a great distance.

Kehr came up close and asked him who were the people. When Karel didn't answer Kehr hit him so hard across the face that it changed the taste in his mouth. Then he went away and the two assistants unshackled Karel and carried him back to his cell.

He lay on the floor feeling his nausea as a kind of acidic chill. He had nothing to fall back on in his attempt to understand what had just happened. He was aware of flies, houseflies and smaller flies with greenish heads. They buzzed and helixed before him when he moved his leg.

He thought, Am I better now? He was always aware of his knee, the pain like metal within it. He came to with a strange man bending over him. The man said he was the doctor and sat him up and showed him his knee. There were petals of flesh curled back from the opening and the whole thing seemed to him like meat on a plate. The man touched a white sponge soaked in something yellow to the area and Karel's whole leg moved independently while he watched. The man held Karel's palm open and tumbled three orange aspirins into it, to get him, he suggested, over the rough patch. He suggested when he left that Karel shake off the past and look to the future.

They brought him back to the torture room while he was still half muddled and he struggled and cried and tried to hold on to parts of his cell door like someone searching a sandy ocean bottom in murky water. Kehr asked him who the people were and he wailed and jabbered and tried everything to keep it from happening again. They leaned him back against the rack with one of the assistants supporting him since he could no longer support himself, and he tried feebly to keep his hands together so they couldn't be shackled. The assistant patiently pulled them apart.

Kehr said, "Long ago we figured out, in laboratories like these, that certain things can be done to human beings without the sky falling in. Most people really don't know that everything's possible. You resist," he said. "So you're back again. Who are the people?"

"I'll tell you, I'll tell you," Karel said, but images and information all milled around in his head and he couldn't think of a name to give or invent.

Kehr had something metal on Karel's thigh and sawed into it and tore back whole sheets of muscle. It was as if his leg had been inverted into fire.

He came to dizzy and weak from the loss of blood. Behind his eyes ovals and whorls of light cascaded. *Somebody save me,* he thought.

"Why are you resisting?" Kehr said. "There's no one left. Do you think there's anyone left?" But Karel couldn't focus on the words, overwhelmed with a suffocating and implacable fear. He refused to think, tried in every way possible to preoccupy his mind: Eski, he thought, and the little dog passed untouched through the darkness.

"Do you recognize this?" Kehr asked, and he held up bloody clothing. Karel didn't.

They started to strip the skin from the soles of his feet. He had the sensation they were trying to separate the skin at the edge of the wound with a pair of pincers. He passed out and came to and slid down a huge slippery tube where he would disappear and it would all stop. When he revived he was fully horizontal on a pallet, still in the room. His feet were on fire and he was howling and whining and his legs galloped weakly in place to make it stop. Something was holding them down. Kehr was over him.

"Let me tell you what you're hoping for," he said gently. "The good that saves the day, that turnaround moment when the point of light expands and drives away the darkness. If Karel was like Kehr, then why couldn't Kehr be like Karel?

"Let me tell you what will happen," he said. His eyes were close to Karel's and Karel closed his own and tried to raise an arm, like a blind man groping to ward off a blow. "We're taking everything. No one is left for you. No one will be sorry. We're taking your life and your death. You're resisting, but I've taken away the world you're resisting for. Your martyrdom is impossible. With no witnesses there's no testimony. Who's going to record your gesture? Who's going to record hers?"

"I am," Karel whispered. He was crying and wanted only to be put out of his agony. "I do."

You should have been born in another time, Kehr was telling him, after it had been quiet. This was a chosen time and a chosen place. What chance did you have? Kehr stood and signaled to someone, and he felt himself being lifted up. So many never fully understood, Kehr was saying from somewhere behind him, the way that in places and times like this it was just a matter of history being let off the leash.

In his cell he lay across his mattress, too weak to move, shivering violently. He thought he could hear the faint scraping and tapping of mortar and trowels and imagined his cell expanding in all directions. His thigh and knee swayed and throbbed in steady waves and he could feel his blood purling out of him. He wrote his name and Leda's name with his finger on the floor. At times he thought to himself, *Now it's time to get ready, now's the time they'll come for me,* or *I'm not ready, I'm ashamed, I'm alone, I'm guilty,* but at other times he could let feelings and sensations from his time with Leda enter him as he might enter shade, and he tried to hold on to parts of her, small memories that faded and wavered unreliably as he tried to keep them still. Maybe they won't come, he thought, and heard them at the door, and he could feel his heart within his chest and the fear of facing this alone like a single transparent hand against his back. They cleaned his cell while he lay there, and when they lifted him to his feet his mattress was dragged away, and even supported as he was by two men he was trembling and unsteady and desired to press his heel against the stone floor to steady himself. He told himself he should be calm and controlled and lucid for this and closed his eyes to shake off the numbness and he felt he wanted to say a measured goodbye to even this world but his breathing would not allow it, and the sensation he felt as they brought him across the cell and laid him on their pallet was that of sliding slowly across warm sheet ice. They settled him into it and tied him down and he registered from the feel of the air and the paleness outside his window that it was sometime before dawn, and he began an incantation of names: Leda, his mother, his father, Albert, Eski, Seelie, David, Nicholas, Herman, Mrs. Fetscher, and Leda, the loop allowing him the sense that his past was there with him still breathing in the darkness, and as they lifted him and rocked him along he felt he was being allowed a dream, David and him at the ocean, David gone, himself on a sandbar surrounded by fog and everything silent except the lapping of waves. There was a nonvisual sense of Leda, a certainty she was there because of the weight of her arms and the warmth of her body, and because he thought Kehr was wrong and the mercy he would be granted had no conditions.

And from that sandbar they could see the offshore Seprides, the Roof of Hell, and as his body tilted on its axis and hands steadied him against the cold iron on his back and other hands fumbled with the shackles around his wrists, some part of him wanted to generate an image of retribution, a smiting and a scouring of the earth: the sea at night in front of the island churning as if stirred from beneath, an explosion, and then the wave of Albert's father's memory: at first a thin phosphorescent line rising higher and higher in the distant darkness, and then the clear silvery-white crest showing the wall of black water beneath it, the air pressure a rising roar before it, the whole sea piling up behind it, and when it hit the hills themselves would seem to capsize, and the ground roll like choppy waves in a rough sea, the cove itself falling away in concentric ranks to expose the bodies of all the tortured and the dead, all forgotten, all buried sitting up and facing the sea, but as Kehr came closer and the world came back to that room, in the end it was Leda, Leda, always and only Leda.